Multi-Vendor Networks
Planning, Selecting and Maintenance

Other books in the J. Ranade Series on Computer Communications

ISBN	Author	Title
0-07-019022-4	Edmunds	SAA/LU6.2 Distributed Networks and Applications
0-07-054418-2	Sackett	IBM'S TOKEN-RING NETWORKING HANDBOOK
0-07-004128-8	Bates	DISASTER RECOVERY PLANNING: Networks, Telecommunications, and Data Communications
0-07-020346-6	Feit	TCP/IP: Architecture, Protocols, and Implementation
0-07-005075-9	Berson	APPC: INTRODUCTION TO LU6.2
0-07-012926-6	Cooper	COMPUTER AND COMMUNICATIONS SECURITY
0-07-016189-5	Dayton	TELECOMMUNICATIONS
0-07-034242-3	Kessler	ISDN
0-07-034243-1	Kessler/Train	METROPOLITAN AREA NETWORKS: Concepts, Standards, and Service

Other Related Titles

ISBN	Author	Title
0-07-051144-6	Ranade/Sackett	INTRODUCTION TO SNA NETWORKING: A Guide for Using VTAM/NCP
0-07-051143-8	Ranade/Sackett	ADVANCED SNA NETWORKING: A Professional's Guide to VTAM/NCP
0-07-033727-6	Kapoor	SNA: Architecture, Protocols, and Implementation
0-07-005553-X	Black	TCP/IP AND RELATED PROTOCOLS
0-07-005554-8	Black	NETWORK MANAGEMENT STANDARDS: SNMP, CMOT, and OSI
0-07-021625-8	Fortier	HANDBOOK OF LAN TECHNOLOGY, 2/e
0-07-063636-2	Terplan	EFFECTIVE MANAGEMENT OF LOCAL AREA NETWORKS: Functions, Instruments, and People

Multi-Vendor Networks

Planning, Selecting and Maintenance

Robert L. Dayton

McGraw-Hill Inc.

New York St. Louis San Francisco Auckland Bogotá Caracas
Lisbon London Madrid Mexico Milan Montreal New Delhi
Paris San Juan São Paulo Singapore Sydney Tokyo Toronto

Notices
Lotus 1-2-3 is a trademark of Lotus Development Corp.
JitterBuster is a trademark of Texas Instrument/Proteon Inc.

FIRST EDITION
FIRST PRINTING

©1993 by **McGraw-Hill, Inc.**

Printed in the United States of America. All rights reserved.

Library of Congress Cataloging-in-Publication Data

Dayton, Robert L.
    Multi-vendor networks : planning, selecting, and maintenance / by
Robert L. Dayton.
      p.   cm.
    Includes index.
    ISBN 0-07-016196-8
    1. Computer networks—Planning. 2. Computer networks—Maintenance
and repair. I. Title.
TK5105.5.D437   1992
621.382'029'7—dc20   92-1738
                                              CIP
For information about other McGraw-Hill materials, call 1-800-2-MCGRAW in the U.S. In other countries call your nearest McGraw-Hill office.

Acquisitions Editor: Gerald T. Papke
Editor: Lori Flaherty
Direction of Productiion: Katherine G. Brown
Book Design: Jaclyn J. Boone

Contents

Part II
Selecting

Part III
Implementing & Maintenance

Appendices

Introduction

There is something about multi-vendor networks that makes me think of an old country and western song. Unfortunately, the singer's name has escaped my memory but the theme of the song lingers on. The male vocalist goes on about how he assembled a car from parts obtained at the junk yard. His accomplishment was a car with parts from a Cadillac, a Lincoln, and so on, until the final product included a part from about every type of car made. Multi-vendor networks can often look like this car. Planning is the secret in obtaining a multi-vendor network that is a thing of beauty; something that runs perfectly without major overhauls. The person in the song connected many different parts together. If they didn't quite match, he had to modify the parts to prevent the car from falling apart on the first test drive.

Creating a new network can be an awesome responsibility. It usually entails a great capital expenditure for the company. Consequently, upper management is concerned that the finished product run like a luxury car but cost no more than an economy car. Unfortunately for too many companies, the initial cost is the deciding factor instead of the costs over the life of the installed network. This book contends that buying intelligently is the only way to buy. It is like buying that 100 percent wool suit versus the suit made from a blend of synthetic fabrics. The wool suit initially costs more, but it lasts longer in nearly new condition. If the suit with synthetic fabric costs a third of the price of the wool suit and lasts nearly as long, there's no question that the synthetic suit will work just fine. It still boils down to making intelligent decisions.

Not all companies have a surplus of geniuses or psychics waiting around to make the infallible decision on the perfect system. Sometimes, a company will assign several groups to make the final decision. While the blame can be spread across a bigger cross section, the results often look like the proverbial camel when their task was to build a horse. Making intelligent decisions is easy—even if you do not possess a doctorate from Princeton or Stanford. In fact, you can get by with just your high school diploma in hand.

Well, how does one go about buying intelligently? One way is gathering a reasonable amount of information on the subject. A reasonable amount of information is just that. You do not have to hunt down every widget made in the world to satisfy a reasonable search. Nevertheless, a reasonable number of products is more than one. Not only does a study of several products show you did a comprehensive job, it also shows an impartial judgment. This book covers ways to ensure you are truly impartial and not influenced by a particular vendor's generosity. As you will read later, you cannot be impartial by accepting gifts from vendors in any fashion. A person's decision process gets very blurry after dinner at a fancy restaurant and then going to the theater later.

After you have made a reasonable search, the next step is determining what parts you really need. Specifying your needs gets categorized into three areas: absolute necessities, desirable features, and extra bonus features, or the "nice but not essential" items. This is similar to entering a new car showroom with the intention of buying some basic transportation. Before you know it, the salesperson has moved you past the basic auto all the way to the deluxe model. The salesperson was able to show you it is just a few dollars more each month to go first class. Many of the items you were talked into fall into the "nice but not essential" category.

When you get into specifying your needs, the absolute needs fall around your basic needs. These needs are explained as much as possible by using the existing standards of the electronic industry. While your task to identify all the standards might seem beyond your capabilities, the vendors have, for the most part, verified their unit will meet some standards. The biggest problem with standards is that they are open to interpretation. Vendors will view the unspecified parts to standards as an invitation for exclusive usage. Simple things go wrong when vendors use the unassigned pins in an Electronic Industry Association EIA-232 interface. One vendor uses an unspecified pin to bring out a test voltage; another uses the same unspecified pin to produce a function when applying a voltage to it. Both vendors did nothing wrong when it came to the standards, but their products would not function when connected. Another thing to watch out for is the very large vendor that has many groups designing things. Each group has a habit of thinking they are the only ones in the company designing things and often introduce incompatible interfaces.

The next step in buying intelligently is to make the best selection. Selecting is a risk adventure. If you make the wrong selection, upper management will never forget you—even after you no longer work there. When you make the right decision, you will be remembered—even if your boss claims responsibility. Reducing risks is the name of the game. If you have to walk over a rope bridge spanning a deep ravine, it lessens the risk if you take reasonable precautions. There is a difference between reasonable precautions and being paranoid about the trip. Being paranoid means one may never put one's foot on the bridge. Nevertheless, if you attached safety ropes before venturing out, you might even have a look of confidence on your face as you cross over the span. Risk analysis is the safety rope you use before making that final selection.

Much like making a final choice of suits or automobiles, you want to try it out to make sure it fits before you pay your money. That car looked good in the showroom, but it might be all wrong after you see how it handles. Unfortunately, a multi-vendor network is more complicated than a spin around the block in a new car. It might be more complicated, but it isn't impossible to do. There are ways to take your multi-vendor network out for a test drive before signing the contract.

This is especially true if there isn't any history of the various products ever working together. Just verifying that the interfaces do indeed work together is essential. Little things like the wrong sex (i.e., male or female) of the interfaces can cause a long delay while new cords are fabricated. Another time, you find one vendor has looped back a particular command lead that turns off the other unit. It is like buying the deluxe electric charcoal lighter. Just before it's time to light the grill, you unwrap the lighter and find that it has only a 2-foot cord—barely enough cord to reach the top of the grill. There is no way to use the product unless you modify the cord or dig up an extension cord. Although some of these analogies sound a bit outlandish, they actually do occur.

Now that you have planned, selected, and verified your choice, the next thing is putting the parts together. This is the critical test—finding out if your planning was thorough enough. It's not the end of the world if there are adjustments to make to the final system to make it work perfectly. There are fine-tuning adjustments that everyone expects. Unfortunately, there are bosses in the world that will think "you blew it" if the entire network wasn't 100 percent fault-free and ran perfectly from day one.

After the network is turned on, it must be maintained. A few years ago, there were various systems to measure and control sections of your network. Some of these systems crossed over boundary lines and claimed to check other portions of the total system. Some made very large claims as to their capabilities. My favorite device was a tester for analog data circuits. With a push of the button it would instantaneously feedback readings on various parameters that had a normal testing period of 15 minutes. Most of the readings were pure garbage, while the rest were circumspect. The one thing it did for the user was to give them a false sense of their network's health. Today, sophisticated network control systems not only check the health of a system but report the troubles to the responsible carrier.

That was a fast trip through the process of successful multi-vendor networks. This book is divided into three main parts: planning; selection; and implementing and maintaining. You can either go from cover to cover or concentrate on a particular main theme. If you have progressed past the point of selecting the equipment, then you will find Part III is more meaningful to you. One thing you will find throughout the book is a recurring message about quality.

Quality is apparent in the best products. It seems to permeate throughout the company. You notice it in the attitude of the employees. It is evident when you take a tour through their manufacturing plant. The good ones jump out at you, and the bad ones become red flags to stop right where you are. After years of selecting telecommunications products for the Bell System, I got to see many manufacturers. You would see manufacturers grow from small companies to very large ones and watch their growing pains. One small company's only quality control was one man who stored all the information in his head. When asked about their quality control, they would point to the man. A problem resulted when the man with all the information in his head retired the next month. Gone were all the mental records. They quickly saw their errors and established a first-rate quality control process.

One company's quality control process was outstanding. Their market was almost 90 percent located in Third World countries of Africa. The product had to work the first time and for a long time under adverse conditions. They almost were to a point of over inspecting the components—if that is possible. One sharp-eyed visitor picked up two identical circuit boards and asked why resistors with different values were in the same location on the boards. Electrically, the boards passed inspection because the resistors were very close in value, but the quality was off. This appalled upper management because they thought they had a good quality program. After that, they added another inspection step that visually checked to see if the components agreed to a standard reference.

Your goal is to get the best product for your money. The way to get it is to make sure an item meets standards and has the highest quality. Quality doesn't mean luxury. People got turned on to Japanese compact economy cars because their quality was better than the luxury cars built in America.

Several features of this book are unique, and are a product of years of making equipment selections. One is a quality check sheet that guides you in learning how to judge the quality of a vendor. It has all the questions you need answers to so you can find out the true quality of a vendor. Another is a process called risk analysis that reduces your selection risks to a minimum. Interspersed throughout the book are things that one learns only after years of specifying and selecting equipment. While the main thrust is about telecommunication equipment, the principles are valid for almost anything you buy.

Part I

Planning

1

Introduction
to planning

Writing about how to plan for every possible multi-vendor network would produce a multivolume series of books. Instead, this part of the book on planning is as generic as possible so that it can cover most network variations. A good portion of this section is devoted to the various standards and what they mean to you. This is important, because these standards become the foundation of your request for proposal (RFP) or quote (RFQ).

The final chapter in Part I covers the end product. The differentiation between RFP and RFQ is used in order to be more factual. If you need someone to propose a solution to your needs, you would write an RFP, which is designed for suggestions. If your mind is set to exactly what you want, however, you would write an RFQ to get a firm idea of the final cost.

Initial planning

Webster's New Collegiate Dictionary defines planning as: "The act or process of making or carrying out plans; specif: the establishment of goals, policies and procedures for a . . . business." If you look up the synonyms for planning, you'll find words like contriving, designing, drafting, devising, and setting out. When you set out to establish a multi-vendor network, you need to approach the process with an idea, or map, of how you are going to reach the final goal of a fully functional network. Some things you should know before you start to establish your goals or design a network are:

- Your present voice and data requirements. This usually breaks down by volume, calling location, called location, and peak hours for traffic.
- Company plans to expand, consolidate, or eliminate locations over the next few years. Most of your investment will take several years to

amortize, and it might not be prudent economically if there are major plans in the future.

If you have records of voice and data volumes over the past few years, you can trend expected increases in the future. If the company has no major forecasts in their five-year plan, don't anticipate an unrealistic growth. Don't be like some market managers who forecast a 30 percent product growth each year even though the product has never grown faster than 10 percent in any one of the past five years.

- A reasonable feeling of the company's desire to include new and different telecommunication services, like video teleconferencing and CAD/CAM services. Don't take it upon yourself to make unilateral decisions to provide for something that might never be used. It's like building that gazebo in the backyard that nobody ever sits in. It just takes up space and adds to your tax assessment.

Now that you know where you are and where you are going, you can start the planning stage. First, you must establish a reasonable schedule for planning, selecting, and implementing your network. Exactly what reasonable means will depend on the size of the network and the complexity of the design. What you really need to establish is a window that will close at a particular time. Without a window for planning and selecting, planning could go on indefinitely. There must be a point that concludes all study and decision-making.

There are times when you will find a newer design at the last minute that costs less. An example of this was the introduction of the NEC 4FG Series monitor that replaced the popular 4DS monitor. The 4FG provided the same viewing area as the 4DS, had improved features, and cost $100 to $200 less. If a change does not directly interfere with your overall schedule, then it is certainly wise to go with the newer equipment. While you can occasionally get away with one change at the last minute, you will run into trouble with two or more changes. The best policy is to stay with the plans and decisions you made within your time frame. Otherwise, you'll never reach a point where you are completely satisfied.

Establishing time frames is best handled by some form of project scheduling software, such as a Gantt chart or a Performance Evaluation Review Technique (PERT) chart. Most scheduling software looks like the Gantt chart shown in FIG. 1-1. You would normally have two rows for each project item: one row for the dates of the planned schedule, the other listing the actual dates of completion. Using two lines is a good way to tell at a glance which item has a scheduling problem.

Figure 1-2 shows a PERT chart that is more of a balloon and string diagram. This type of chart is not really adaptable to a time schedule, although here it is shown with week numbers associated with each balloon. You could write the start and completion dates next to each event to aid in maintaining your schedule. A PERT chart's main strength is developing critical paths where it is evident that certain functions cannot take place until a previous one is completed.

Project Item	Week 1	Week 2	Week 3	Week 4	Week N
Define goals of network	X———X				
Outline total system		X———X			
Review standards		X ————————X			
Develop the various RFQs			X————————————X		

Fig. 1-1. Gantt-type project schedule.

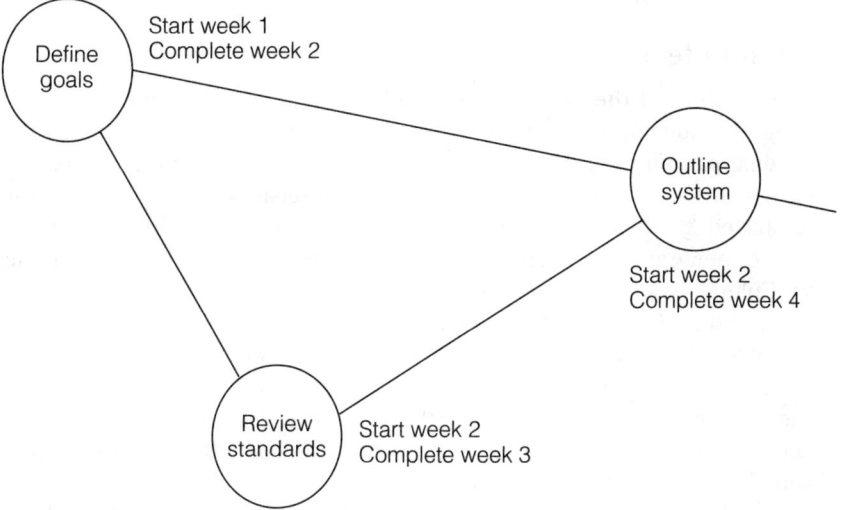

Fig. 1-2. PERT chart.

You'll find yourself missing critical dates throughout implementation without some form of scheduling tool. Things fall into the cracks because they slipped the mind. A schedule helps you to keep track of all events. Don't worry that your schedule might not cover all things from the first day. There are always unforeseen things that cause additions and changes. The intent is to adjust internal time frames so you can still meet the final date for turning up the network.

Assembling the principals

A principal person is an individual that has a proprietary interest in planning and selecting the network's configuration. These people have a vested interest in the network and feel they are the owners. Principals might have subordinates working for them, but they are considered secondary personnel. Indeed, they might be instrumental to a principal's input, but the principal player is the one who must bear the accountability and responsibility.

Principal personnel should be limited to the least number of people needed to do the job. Assembling a "cast of thousands" only leads to delays, and often results in the wrong conclusion. It is far better to have only a few good people as the inner core of principal participants. Secondary personnel can do much of the work, but do not make any final decisions.

Later in the chapter, the length of time it takes to issue a final standard is discussed. Interestingly, the main cause for its delay is the number of people that have their oar in the water and are rowing in different directions. Smaller groups are much more effective.

Planning techniques

If you are sure of the direction your network should take, then it is only a matter of producing the various RFQs with the necessary standards so that individual parts fit into the total system. This assumes you have approached your network as a system when combining the separate parts. One company that started an alternative to the Bell System seemed to follow what is the Chinese menu approach. They picked one product from Column A, another from Column B, and so on. There appeared to be no concern for what was put together other than the data operating speed. There wasn't a shred of system analysis to figure out how the sum of the parts would work.

One way to plan your network is to let other organizations propose a system for you. You can issue an RFP to several telecommunication companies, such as various telephone companies (telcos). Because telcos have diversified equipment, a finished system generally results in a multi-vendor network. Telcos can also do much of the work your company is not capable of (i.e., not enough personnel, lack of training, etc.). The only drawback is that telcos will normally just tell you the cost, revealing little information about the equipment or facilities. Years ago, they would tell you everything about their proposal, but then they found that this information got into the competition's hands or the RFP issuer used the information themselves.

Another approach is to use a telecommunication consultant to propose the network, work with you in the design, or bless what you have done. As you will read in Part II, consultants have varying degrees of abilities. Follow the advice in chapter 7 about consultants, and you'll stand a better chance of having things work out to your benefit.

Systems planning approach

Because the heralded Integrated Services Digital Network (ISDN) remains a telco offering or network, the integrating of voice and data from one common unit has not progressed as quickly as some people predicted. Most networks are frequently divided between the voice realm and the data. This is due to the split between telecommunications and information services groups within a company. Joining these two entities is accomplished within a digital telecommunication network where both data and voice look the same.

When you begin to plan your network, you must look at the total system or the multi-vendor network as a whole entity. Define what your needs are and then shape the system in general specifications. The system approach looks at the broad picture and then concentrates on the parts of the puzzle. This allows you to find the parts that fit the network instead of trying to make the network fit the parts. Without a system's approach, you could end up with a network much like the car mentioned in the Introduction.

Some network managers have opted for loading much of the transmission requirements over high-speed transmission lines for economy of scale. If your system can survive a catastrophic failure of the transmission line, then you can justify the savings. Putting all your eggs in one basket is not for a network that must operate without any interruptions, however. At times, survival calls for a diversified network that spreads the telecommunications flow over many routes.

After you have your picture of the system, it is time to put the parts together. Each time you add a part, you need to check to see how it interacts with what is already in place. This is especially true when you are dealing with a digital telecommunications system. One of the most important things to keep in mind is that you must follow just one master clocking system. If your network has more than one master clock in the system, you will have bit errors occurring on a cyclic basis. If you adhere to the standards in the following chapters, however, you'll have fewer problems in the future.

Need for standards

Standards are the closest thing to having everybody playing the same tune in the band. The originators of the various standards start out with very good intentions. They do not always hit the bull's-eye but they at least hit the target. While standards might not be 100 percent correct, they are your only place to start planning. Once you know about the various standards, you're ready to ask very pointed questions from vendors.

Standard originators

Standards go through many organizations before they are universally accepted. They usually start out in subcommittees of larger organizations. That is not to imply that the subcommittees are just a couple of people laboring over some ideas in the back room. These subcommittees have worldwide representatives from the telecommunications industry and most telephone companies.

Because these organizations provide a wide cross section of the entire industry, there is a very long interval between the original work and the acceptance of the standard. Months go by just to review the document, which allows time for members to comment on the words. Another period goes by to review all the comments and modify the document again. If the proposed standard is controversial, it will be several years before a conclusion is reached and a standard is accepted.

While some standards are being accepted over this long time frame, new ideas are introduced that are different from the ones being considered. The terms *bis* or *tres* can often be found behind a designation to show a second or third variation of the original standard. This is common with the various modem standards adopted by the International Telegraphy and Telephony Consultative Committee (CCITT) of the International Telecommunication Union (ITU) in Geneva, Switzerland.

Other major standards groups are the Electronic Industries Association, the Institute of Electrical and Electronic Engineers (IEEE), and the Federal Communications Committee. The American National Standards Institute furnishes a service by verifying that the various standards are correct. Both AT&T and Bellcore have extensive technical references that supply information about telephone company standards. Companies like US Sprint, GTE, and regional Bell companies also issue references, although on a much smaller scale.

De facto standard originators

There is often a rush to introduce a corporation's idea about what a new standard should be. They are trying to be in the leadership position to have their idea become the universal standard. It works so well that the original document becomes the de facto standard because it was the first. In the case of ISDN, AT&T quickly issued the first document on the Primary Channel as Bellcore was pushing out their version of the Basic Channel. There were some minor changes to these documents before they became a national standard, but they were, for the most part, adopted from the original writings.

The other case of de facto standards is when groups like AT&T and Bellcore issue documents that might never be considered because of lengthy standard adoption proceedings. This type of document becomes the accepted benchmark for the rest of the industry.

Understanding the verbiage

Lewis Carroll wrote a poem called Jabberwocky that has come to mean meaningless speech or writing. Standards tend to apply too many words to explain some simple operation. Lawyers and engineers have a great similarity in being able to write about one little item and include every conditioning phrase they can think of. Bellcore TR-TSY-000418 explained availability in the following manner.

Availability—The ability of an item to be in a state to perform a required function at a given time or at any instant of time within a given interval, assuming the external resources, if required, are provided. Notes: (1) This ability depends on the combined aspects of the reliability performance, the maintainability performance and the maintenance support performance of an item. (2) In definition of the item the external resources required must be delineated. (3) The term availability is used as an availability performance measure.

Needless to say, this could be reduced to something simple. For example, "A unit is considered available if it functions properly when actively connected to a network. When it does not work, it is considered unavailable." Longer definitions tend to lend themselves to misinterpretation. If you are confused about a standard, read it again in short sections instead of whole paragraphs. The crux of the statement might be confined to a few short words in one sentence with the rest of the verbiage modifying the specifics.

Things that get you into trouble

While standards are your greatest tool to putting a successful network together, there are several things about them that can get you into trouble. The most prevalent trouble is the unassigned pin of an interface. Manufacturers tend to assume that an unassigned pin means they can use that position for their own use. One example of this is the unassigned pins in the Electronic Industries Association EIA-232 interface. Pin 11 is probably the most misused pin of all. There are other pins, like 9 or 10, that often have test voltages on them.

You should know every interface pin assignment on each piece of equipment. You should then either remove the unassigned interface pins, or make sure the wires do not connect to them. It is important to fully understand what appears on each interface. A part of your RFP or RFQ should specify that the responder tell you what is on each pin assignment. Even if they list a pin assignment as unassigned, they should verify that there isn't any internal connection to the pin.

If the interface has more functions than specified by the standard, you run the risk of trouble. A vendor should also explain all nonstandard pin assignments and the reason for their function. Don't rely on a marketing department's answer. Insist on the design engineers' input as to what exactly is on each pin.

When you mix and, hopefully, match different modems on your network, you run the risk of small nuances that conflict with each other. Simple things like differences in software versions of the Microcom Network Protocol can cause major problems unless they are completely compatible with each other. Just because the modem's data speed is 9600 b/s does not mean it will work with another 9600 b/s modem. There are different modulating schemes that will not talk to each other. They might use the same modulating method, but it does not mean different manufactured products will function together. Here, the handshaking between units will suffer the greatest amount of problems. Standards are not infallible and manufacturers take liberties with their interpretation, so caveat emptor!

Summary

Planning should be based on a systems approach. The total system should be examined to determine how the individual parts will fit into the system. A network made up of a batch of individual parts leads to problems when it is implemented as a system. Before a new part can be added to a system, you must verify that it will not negatively impact the system in any way. The new part might affect parts of the system other than just at the local connection.

Standards are your lifesaver when requesting proposals from vendors. Use liberal amounts of standard references when dealing with any vendor. One word about planning is that you should allow several weeks just to get all the standards you need. Some suppliers can expedite your order, but others require cash in hand before filling your request.

2

Telecommunication transmission requirements

Before you start your planning period, you must be aware of all the various standards available that will provide the best possible chance that system parts will interconnect. This chapter reviews the various transmission standards that become part of your request for proposal (RFP) or request for quote (RFQ), which is covered in chapter 6. There are many transmission standards around the world. In the United States, the American National Standards Institute (ANSI) is the final word on transmission. Europe follows the standards issued by the International Telegraph and Telephone Consultative Committee. (CCITT). Years ago, there were major differences between the two standards groups, but they are getting closer in the context. Today, the difference between the groups is mainly in the wording of the newer standards.

This chapter covers the ANSI standards and telephone company technical references in greater detail. European readers should double-check with the CCITT and their individual country's standards to ascertain what is appropriate. Some major differences between the two standards groups are:

- Jitter tolerance requirements.
- In-band signaling and digital framing locations.
- Digital signal hierarchy structure.
- Analog noise measurements (i.e., C-Message vs. Psophometric)
- Analog circuit conditioning gauges or operating ranges.

Clocking accuracy

Too many people lump synchronization and timing together as if they were the same. While the band leader uses the baton to keep time, he also synchronizes the start of the music by saying "a one, a two, etc." Both items are critical to the successful start of the music, but are separate functions. Terminal equipment depends on synchronization to remain in step with remote devices and it is a function of the framing pattern. Synchronization lets each end know exactly where to find data locations. Another way to look at the difference between the two is to think of timing as a hardware item and synchronization as a software item.

Nevertheless, timing controls the internal operation of the terminal and it relies on a master clock source. It is critical to have just one clock source for digital data to reduce bit slips. Network clocks are in a hierarchy structure called Stratum Levels and originate from one source. Interconnecting between different telephone companies produces two or more different clock sources. Even worse, some telephone companies (telcos) have installed several source clocks within their own networks. Two master Stratum Level-1 clocks are very close, but they have differences. Nevertheless, the differences widen as you go down the clocking ladder. If the telcos feed the majority of their offices from high-level clock sources, there are only minor bit slips to your data.

Stratum Level-1

Stratum Level-1 is a cesium atomic clock source known for its accuracy. Once, there was just one Stratum Level-1 clock for the entire Bell System. Even after the split of the Bell Companies away from AT&T, they continued to use the same source for many years. Over the years, the various Bell companies have installed one or more Stratum Level-1 clocks to replace the AT&T source. After you place an atomic clock and a hot spare on line, you combine their outputs to produce one averaged clock.

A Stratum Level-1 has an analog clock frequency of 2,048,000 Hertz (Hz), and you shouldn't see any drift over 10 or 20 years. Its accuracy is as fine as one part in 100 billion or ±0.00002048 Hz.

Stratum Level-2

After the telcos implement their Stratum Level-1 clock source, they distribute the 2,048,000 analog clock frequency to the first working level. Stratum Level-2 is really the first clock source the network sees. The initial clock frequency phase locks the less accurate frequency generator at main distribution points. This clock source drops down to 1,544,000 Hz but is still very accurate. In fact, its accuracy is 1.6 parts out of 100 million, or ±0.024704 Hz minimum frequency accuracy (long-term deviation without an external frequency reference).

Stratum Level-3

Getting from a Stratum Level-2 to a Level-3 telco office is done primarily over the digital network. The accuracy of a Stratum Level-3 clock relies on averaging several incoming digital lines, which results in a nodal clock. Its accuracy has dropped to a minimum frequency accuracy of 4.6 parts out of a million, or

±7.1024 Hz. Bellcore's Switched Multi-megabit Data Service (SMDS) uses a Stratum Level-3 clock on services toward your premise.

Stratum Level-4

Other digital services will normally use a lower level of clock accuracy. Stratum Level-4 is the worst clock frequency in the entire telco network and appears at the last or end-office in the chain. Now, the accuracy has dropped to 32 parts out of one million, or ±49.408 Hz. At this point, the standard clock reference rounds off to read ±50 Hz for the minimum frequency accuracy. The internal clock accuracy of SMDS terminal equipment must be able to meet the free-running clock accuracy of a Stratum Level-4 source. During normal operating conditions, the transmission rate of the DS-1 signal is 1.544 Mb/s ±0.00001. This is an absolute requirement in your specifications for any equipment running at the T1 rates.

T1 line requirements
Ones-density

Old-time digital repeaters were infamous because they developed a voltage imbalance very quickly if they were not fed enough 1-bits. The circuit would get noisy and the clock recovery would go to pot. They never did away with the requirement even though the equipment got better. Digital facilities in North America always had a requirement for a thing called ones-density. That says the terminal equipment must furnish the transmission lines a healthy diet of 1-bits to maintain the integrity of the system. AT&T PUB 62411 technical reference states the following requirement for ones-density:

The terminal equipment must not transmit more than 15 'zeros' in a consecutive row, and in each and every time window of $8\times(n+1)$ bits (where n can equal 1 through 23), there should be at least 'n' ones present.

This is confusing and, in fact, has caused many vendors to misunderstand the meaning. TABLE 2-1 shows the breakdown of the number of 1-bits that must be distributed within the window to prevent 15 zeros in a row.

Table 2-1. Ones-density rule.

Window (bits)	n=1	Ones needed
16	1	1
24	2	2
32	3	3
192	23	23

Bellcore's TR-TSY-000191, Alarm Indication Signal Requirements and Objectives, goes on to define a good signal definition as: ". . . declare a DS-1 signal good when the ones density is at least 12.5% with no more than 15 consecutive zeros." This definition is different, but is saying almost the same thing. A good signal has an additional 1-bit included in the window to make it better than the minimum.

Clear channel capability

Clear Channel Capability (CCC) comes in two forms—restricted and unrestricted. Restricted CCC allows that the end user can send 64 Kb/s over the basic time slot of a digital signal but they must control the ones-density rule internally within their data stream. In other words, you can send 64 Kb data as long as you find a way to eliminate strings of zero bits. One way to do that is to add a pseudo-random scrambler stage to reduce the chance of a string of zeros. Obviously, the chance of your actual data adding to the random signal to produce a long string of zeros is possible, but very remote.

The other CCC is the unrestricted signal where the transmission equipment handles the ones-density requirement, and the user can send long strings of zeros. One example of having long periods of consecutive zeros is when you send uncompressed graphics or video. The best way to get around this is to insist on Bipolar 8-Zero Substitution (B8ZS) on all T1 facilities.

AMI, ZBTSI, or B8ZS

The Alternate Mark Inversion (AMI) signal is the original type of digital signal. Figure 2-1 shows an alternating mark inversion pattern of 1-bits. A zero or Space bit has zero voltage and only occupies a space in time. Alternating the Mark or 1-bits accomplishes several things. Too many pulses of a positive or

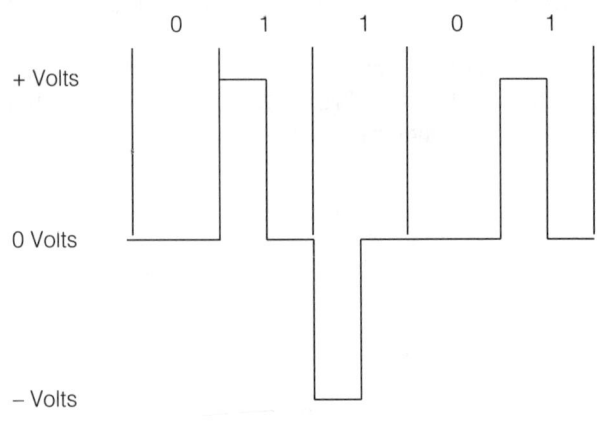

Fig. 2-1. Alternating mark inversion.

negative polarity produces an electrical voltage imbalance or difference. If this happens, a noise signal develops to degrade the transmission. By alternating the pulses, it neutralizes the average potential or voltage and reduces inter-symbol interference.

As you can see in FIG. 2-1, the only signals on the line are the 1-bits. Today, the trend is to transfer the ones-density rule by installing either Zero Byte Time Slot Interchange (ZBTSI) or B8ZS on the 1.5 Mb/s transmission lines.

The preferred method is B8ZS because it is a better system than the ZBTSI way. Zero Byte Time Slot Interchange was implemented in isolated areas in the country because it was expedient and economical at the time. The rationale was that individual telephone companies would spend less money in the short term. As a long-term investment, it was a loser. Nevertheless, ZBTSI adds additional delay, the out-of-frame alarm triggers quicker, the data link within the Extended Superframe Format (ESF) reduces to 2 Kb/s, and the signal cannot go through a Digital Access Cross-connect System (DACS). ANSI T1.403-1989 DS1 Metallic Interface covers ZBTSI if your network must go through an area that still has that method.

B8ZS is the recommended way to pass the responsibility of ones-density to the composite 1.5 Mb/s digital stream. Figure 2-2 shows the replacement code (Line B) for a string of eight consecutive zeros (Line A). For the sake of this example, only one code variation is shown. The other code depends on the polarity of the previous AMI pulse, which switches the pulses in polarity while maintaining alternating violation codes.

Your requested needs should include a statement that the provider of the equipment and transmission services use the B8ZS method of coding. It will be the standard in the future and it should be in your plans now.

| A | 0 | 0 | 0 | 0 | 0 | 0 | 0 | 0 |
| B | 0 | 0 | 0 | +1 | −1 | 0 | −1 | +1 |

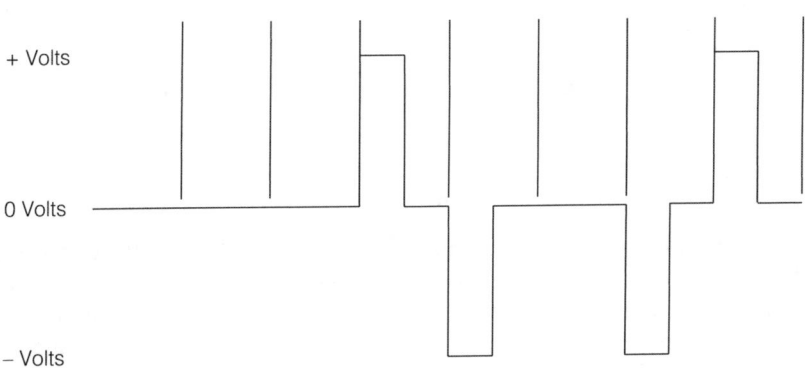

Fig. 2-2. Bipolar, 8-zero substitution.

Jitter

Each terminal has an internal clocking system but the frequency is based on the incoming signal, which feeds the receive data stream to a circuit called a phase-locked loop (PLL). The PLL circuit swings back and forth like a pendulum, averaging the frequency of the receive digital signal. How well the PLL performs is up to the individual designer. Simple changes in resistor and capacitor values alter the operation. Variations of the digital signal from its ideal position in time greater or equal to 10 Hz is jitter. Under 10 Hz, variations are called wander.

Jitter is a great concern in most digital systems. Digital networks, like Token Ring equipment, get a timing reference from the incoming pulses and then use this "recovered" clock to send the data out in the next span. Clock recovery is a task for the PLL because incoming data pulses do not have sharp rise times to their leading edge, but look more like an analog signal at this point. It is a guessing game for the equipment to decide the real location of the original pulse. Figure 2-3 depicts what happens to the transmitted pulses timed by a recovered clock. A digital signal is in the time domain; an analog signal is in the frequency domain. If the analog signal changes the time phase of the digital signal, there is jitter. The phase jitter moved the second pulse out of its normal or expected position. Pulse #4 has a phase shift greater than 50 percent of a Unit Interval and does not meet specifications.

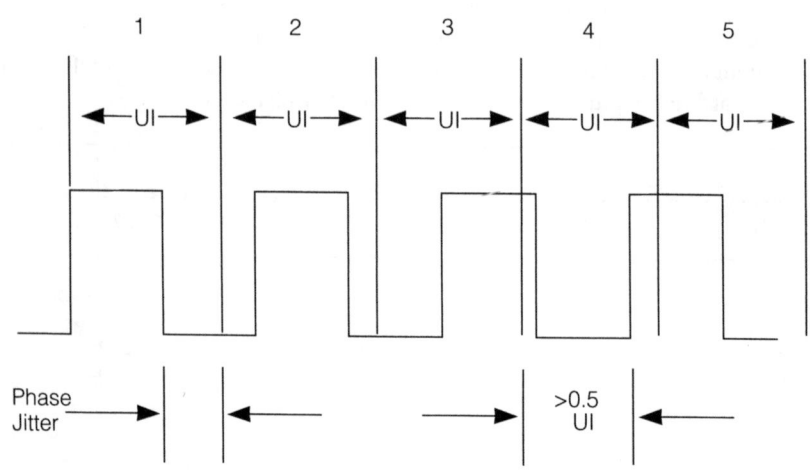

Fig. 2-3. Jitter effect.

When systems develop too much jitter, a unit called a *dejitterizer*, or a *JitterBuster*, is installed. A dejitterizer is a buffer that reads in data by the receive clock and reads out data with a new stable clock. The JitterBuster approach filters the analog influence. Nevertheless, your specifications for standards should include a statement about jitter tolerance.

ANSI T1.403-1989, Section 5.7.6, specifies the maximum permissible levels of jitter from the terminal equipment. Jitter must not exceed 0.5 Unit Intervals (UI) peak-to-peak (p-p) in the frequency range of 10 Hz to 40 kHz, and 0.07 UI p-p between 8 kHz to 40 kHz. Again, the last pulse in FIG. 2-3 is out greater than 0.5 UI and does not meet requirements.

T1 (DS1) signal format—D4 or ESF

For years, the T1 framing pattern was the D4 framing pattern named after a series of digital channel banks. This pattern is the same one as the framing pattern used for D2 to D5 channel banks. It has a simple bit sequence of 100011011100 and locates each frame pattern bit at the beginning of a 192-bit frame. The terms format, frame, and pattern tend to be combined as meaning the same thing. The following describes the correct meaning of format, frame, and pattern:

Format A contiguous sequence of bits or bytes formed serially in a periodic structure.

Frame One period of the format structure identified by a start (beginning) and stop (end) framing pattern bit. The stop bit of one frame is the start bit of the next frame in the T1 or DS1 frame.

Pattern A pattern is a sequence of bits that appear at the start-stop bit positions of the frame (one bit each time). In the D4 and Extended Superframe Format (ESF) patterns, every 193rd bit position belongs to a framing pattern bit. The CCITT frame pattern appears as an 8-bit byte in the first time slot of 32 frames.

If you went back and counted the frame bits for a D4 frame pattern, you'd see that it sends 12 frames before the pattern replicates. The ESF pattern is referred to as an extended pattern because it uses 24 frames before its pattern repeats. The difference between the two patterns is shown in TABLE 2-2.

Most offerings today, like SMDS, will specify using ESF because of its data-carrying capability and the CRC-6 error-detection code. The logical place for this activity is in the customer service unit (CSU) function. This could be either a separate unit or an internal CSU circuit. While some vendors continue to talk about a T-1 digital service unit (DSU) combined with the CSU, it is not correct unless they furnish clock leads and a nonstandard interface.

In addition to the error-detection and record-keeping capability of the CSU, there is a data link that transfers the error performance reports and alarms. One format uses a 14-octet packet to send performance information on a scheduled basis. ANSI T1.403-1989 describes the message structure (CCITT Q.9212/LAPD). The other format is an unscheduled message that uses 16-bit code words. Because unscheduled messages are alarms, they will preempt scheduled performance messages.

Although the 4 Kb/s data channel is an overkill for very short packets, telephone companies are reluctant to open it to vendors. It could have tremendous benefits for everyone, as proposed several years ago in *Guide to Integrating Digital Services*, McGraw-Hill.

Table 2-2.
Framing patterns.

Frame bit	D4	ESF
1	1	D
2	0	CRC1
3	0	D
4	0	0
5	1	D
6	1	CRC2
7	0	D
8	1	0
9	1	D
10	1	CRC3
11	0	D
12	0	1
13	1	D
14	0	CRC4
15	0	D
16	0	0
17	1	D
18	1	CRC5
19	0	D
20	1	0
21	1	D
22	1	CRC6
23	0	D
24	0	1

Where:
D = Data Bit
CRC = Cyclic Redundancy Check

Nevertheless, the ESF framing pattern has produced a robust digital system that is better than the D4 and CCITT versions. You should make this one of your absolute needs when you write your RFP or RFQ. A desired requirement for the CSU is an audible alarm that sounds when errored seconds exceed a preset point. Another desired feature is the ability to connect the CSU to network management equipment to centralize the alarm activity.

Error performance

Bellcore TR-TSY-000499, Transport Systems Generic Requirements, specifies the maximum error performance a vendor's transport equipment can introduce. Before getting into that specification, you should know that digital signal transmission is perfect for long periods and then there are bursts of errors. Analog signal transmission has random bit errors distributed over a long period. Consequently, the error performance for digital transmission uses a burst of errors in a given, one-second time frame.

Understanding the terminology used with the various standards or technical references is confusing. Another term used with digital transmission is *burst errored second*, which is any one-second interval that has at least 100 bits in error. If you measured 99 bits in error during the one-second interval, it is just a bit error ratio (BER). One more bit in error and it is a burst errored second.

Bellcore also specifies that burst errored seconds average no more than 100 per day and that a long-term percentage should not be greater than 0.75 percent. They expect to see something better than a 10^{-9} (excluding burst errored seconds) on fiberoptic services like SMDS during the measurement period. This says the BER is between a 10^{-9} and 10^{-10} error performance. Remember that services like SMDS are designed around switching nodes with a probable facility limit of 125 miles. Long-haul, 1.5-Mb services support a lower number because of the distance and equipment involved with the service. It is reasonable to expect an error performance of 10^{-8} or a 98.5 percent error-free second (EFS) on 1.5-Mb facilities under 1,000 miles. Figure 2-4 shows the correlation between BER and EFS error performance for 1.5 Mb and 45 Mb digital rates.

The vertical axis is the percent of error-free seconds; the horizontal axis is 1 bit error out of 10^{-x} bits sent (i.e., $1/10^{-x}$ Bits). Typical BER values are 10^{-6}, 10^{-7}, or 10^{-8}, which means 1 bit error in 1 million, 10 million, or 100 million bits sent. If you look at the 10^{-9} BER vertical line, you see it intersects with a

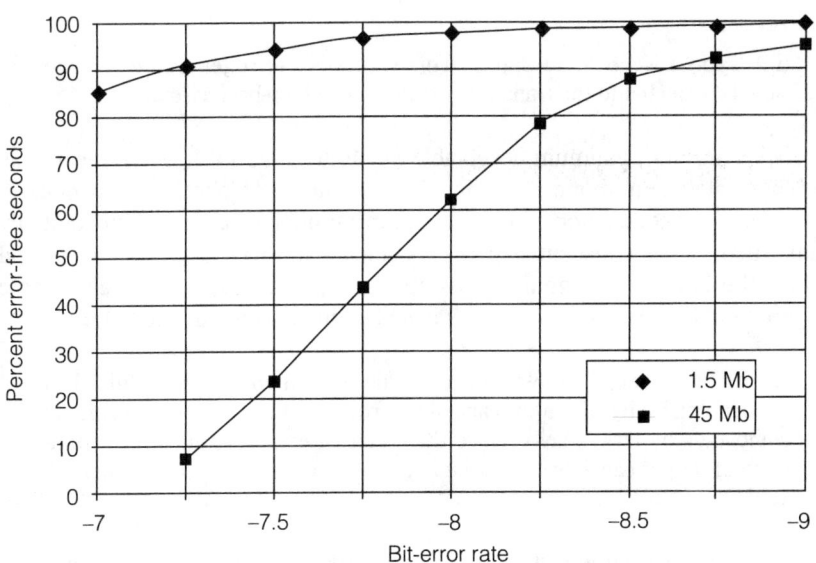

Fig. 2-4. Bit error performance versus percent error-free second.

horizontal line better than 99 percent EFS for the 1.5 Mb rate and 95 percent for 45 Mb. Going back the other way, you can trace a 95 percent EFS and see that it approximates a $10^{-7.5}$ BER for the 1.5 Mb and 10^{-9} for the 45 Mb rate.

It is important to note that error-free-second rates exhibit different bit-error rates for the various digital speeds. A 99.5 percent EFS for a 56 Kb rate is not better than a 92 percent EFS rate for 1.5 Mb.

Continuity of output signal

Continuity of the output signal indicates that there must be a ones-density and a keep-alive signal. The following excerpts from the Federal Communications Commission, *Code of Federal Regulations (CFR)*, Title 47, Part 68, Section .318 (the Federal Register cites this as 47 CFR 68.318) and defines continuity of output signal as:

The minimum acceptable pulse density is 0.125. The maximum acceptable length of a continuous sequence of 'zeros' is 80 pulse positions. The keep-alive signal inserted when the pulse density drops too low shall be one of the following:

(i) Type 1 Keep Alive Signal. This signal is a consecutive sequence of all 'ones'.

(ii) Type 2 Keep Alive Signal. This signal is a sequence of 193-bit frames consisting of a framing bit plus 192-bit sequence of consecutive 'ones'. The framing bit executes the following repetitive pattern every 12 frames:

100011011100

(iii) Type 3 Keep Alive Signal. This signal is the regenerated receive signal connected to the transmit port through a loop-back circuit.

Note that the minimum acceptable pulse density of 0.125 is the same as Bellcore's statement that a good signal had to have 12.5 percent pulse density. However, the requirement for a maximum number of zeros is substantially higher than the 15 consecutive zeros specified elsewhere. This allows a period before the keep-alive signal is introduced. The FCC paragraph also has a requirement for 1.544 Mb/s services installed up to December 18, 1992:

As of December 18, 1989 such terminal equipment is not required to contain continuity of output capability, provided, however, that telephone companies by tariff may require that such equipment contain the continuity of output capability described in this paragraph up to December 18, 1992.

While not explained, it appears that after December 18, 1992, all new installations must have B8ZS to maintain the pulse density.

DS-3 or 45 Mb/s digital service

Digital Signal Level-3 is fast becoming a service of choice for the mid and large networks. The amount of bandwidth is surprisingly inexpensive in comparison to an equivalent number of T1 lines. Usually, the crossover point is around 5 to 7 T1 lines. Services like AT&T's Accunet T45 Service and Bellcore's planned SONET and SMDS services are just a couple of examples using DS-3 signals.

There has been a major rethinking about the structure of DS-3 in how to format the frame. A problem with the older version of DS-3 is that you cannot separate individual circuits without breaking it down into DS-1 signals. The basic DS-3 signal is a bit-interleaved signal that makes it difficult to take apart at some point in the middle without an embedded operating system. Both SONET and SMDS-type services rely on the capability of rearranging parts of the DS-3 signal without going through several layers of demultiplexing (i.e., DS-3 to DS-2 to DS-1). Bellcore TR-TSY-000499, Transport Systems Generic Requirements, and ANSI T1.404-1989, Carrier to Customer Installation, are two good standard DS-3 signal references. The newer format, called the Physical Layer Convergence Procedure, should appear as Bellcore TR-TSY-000773 after the final agreement on the technical advisory and in IEEE 802.6 DQDB subnetwork of a Metropolitan Area Network (MAN).

Voiceband applications

The following is a list of standards and references for voiceband applications. Because the voiceband and analog requirements are so diverse in levels and signaling, you must rely on the references for assistance. However, you shouldn't get into deep trouble with a subject that is as old as this. Other than the rules for ISDN, there have been few changes to voiceband in the past 50 years. Your specifications should note the various standards and that all services and equipment must meet the transmission levels, bandwidth, and signaling requirements.

- ANSI/EIA/TIA - 464A Private Branch Exchange (PBX) Switching Equipment for Voiceband Applications.

- 47 Code of Federal Regulations, Part 68 — Connection of Terminal Equipment to the Telephone Network.

- ANSI/EIA - 470-A-87 Telephone Instruments with Loop Signaling.

- EIA-478 Multi-line Key Telephone Systems (KTS) for Voiceband Applications.

- Bellcore Technical References (Catalog # SR-NWT-000264).

- AT&T Technical References (PUB):
  10000 Catalog of Communications Technical Publications

43202 Analog Voice-Total and Coordinated Services
41004 Data Communications Using Voiceband Private Line Channels
41009 Transmission Parameters Affecting Voiceband Data

Summary

To make sure you have a better than even chance of connecting a working multi-vendor network, you must lean heavily on existing standards and technical references. Standards do change and what was a rose yesterday might not be a rose today. For example, the vendor's continued use of EIA RS-232C interfaces when the standard is now up to EIA-232E. It is either a case of the vendor not being aware of changing times or not knowing any better.

Analog transmission is forgiving while digital requires strict adherence to timing and jitter requirements. Don't take on the problem of more than one timing source for digital networks. It will not function properly.

3

Interface & cable requirements

Some of the basic data interfaces have recently undergone major changes. While all standards play a big part in your planning process, it is important to fully understand all your interface requirements, because these present the biggest problem to a successful installation. Therefore, it is imperative that they represent a large part of your planning.

The Electronic/Telecommunication Industries Association EIA/TIA and the Institute of Electrical and Electronic Engineers (IEEE) provides most engineering standards for telecommunication equipment used in the United States. The American National Standard Institute (ANSI), in turn, validates that the document is sound and does not conflict with other standards. Over the years, terminology has changed to reflect international standards, but the International Electrotechnical Commission (IEC) activity has not progressed far enough to make a comparison between documents. While the purpose of standards is to reduce problems when connecting multi-vendor products, the EIA/TIA also recognizes that vendors might stray by issuing the following caveat.

> Existence of such Standards and Publications shall not in any respect preclude any member or nonmember of EIA/TIA from manufacturing or selling products not conforming to such Standards and Publications, nor shall the existence of such Standards and Publications preclude their voluntary use by those other than EIA/TIA members, whether the standard is to be used either domestically or internationally.

As mentioned in chapter 1, vendors do take liberty with interpreting standards. The preceding EIA/TIA statement is a good example that the industry does recognize the inability to control vendors from making unilateral decisions. One possible interface configuration shown in EIA-232-E is the Z interface type, which allows the vendor to specify any circuit except the signal common ground. Your task in the selection process is to find what the individual vendors did that was different from the accepted norm.

Data interfaces

EIA/TIA-232E interface (25 pins)

In July 1991, the basic EIA-232 standard was revised to accomplish several things. One was to eliminate the EIA-232D (a 9-pin interface) standard because there was widespread misunderstanding that it was a replacement for the older EIA RS-232C. Its origination stemmed from the telecommunication industry using a smaller interface that had the same electrical characteristics as EIA-232. The replacement standard for the 9-pin interface is ANSI/EIA/TIA-574-1990, or just EIA-574 for short.

The other major revision with EIA-232E is the introduction of a smaller interface called EIA-232E Alt A—a 26-pin interface. This interface could well become the interface of the future because it is similar than the 9-pin interface but has more capability.

EIA-232-type interfaces have a data speed limitation of up to 20 kilobits per second (Kb/s). For data speeds over 20 Kb/s, it is recommended that the standards EIA-530 (a replacement for EIA-449), EIA-561 (8-position miniature or RJ-45 type), and the EIA-574 (9-pin replacement for EIA-232D) interface be used.

Over the years, the EIA-232 standard showed a male interface for data terminal equipment (DTE) and a female connector for data communication equipment (DCE). Figure 3-1 depicts the usual graphics used in literature to show male and female interface connectors. Don't trust that the vendor has followed the normal convention strictly by their graphics. You need to verify everything.

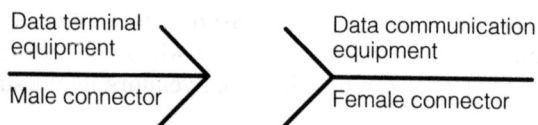

Data terminal equipment
Male connector

Data communication equipment
Female connector

Fig. 3-1. Connector graphics.

Vendors often stray from the conventions used for the gender of the interface. It is simply a matter of economics to stock only one type of interface instead of two. We included the pin numbers for the EIA-232 female jack (FIG. 3-2) because it is a near impossibility to read them on the connector. The male connector's numbers run in a left to right direction.

The two-gender convention remains for the EIA-232E 25-pin interface, but goes away with the Alt A 26-pin connector. The EIA-232-E Alt A connector is female for both the terminal and communication equipment, and the cable has

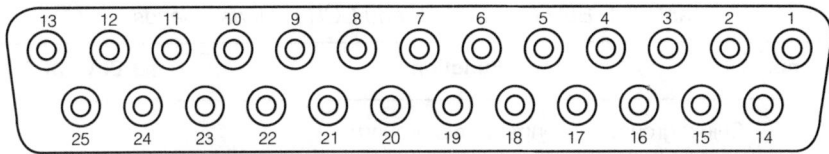

Fig. 3-2. EIA-232E data communication equipment interface (female).

male connectors on both ends. This is a very logical approach that, hopefully, is the direction for all future standards. It does not make any sense to have three different types of cables when one would suffice. Also, it eliminates the guessing game of what gender the connector is.

While the EIA-232 series describes the physical characteristics of the interface, EIA-334A specifies signal quality for synchronous systems and EIA-363 for nonsynchronous systems. The transmitted data must be between 5 and 15 volts when measured over a test load of 3000 to 7000 ohms, and the received data must be between 3 and 15 volts. An open-circuit voltage on the transmitter cannot exceed 25 volts with respect to signal ground. The other notable thing about the electrical signal is the rise and fall time of the signal that sets it apart from other interfaces.

TABLE 3-1 lists all the circuits associated with EIA-232E and Alt A interfaces. Over the years, the EIA tagged the various circuits with letter designations. Meanwhile, the CCITT used a three-digit code. The trend today, as true international standards are developed, is toward the CCITT nomenclature. Note that your particular network will not use all these leads. Some are very specialized for modems that are rate-selectable, used with switched services, or have external timing. A brief description of the various interface circuits follows. See the actual EIA standard for a detailed description.

102 signal common: This is the common ground return for all other circuits. It normally connects to the protective ground of the equipment, but sometimes it is not for design reasons. In these cases, it will have an impedance connected between the two to provide a path for static discharge. Chapter 4 on electrical and safety standards covers static discharge.

103 transmitted data: For many years, this circuit was called *send data*. It is the data stream from the terminal toward the communication's equipment. If the terminal is in an idle mode (i.e., not sending data), it has to send steady marks or negative voltage signals.

104 received data: This is the data from the DCE toward the terminal. It also is held to a steady marking when nothing is received from the other end.

105 request-to-send: This circuit alerts the DCE that the terminal wants to send data. A multi-point network will have a permanent request to send at the local end and use switched (i.e., ON—OFF) at the remote ends.

Table 3-1. EIA/TIA - 232 - E and CCITT interface leads.

Pin no.	Function	EIA	CCITT
1	Shield ground (no longer frame ground)	-	-
2	Transmitted data	BA	103
3	Receive data	BB	104
4	Request-to-send (CA) - Ready for receiving (CJ) (Note: When hardware flow control is needed, the CA may have the function of CJ)	CA CJ	105 133
5	Clear to send	CB	106
6	DCE ready	CC	107
7	Signal common	AB	102
8	Receive line signal detector	CF	109
9	Reserved for testing (usually + volts)	-	-
10	Reserved for testing (usually – volts)	-	-
11	CCITT select transmit frequency	-	126
12	Secondary received signal detector (SCF) DCE data signal rate selector (CI) (Note: If SCF is used, then CI is assigned to pin 23 (CH)).	SCF CI	122 112
13	Secondary clear to send	SCB	121
14	Secondary transmit data	SBA	118
15	Transmitter signal element timing (DCE source)	DB	114
16	Secondary receive data	SBB	119
17	Receiver signal element timing (DCE source)	DD	115
18	Local loopback	LL	141
19	Secondary request to send	SCA	120
20	DTE ready	CD	108/1 108/2
21	Remote loopback (RL) Signal quality detector (CG) (The use of CG is no longer recommended)	RL CG	140 110
22	Ring indicator	CE	125
23	Data signal rate selector (DTE\DCE source) (Note: See pin 12 for CI usage)	CH CI	111 112
24	Transmit signal element timing (DTE source)	DA	113
25	Test mode	TM	142
26	No connection on EIA-232 ALT A interface	-	-

Source from ANSI/EIA/TIA - 232-E-1991

106 clear-to-send: If everything in the communication path is operational, the DCE will normally provide an indication to the terminal that it is alright to send data.

107 DCE ready: While this seems like circuit 106, it tells the terminal that the DCE is alive and is ready for transmission or testing.

108 DTE ready: This is normally only used with switched services. When an incoming call activates the ring indicator circuit, the terminal responds with an on condition to indicate it is ready to receive data and to answer the telephone call.

109 Received line signal detector: Old-time data people still call this lead *carrier detect*. It tells the terminal that it is receiving a carrier signal and that, at least, the receive side of the circuit is still working.

110 Signal quality detector: No longer recommended. This attempted to evaluate the quality of the signal and indicate that errors were likely. Newer modems automatically shift speeds when the error rate goes up instead of notifying the terminal it is having trouble with errors. Circuit 112 replaces this function.

111 Data signal rate selector (DTE source): Used to select multiple rate synchronous DCE data speeds. Because it has only two states of on or off, it can tell only two speeds or ranges of rates.

112 Data signal rate selector (DCE source): This is the reverse of circuit 111 in that the DCE tells the DTE what data speed or ranges it is receiving.

113 Transmitter signal element timing (DTE source): Another name for this circuit is external timing. It is a better name because it reduces the confusion to circuit 114. It is normally used only with tail circuits off another modem or multiplexer and is never used with digital services.

114 Transmitter signal element timing (DCE source): The normal transmit clocking that tells the terminal when the DCE expects to see signal transitions.

115 Receiver signal element timing (DCE source): Using the terms *receive clock* or *timing* seemed much easier. It is the recovered clock developed in the DCE that allows the DTE to gate the incoming data.

118 Secondary transmitted data: Information on this circuit is the send data for secondary channels (i.e., the DCE transmits another data stream under or over the main modulation). It is usually used for network and maintenance control systems.

119 Secondary received data: Data on this circuit is the information coming back on the secondary channel.

121 Secondary clear-to-send: This tells the DTE it is all right to send on the secondary channel.

122 Secondary received line signal detector: This tells the DTE that the receiving secondary channel is functioning.

125 Ring indicator: A ring indicator is needed only with switched services. The normal 20 Hz ring current on the telephone line triggers the indicator circuit, which, in turn, tells the terminal a call is coming in.

126 Select transmit frequency: Only found in the international ISO 2110 standard, it is not used with EIA standards.

140 Remote loopback: Used to control a loopback in the distant or remote DCE. Activating this lead causes the local DCE to send a special code to the distant end to make a loopback.

141 Local loopback: This causes the local DCE to loopback its final transmit section to its first receive section. Local loopback also serves as the old "busy out" used in switched services to take circuits out of service.

142 test mode: When either the local or remote loopback activates, this circuit tells the terminal that the DCE equipment is in a test mode and that it cannot send information.

EIA/TIA-232E Alt A interface (26 pins)

While the confusion about the EIA-232D is cleared up, the standards committee also did everyone a service by initiating the Alt A. The Alt A answers the industry's desire for a smaller interface while maintaining the electrical characteristics of existing circuits. Figure 3-3 shows the size and pattern of two in-line rows of 13 contacts. The size difference between the old EIA-232D and the new Alt A is an increase in length and a reduction in width of approximately 7/64 inch in each dimension.

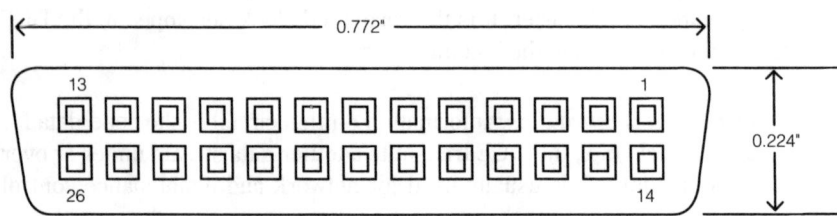

Fig. 3-3. EIA-232E ALT A data equipment interface.

EIA/TIA-574 interface (replaces EIA-232D)

The EIA/TIA-574 interface replaces the EIA-232D reference but, in a sense, it creates a new 9-pin connector. It is no longer electrically compatible to the older EIA-232D that used basic 5- to 15-volt transmit signals and was limited to under 20 Kb/s data speeds. The newer 9-pin interface is capable of faster data speeds and is driven from a ±5 volt supply. What is interesting is that they kept the same conventions of the female (FIG. 3-4) for the DCE, and the male (FIG. 3-5) for the DTE. TABLE 3-4 lists the various circuits available on this interface. See the definitions under EIA-232E for a description of the circuits.

Fig. 3-4. EIA/TIA-574 data communication equipment interface (female).

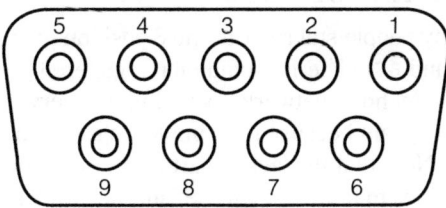

Fig. 3-5. EIA/TIA-574 data terminal equipment interface (male).

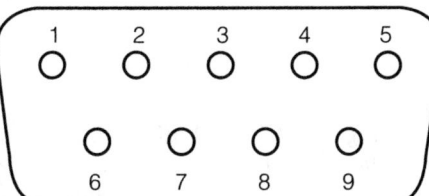

Table 3-2. EIA/TIA - 574 interface (9-pin replacement for EIA-232D)

Contact number	CCITT circuit	EIA/TIA - 574 designation	Transmit towards DTE DCE
1	109	Receive line signal detector	◄ - - - - -
2	104	Receive data	◄ - - - - -
3	103	Transmit data	- - - - - ►
4	108/2	DTE ready	- - - - - ►
5	102	Signal common	- - - - - ►
6	107	DCE ready	◄ - - - - -
7	105	Request to send	
	133	Ready for receiving (Note: Circuit 105 may take on the role of Circuit 133 if hardware flow control is needed)	- - - - - ►
8	106	Clear to send	◄ - - - - -
9	125	Ring indicator	◄ - - - - -

Source ANSI/EIA/TIA - 574 - 1990

Remember, the EIA-574 connector cannot work with the older EIA-232-D interface because the voltages and rise times are different. You should be certain which 9-pin connector the vendor is offering. It makes sense to request the EIA-574 interface because it can operate at higher data rates and has lower power requirements.

EIA/TIA-561 interface (8-pin)

Many people still refer to the 8-position plug and jack as *RJ-45 connectors* (FIGS. 3-6 and 3-7). The RJ stands for registered jack and had greater meaning when the telephone network opened up to everyone. It will probably stick around for many years because it is simpler to say than EIA-561 interface.

Note that the jack is part of the equipment, and the plug or male connector attaches to both ends of the interface cables. While eliminating some confusion about the gender of the interfaces, the connectors find their way into totally different services. TABLE 3-3 lists just three of the possible types that use the 8-

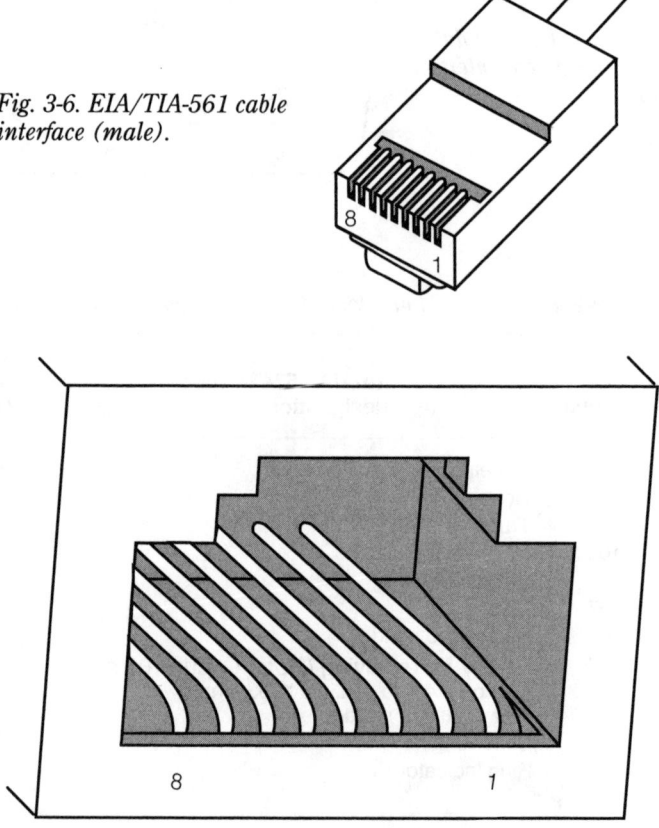

Fig. 3-6. EIA/TIA-561 cable interface (male).

Fig. 3-7. EIA/TIA-561 equipment interface (female).

Table 3-3. EIA 561 interface (8-position RJ-45 type).

Contact number	EIA/TIA - 561 designation	10 Base-T (UTP) designation	T1 designation
1	Ring indicator	+ Receive data	Transmit (ring)
2	Receive line signal detector	– Receive data	Unassigned
3	DTE ready	+ Transmit data	Unassigned
4	Signal common	Unassigned	Receive (ring)
5	Receive data	Unassigned	Receive (tip)
6	Transmit data	– Transmit data	Unassigned
7	Clear to send	Unassigned	Unassigned
8	Request to send Ready for receiving	Unassigned	Transmit (tip)

pin connectors. It is easy to see that the pin assignments are different, but might not be obvious that the electrical characteristics are also different.

ANSI/ EIA-530-1987 interface (25-pin replacement for EIA 449)

The EIA-530 is the answer to the complaints about the large size of the old EIA RS-449 37-pin interface while retaining the frequency spectrum of up to 2 Mb/s. Just when the world was moving toward miniaturization, the EIA RS-449 was introduced. AT&T was one of the very few companies that used this interface with their DATAPHONE II series of modems.

Today, the EIA-530 interface uses the same mechanical size connector as the EIA-232 (FIG. 3-2), but uses EIA-422A balanced voltages or EIA-423A unbalanced voltages. While physically possible to connect an EIA-530 to an EIA-232, they are not compatible. TABLE 3-4 describes the pin designations for the EIA-530 interface, and TABLE 3-1 covers EIA-232E. In addition to not having the same lead designations, the voltages are different. When using the balance voltages, the leads marked A and B are used with each corresponding circuit. If you use the unbalanced, your interface will be only the leads marked with the letter A and the common signal ground lead.

V.35-type interface

Some vendors mislabel the V.35-type interface by calling it a CCITT V.35 interface. It is a combination of V.35 and EIA-232 and is not a true CCITT V.35 connector. All the data and timing leads adhere to the V.35 specifications (balanced circuits) and low voltages. However, all the control leads are EIA-232 voltages (unbalanced). Some vendors have included CCITT leads in their descriptions of V.35, but they are not used with 56 Kb/s DDS. Things like external transmit timing, loopbacks, DTE ready, and test mode are not available.

Table 3-4. EIA/TIA - 530 replacement for EIA-449 interface.

EIA 530 Pin no.	EIA 530 function	EIA RS-449 equivalent pin
1	Shield	—
2	Transmitted data A	SD-4
3	Receive data A	RD-6
4	Request-to-send A	RS-7
5	Clear to send A	CS-9
6	CDE ready A	DM-11
7	Signal ground	SG-19
8	Receive line signal detector A	RR-13
9	Receive signal element timing B (DCE source)	RT-26
10	Received line signal detector B	RR-31
11	Transmit signal element timing B (DTE source)	TT-35
12	Transmitter signal element timing B (DCE)	ST-23
13	Clear to send B	CS-27
14	Transmitted data B	SD-22
15	Transmitter signal element timing A (DCE)	ST-5
16	Received data B	RD-24
17	Receiver signal element timing A (DCE source)	RT-8
18	Local loopback	LL-10
19	Request to send B	RS-25
20	DTE ready A	TR-12
21	Remote loopback	RL-14
22	DCE ready B	DM-29
23	DTE ready B	TR-30
24	Transmit signal element timing A (DTE source)	TT-17
25	Test mode	TM-18

Figure 3-8 shows a male connector and the letter positions. Note that the actual CCITT V.35-type functions are on the right-hand side and the EIA-232 functions are on the left. TABLE 3-5 lists the lead functions. While there are separate transmit and receive timing leads, they are actually tied together internally in the DCE. It would be reasonable to expect this type of interface to disappear in the future because of the size, cost, and newer high-data speed interfaces.

Voice interfaces

Telephone interface

Telephone equipment connectors are mini-modular 4-and 6-pin registered jacks (RJ-11 and RJ-12 respectively), and the connecting cables have the male plugs on each end. Because most telephone operations are only two-wire

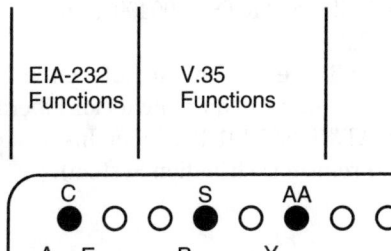

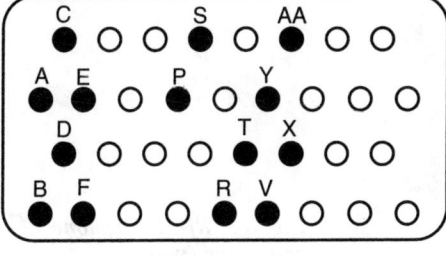

Fig. 3-8. V.35-type male connector (56 Kb/s DDS service).

Table 3-5. V.35 type
interface for 56kb/s DDS.

Pin letter	V.35 interface
A	Protective ground
B	Signal common
C	Request to send
D	Clear to send
E	DCE ready
F	Received line signal detector
P, S	Transmitted data
R, T	Receive data
V, X	Receiver signal element timing
Y, AA	Transmitter signal element timing

devices, some connectors might have only four contacts (contacts 1 and 6 are missing). Four is an overkill for a two-wire operation, but is correct for a four-wire device. Figure 3-9 shows the pin positions for the male RJ-12 connector.

Cabling standards

When it comes to fiberoptic cabling, there are many standards to rely on. The following standards and technical references are just a few of the documents that you can look to for help:

- ANSI/EIA-455 & 472 series of standards covers just about everything you ever wanted to learn about fiberoptic cabling.
- ANSI/IEEE 812-1984 defines the terms relating to fiberoptics.

- Bellcore TR-TSY-000409 Generic Requirements for Intrabuilding Fiber Cable.
- Bellcore Technical Reference TR-TSY-000418 Generic Reliability Assurance Requirements for Fiberoptic Transport Systems.
- AT&T 555-401-102 Fiber Installation Manual (how to install fiber in a Premise Distribution System).

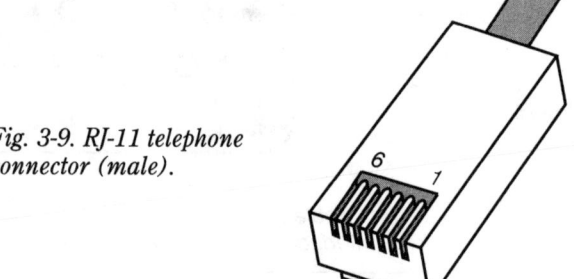

Fig. 3-9. RJ-11 telephone connector (male).

Fiber has many advantages, but the expertise needed to install it and the need for straight runs are its two drawbacks. Even minor turns in a fiber cable cause more light to be lost, and you will lose power from your total light budget. Figure 3-10 shows a straight section of fiber and one with a bend in it. Angle C is the critical angle that the light or optical beam will still bounce off the cladding, almost like a mirror. Because the cladding is not reflective but refractive, however, there is a minute amount of light loss. When the critical angle is reduced because of a bend in the fiber, there is a greater loss of light in the cladding.

The IEEE 10-Base F working group approved implementing 62.5 micron glass fiber for Ethernet (IEEE-802 Standard). This standard breaks down into three subcategories. A link standard (10-Base FL) is for up to 2 km and is used for connecting terminals or repeaters. The backbone standard (10-Base FB) relies on a synchronous clock and allows cascading of up to 15 repeaters. The last category is the passive standard (10-Base FP), which provides connections between passive hubs and workstations or PC interface cards. As the cost of fiber products decrease, this new standard might become cost-effective as compared to twisted-pair cabling.

Twisted-pair cabling

Shielded (STP) and unshielded (UTP) twisted-pair wires are, by far, the most popular because of installation ease and cost in comparison to fiber and coaxial cable. Just when great strides were made in the Fiber Distributed Data Interface (ANSI X3.166-1990), various vendors made equally great strides in pushing the

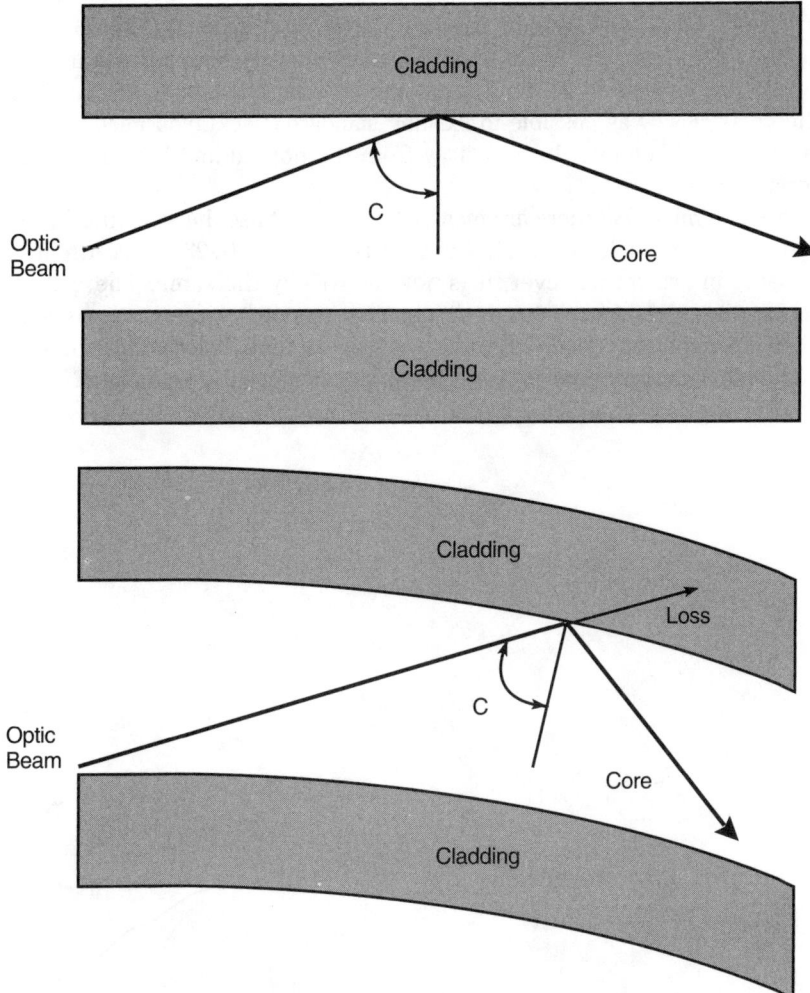

Fig. 3-10. Light loss in fiberoptic cable.

limits of twisted-pair wires. The only stipulation of using UTP wiring is that wiring runs be no greater than recommended. Also, you must avoid running wires in the same cable ducts as high-power cables and other noise-generating cables. If you cannot avoid noisy areas, then you need to use shielded, twisted-pair cabling. Two other standards you might want to review are:

- ANSI/IEEE 802.5-1989 LAN: *Token Ring Access Method and Physical Layer Specifications.*
- ANSI T1.102-1987 *Telecommunications-Digital Hierarchy-Electrical Interfaces.*

Summary

There are standards and references for just about everything you can think of. Your first goal is specifying that the equipment that you need in your network adheres as closely as possible to existing standards. Next, you need to verify that individual vendors did not stray from the normal and include strange interface leads.

Keep in mind that there are many interfaces that use the same mechanical interface. For example, an EIA-574 can replace an old EIA-232D because it fits the same interface, however, it is not electrically the same. The EIA-561 interface fits at least four distinctly different type services. If there is a possibility of having similar interfaces and different type services, color coding or some other method is required to prevent connecting incompatible equipment.

4

Electrical & safety requirements

Some of the most important planning requirements are electrical and safety ones. While the reasons for some might seem as if they could only occur during a stampede of elephants through an eye of a needle, you must make sure that no one gets hurt during the stampede. It is like using seat belts, you never really need them until the moment you have an accident.

Over the years, both AT&T and Bellcore have made extensive safety and harm tests on any product they planned to put into a customer's location. Things like checking to see what happens if 220V crosses over to the interface leads in a cable run. One of the tests they make is to connect all the leads, other than ground connections, and then connect a power supply between the leads and the ground lead. They start with a low voltage and increase it until something happens. They know a high voltage will destroy an interface that only expects 5 to 15V on the leads. The test checks to see that it does not catch fire or emit toxic fumes as it smolders or burns. Neither possibility is a good thing to happen—on their own property or on someone else's.

In many countries, the equipment connected to various telephone networks must pass certification testing. Whereas, equipment behind the ones connected to the telephone network does not have to meet any standard. Therefore, these are the ones that are the weak links in your network and demand greater attention.

When you write an RFP or RFQ, you need to specify these standards as an absolute requirement. If the vendor has not taken the trouble to test their equipment for safety and electrical standards, then you have every reason to eliminate them from further review.

The rest of this chapter will first cover the reason for a particular standard and then either go over the actual standard, or refer you to the standard if it is lengthy. Appendix A lists the locations where you can obtain copies of the various standards. The standards are divided into two groups—electrical and environmental.

Electrical

Electromagnetic interference

Radio frequency (RF) interference is a two-way street. Outside sources can interfere with the electronic equipment or the equipment itself can generate RF signals. Either way, it is not desirable. Power tools usually generate static when sparks jump between the brushes and the rotor. You do not want your equipment to be erratic if a vacuum cleaner or power tool comes near it. On the other hand, you do not want your equipment radiating your information to the world, or interfering with your other equipment.

Electrostatic discharge

Static builds up on individuals, whether it is from walking across carpeting or just shifting around in their chair. You have experienced this when you walk across the room and touched something. There is a zap sound and a sharp pain as 5–15,000 volts cross between you and ground. Experienced technicians always ground themselves before working on any equipment. On the other hand, non-technical people do not think about the possible damage from electrostatic discharge and touch or grab things without concern. Had that person built up a static charge, there is a good chance he could discharge the potential to a piece of equipment. If the equipment does not provide a shunt for this voltage to ground, it can destroy components as it seeks a path to ground. It *will* find ground in some way.

Lightning protection

When your network connects to metallic facilities, you run the risk of a lightning surge wiping out your equipment. Don't overlook the fact that some fiberoptic cables include a metallic runner or have metallic facilities collocated in the same sheath. There is also the risk of lightning running through the regular electric service if it hit the electric line entering your building. Therefore, the alternating current side of the unit should be protected as well as the telecommunication line connector.

Potential differences

A grounding system should minimize the possibility of a voltage difference between the particular unit and other units connected to it. Sometimes, the electronic gear is designed to use an isolated ground where it does not connect to the enclosure and earth ground. Another term for this is *floating ground*. If there is a slight potential difference between one unit and another object, a person would feel a tingle when they touched both objects. While the amount of current and voltage is usually not significant enough to cause harm, a person's reaction might result in an injury. Another cause of concern is the possible noise currents between ground planes, which cause interference.

Power supplies

Most vendors use another company's power supply instead of building their own. It is simpler to purchase rectifiers that passed an Underwriters Laboratories (UL) inspection than to build their own. Just because a unit has a UL sticker near the power supply does not mean the entire unit was tested.

Power supplies are often the part of the total equipment with the shortest expected life. Usually, units are rated at 50,000 hours for the average failure. This does not mean that all devices will last that long. Instead, you can expect 63 percent will fail in that period. If you select equipment with a low-wattage power supply, it might be working at its peak and generate excessive heat. Heat will take its toll and hasten the end of the unit. Using a power supply that is rated twice the actual needs of the equipment will produce little heat and have a longer life.

Environmental
Flammability

A vendor should provide evidence that they performed tests on their equipment to guarantee it will not burst into flames. A vendor will not know this unless they have made destructive tests, such as a lightning surge or other high-power test on the interfaces. While it is expected that components will be destroyed during such a test, they should not catch on fire or cause the rest of the equipment to burn.

Noxious fumes

When components undergo a destructive test where components melt or smolder without bursting into flame, it is likely they will emit some fumes. It is important that these fumes not be noxious or cause harm in any way.

Temperature and humidity

Both AT&T and Bellcore specify a wide range of temperatures for all their equipment. However, equipment will sometimes end up in a harsh environment where it must work in extreme temperatures. Nevertheless, you should expect that all equipment function in a 40–100 degrees (4°C–38°C) temperature range and in a relative humidity range of 20 to 80 percent. Equipment that only operates in a limited range between 70–90 degrees and a controlled humidity level requires a special air-conditioned environment.

Acoustic noise

The last thing you want next to your desk is a device that sounds like a wind tunnel. Not only will you have difficulty talking, but by the end of the day, your stress level will peak to an all-time high. Also, the equipment should not emit any high-pitched sounds that have the same stressful capability.

Other needs

Rounding out electrical and safety needs are the practical ones. Check to see that equipment does not have any sharp edges that a person can catch their clothes on or cut themselves. If the item is portable, it should not take a strong person to move it from one place to another.

One test that found its way into the FCC Part 68 registration program was an offshoot of telephone company policy. This test requires dropping the equipment from different heights, depending on the weight and how the equipment is used. While this seems a little vague as to its value, it does make sense. Just consider that anything that can move can also drop on the floor. Component parts (e.g., fuse holders) that project past the side of a surface, will pop right into the equipment when dropped on that particular face. The unit also should have adequate protection in a package because a drop or rough handling during shipping will cause damage.

One well-known data switch manufacturer changed their design of an A-B switch after showing them that a 3-inch drop popped the covers off the unit. This type of equipment should have withstood six random drops from a height of 30 inches. It is reasonable to expect equipment to fail under unusually harsh punishment, but it should not break apart if inadvertently dropped. AT&T and Bellcore take this type of testing another step and test the units in their normal packaging. Not all shippers handle packages or crates with tender loving care, and AT&T and Bellcore want to receive working units. After it gets to the telephone companies (telcos), they are concerned about equipment bouncing around in the back of the installer's truck. By making drop tests of the packaged unit, they are able to find out if the unit will survive rough handling. When testing discovers poor packaging, the vendor has a choice of changing their packaging or not selling to the telcos.

One last thing about packaging. Electronic equipment requires special handling to prevent static electricity from wiping out circuitry. Material such as the white plastic "peanuts" generate static electricity. Individual circuit boards should have special electrostatic protection bags to prevent damage. The boards should only be taken out of the bags when they are ready to be installed and after you have grounded your body to remove any static electricity. Be sure to save several bags in case you must return items. Always place circuit boards in electrostatic protection bags even if the board is defective. This prevents the circuit board from acquiring another trouble before the vendor tries to fix the unit.

Standards

Electromagnetic interference

Electromagnetic interference is radio frequency radiating emissions either from, or to, a piece of electronic equipment. The concern is that a piece of electronic gear might interfere with a nearby radio transmitter or that it might not function properly if a power tool is in proximity. Because of these emissions, the Federal Communications Commission (FCC) Rules, Part 15 of Chapter 1 of Title 47 of the Code of Federal Regulations, specifies the limits for Class A and Class B digital devices. The FCC defines a digital device in the following way:

> A digital device is an unintentional radiator (device or system) that generates and uses timing signals or pulses at a rate in excess of 9000 pulses (cycles) per second and uses digital techniques . . . for the purpose of performing data processing functions . . .

Class A digital devices are those used in commercial, industrial, or the business environment and are not sold to be used in the home or used by the general public. Class B devices, such as personal computers, have a market for both the home and the business environment. The main differences between the two classes are the emissions levels and who certifies the equipment meets the levels. Class A has fewer stringent requirements than Class B and only requires the vendor to make self tests. On the other hand, Class B equipment must be tested by an independent laboratory and carry an FCC certification number.

These rules appear too restrictive. It assumes that all devices are chronic radiators of RF signals that might interfere with police and fire department radios. Nevertheless, the idea of an independent laboratory verifying that the equipment met the RF standard is an advantage in your network. When you write your request for proposal or quote, you should list meeting a Class A standard as an absolute requirement and a Class B as desirable. Of course, electromagnetic fields from radio frequencies can take on an even greater dimension. ANSI C-95.1 1982, *Electromagnetic Fields, Safety Levels with Respect to Human Exposure to Radio Frequency*, covers other hazards other than 47 CFR Part 15. FCC requirements for measuring RF emissions are in FCC/OET MP-4, *FCC Procedure for Measuring RF Emissions from Computing Devices*, and is available from the following address:

NATIONAL TECHNICAL INFORMATION SERVICE (NTIS)
5285 Port Royal Road
Springfield, VA 22161

Electrostatic discharge

Electrostatic discharge can wipe out a lot of circuitry unless the electronic equipment is designed to shunt the energy to ground. These tests are made when the equipment is under load, or in use, to see what happens when an electrostatic discharge touches the equipment. The equipment should continue to function after voltages of Severity Level 2 (4 Kv) and Severity Level 4 (15 Kv) are applied to all areas that are normally exposed to humans. These levels and testing methods are covered under Publication 801-2, First Edition, 1984 of the International Electrotechnical Commission (IEC). Another reference is Bellcore TR-EOP-000001, *Lightning, Radio Frequency and 60-Hz Disturbances*, and TR-TSY-000499, *Transport Systems Generic Requirements*. See Appendix E for registration requirements.

Potential differences

The minimum protection is ensuring that the safety (green) wire of the power cord is firmly connected to the mounting frame and metal enclosure. According to the ANSI #C-2 National Electrical Safety Code, 1990, you should verify that the electrical outlets in your building are properly wired and that there is a common ground connection.

You also should verify that the green or safety wire of the power cord does, indeed, have a solid connection to bare metal. If the metal is painted, the paint should be scraped or sanded away to provide clean metal. The manufacturer should not rely on lock washers to cut through the paint. Figure 4-1 shows how a nut and bolt should attach the ac power cord's green wire to the metal frame. Manufacturers also must use star lock washers (outer-edge cutting points) on both sides of the metal frame to make sure there is a solid contact with the metal and the connector at the end of the green wire. You also should check to see if the nut and bolt are as tight as they can go, and that the sole purpose of the bolt is to secure the ground wire. If the bolt shares functions, like a mounting, there is the remote possibility someone would loosen the nut and bolt inadvertently.

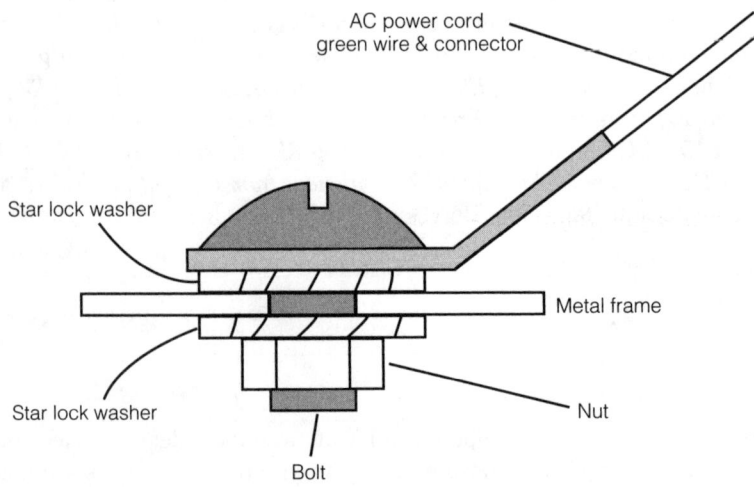

Fig. 4-1. Attaching the green safety wire.

Power supplies

Most manufacturers of power supplies will meet the UL-1012-1988 power supplies standard as a minimum requirement. Your main thrust for safety and equipment longevity is to find equipment with an overrated (i.e., 200 watt vs. 100 watt) and UL-tested power supply. Some large cities have stringent fire codes and will not permit using equipment without UL testing of the power supplies. Chapter 6 on writing RFPs and RFQs explains the rationale of the power supply rating under the power and space considerations section.

Flammability

Title 47 of the Code of Federal Regulations, Part 68.302,(d), (e), and (f) (see Appendix E) describe the various voltage surge tests for the interface leads. These are the least tests necessary for registration. It does not get into fire prevention, but instead, refers only to shunting devices. The real problem is when there is not adequate shunting of the voltages and the components burn. Other possible reference sources for fire resistance are the National Fire Prevention Association (NFPA) - 70 National Electrical Handbook and Bellcore TR-EOP-000063.

Temperature, humidity, and acoustics

See Bellcore TR-EOP-000063 for references on temperature, humidity, and acoustic noise. While it deals with requirements for telephone offices, the specifications are valid for customer premise equipment. The only difference is in the level of acoustic noise. A telephone office has a higher level of additive noise because of ventilation equipment and the extensive rows of equipment that hum, click or whir. Your requirement for an office environment is 10 to 20 dBa lower than a telephone switching center.

Registered equipment must pass the following FCC requirement listed in 47 CFR Part 68.302. The reference to cycling means raising and lowering the testing limits in a controlled atmospheric chamber.

> (b) Temperature and Humidity. Cycling at any convenient rate through the following temperature and humidity conditions three times: 30 minutes at 150°F and 15 percent relative humidity, followed by 30 minutes at 90°F and 90 percent relative humidity, followed by 30 minutes a –40°F and any convenient humidity.

Testing electronic equipment at –40°F is a little extreme and is better suited to electrical components. The one advantage of cycling temperature and humidity over these extremes is to stress the equipment. If it can function over these ranges, it stands a good chance of working under normal conditions.

Other needs

Another FCC-Part 68 registration requirement is the drop test. The necessity for a drop test is is not readily recognized until you receive defective equipment. It is unbelievable how a drop from the back of a delivery truck can bend heavy equipment frames.

Figure 4-2 pictures three of the four types of tests made. A face drop test is perpendicular to each of the six flat areas or sides. A corner drop test puts a perpendicular line between the center of gravity and each corner. An edgewise drop test puts one edge of the rest face on a block to lift it at a 20-degree angle with the test bed. The opposite edge is raised horizontally and then dropped. The last test (not shown) is the corner drop where the equipment is raised at a 20-degree angle from a corner instead of the edge.

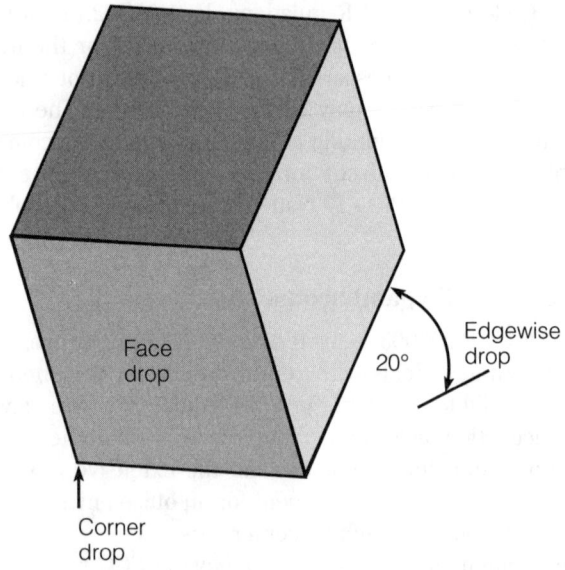

Fig. 4-2. Drop test points.

FCC-47 CFR 68 regulations specify the following tests for equipment not normally carried. These tests are made on concrete covered with ⅛-inch asphalt or similar tile covering.

- 0–20 pounds: One 6-inch face drop on each normal or designated rest area; one 3-inch drop on all other faces; and one 3-inch corner drop on each corner.
- 20–50 pounds: One 4-inch drop on each normal or designated rest area; one 2-inch drop on all other faces; and one 2-inch corner drop on each corner.
- 50–100 pounds: One 2-inch drop on each normal or designated rest area; one 2-inch drop on all other faces; and one 2-inch corner drop on each corner.

FCC-47 CFR 68 regulations specify the following tests for equipment normally carried and hand-held items used near the head. These tests are also made on concrete covered with ⅛-inch asphalt or similar tile covering. A random drop is a positioned release to increase the chances of an impact of six different major areas.

- Hand-held equipment: 18 random drops from a height of 60 inches.
- Customer-carried equipment: six random drops from a height of 30 inches.

Summary

Electrical and safety standards are necessary to ensure the safety of employees or company property. Many of these concerns are covered under equipment registration when it is connected to the public telephone network. Unfortunately, standards are not specified for equipment that has a buffer of some sort between it and the network. This is the area that gets the least attention because manufacturers do not have to test their products. Often, companies getting into the communication business will start with this type of equipment because they cannot afford the cost of independent laboratory testing to qualify their product.

Your primary responsibility in planning equipment is to specify basic electrical and safety standards. The vendor then has the responsibility to guarantee that their product meets these standards. While this chapter discussed a few items contained in FCC Part 68, review appendix E for greater detail concerning safety and electrical requirements.

5

Vendor quality & reliability

The type and amount of quality control by manufacturers makes a large difference in their final product. I have stressed throughout this book that quality does not mean you must buy the most expensive product. The design (i.e., number of components) and the quality level (i.e., I, II, or III) of the parts help to determine the cost. Of course, the other major portion of the cost is a reflection of the overhead, profit, and sales commissions of the manufacturer.

While there are several groups in North America that are concerned about quality, there is greater emphasis on quality in many European and Asian countries. Before certain countries allow products to cross their borders, they certify them similar to the FCC registration. This certification not only checks the usual electrical and safety needs, but also checks quality and operational characteristics. Groups like the Deutsche Bundespost must approve equipment before it can be used in Germany. There are some countries that make type acceptance so tough that it only serves to restrict imports.

You should be cautious about spending time and money learning about quality from a seminar or school. Quality assurance programs usually spend more time developing sampling statistics than teaching skills on how to look for quality. While sampling techniques are very good for testing large quantities of parts, they do not address the issue of what to look for in finished products. Quality assurance reduces the chances of defective components, and final inspection reduces the problems with the finished goods.

Manufacturing quality

This chapter on quality and reliability covers physical quality and not quality assurance. The reliability part addresses the methods used to improve the chances that a product is not dead-on-arrival (DOA) or that it does not die during the infant mortality period.

Circuit boards

Printed circuit boards (PCB) come in many sizes and shapes. Motherboards are large PCB, typically the major board in your personal computer. Daughterboards are smaller PCB that attach to the motherboard with some permanency (i.e., not a plug-in). Probably the largest group of PCB is the plug-in board, which is also the easiest to inspect.

PCB have changed over the past few years as developers increased the complexity of the integrated circuit. As they shrink the size of the conducting foils to cram more parts on a board, the testing becomes more complicated. Very large companies can afford the $500,000 plus cost for sophisticated testing devices. Small companies do not have the funds to purchase such devices and limit their board testing to their expertise level.

The methods used to insert and secure component parts into PCB depends on a company's size. If a company is very small, parts are inserted by hand and then soldered with a hand-held soldering iron. Once a company grows a little, they might buy an inserting device. Soldering might still be by manual labor or by soldering machine. Buying a used soldering machine is like buying a used taxi cab. Both have seen many miles and cost more to keep them running.

When a manufacturer gets a little bigger, they usually have a bigger and better soldering machine and insertion machines get a little more complicated. Very large companies will automate as much as possible. They also have the best testing devices on hand.

The smaller the company, the more you must inspect their product and manufacturing plant. Nevertheless, you need to check the quality of even the largest company. Just because these companies are large, does not mean they are perfect. As the global economy grows, these very large companies are doing business with countries with limited technical knowledge.

Foils

Foils are the conducting paths on PCBs. Today's designers have the benefit of the computer and graphics programs to lay out the circuit board. These wonderful devices produce the artwork for the mask used in etching the copper coating off the base material. Etching is the most common way of producing circuit boards. Other terms and definitions can be found in Appendix B.

The artwork or mask lays out the final foils with a special ink to prevent the acid from etching the desired conducting paths. This process is very critical to produce smooth edges and prevent pitting in the remaining foil. Pits are holes in the conducting material that do not go all the way through the board. Pinholes go all the way through to the other side. While some pits and pinholes are permissible, they are a sign of lower quality in the etching process.

After etching the boards, manufacturers drill holes to hold components or as conducting paths between the board's sides (plated-through holes). Hole drilling is a critical step because they must be drilled in the proper places. Drilling must be exactly in the center of the soldering location without breaking through the edge of the foil. Plated-through holes either connect a conducting path on one side to a path on the other side of the board or they are used to simplify soldering.

After holes are drilled, the boards go through a cleaning process to prepare them for plating the main conducting foils. The plating process should produce an almost mirrorlike appearance. If it is dull or gray in appearance, the solder will not flow properly. There should not be any excess plating that would cause bridging between foils. This is especially true with higher-density PCB that have very close parallel foils.

Bridging

Bridging is usually the result of excess solder. It can also occur when etching is not done properly, leaving a portion of copper that spans or almost spans between two conductors. The "almost span" shown in FIG. 5-1 is worse, because it might not be caught during manufacture and can cause problems later. If a card does not have an insulating protective coating over the foils, dust and moisture can accumulate over time. This can complete the span and provide a shunting path.

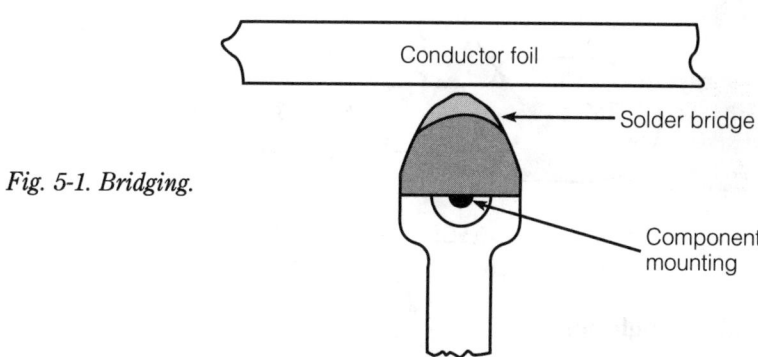

Fig. 5-1. Bridging.

Hole breakout and misdirected holes

Hole breakout is the result of not drilling the hole in the proper location. Figure 5-2 shows a hole drilled at the edge of the conducting path and not in its true location. A hole breakout is permissible if the breakout is less than ¼ of the hole's diameter. It is still a sign of lax quality and can cause trouble when soldering the component part. A standard for drilling holes is covered in *ANSI/Institute for Printed Circuits (IPC), Drilling Guidelines for Printed Boards.*

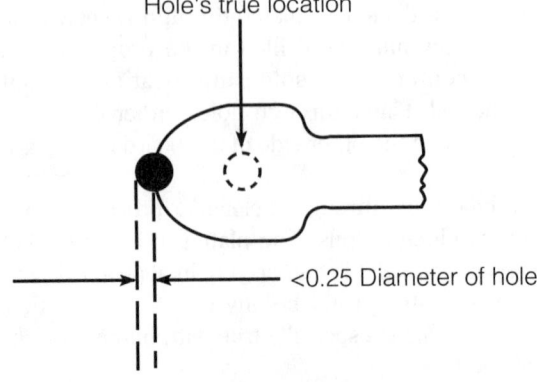

Hole's true location

Fig. 5-2. Maximum hole breakout.

<0.25 Diameter of hole

The other concern with hole drilling is the misdirected hole. Other than drilling in the wrong place, this can occur with misaligned artwork on double-sided boards. While the hole might be perfect for one side of the board, it is not correct for the other side. Figure 5-3 is the reverse of a hole breakout, and is now toward the conducting path. If the hole is too close to the minimum dimension of the conducting path *(C)* it will reduce the size of the path. Here, the combined conductor path *(A + B)* must be greater than 50 percent of the distance *(C)*.

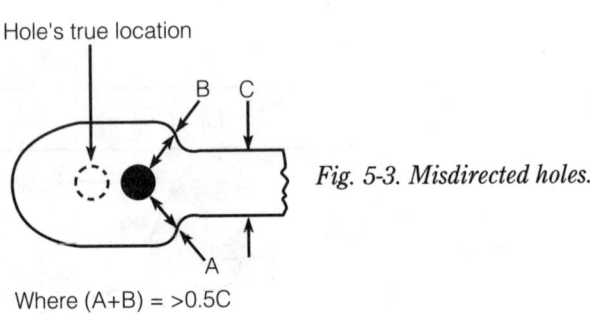

Hole's true location

B C

Fig. 5-3. Misdirected holes.

A

Where (A+B) = >0.5C

Plated-through holes

Plated-through holes are conductive paths through a base material. Normally, they connect foils on either side of the base material as shown in FIG. 5-4. After holes are drilled in the etched board, a metallic coating is applied to the sides of the holes, which allows the plating process to adhere to the sides. When the component-mounted board enters the soldering bath or machine, the solder creeps up the hole in a capillary fashion. Depending on the soldering process, the finished product will either have a convex or concave appearance. Figure 5-4 shows the concave that is typical of capillary action.

Holes should be completely filled with solder, and if the holes have problems, the solder will not pull up into the hole. Partially filled plated-through holes suggest a lower-quality PCB process. Drilled holes that appear on one side of the base material without any foil are not plated-through and do not require that solder be pulled up through the hole. Instead, the soldering is made on the other side where there is foil.

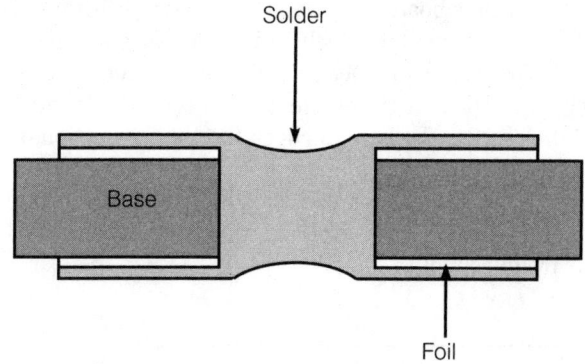

Fig. 5-4. Plated-through holes.

Component mountings

Mounting parts like the one shown in FIG. 5-5 is ideal. Will components work if they don't look like this? Yes, of course, but it is a sign of lower workmanship. Component mountings should be flat on the surface of the board unless there is a problem with heat. If a part generates excessive heat, it should have a standoff to protect the board. It must, however, still be parallel with the board.

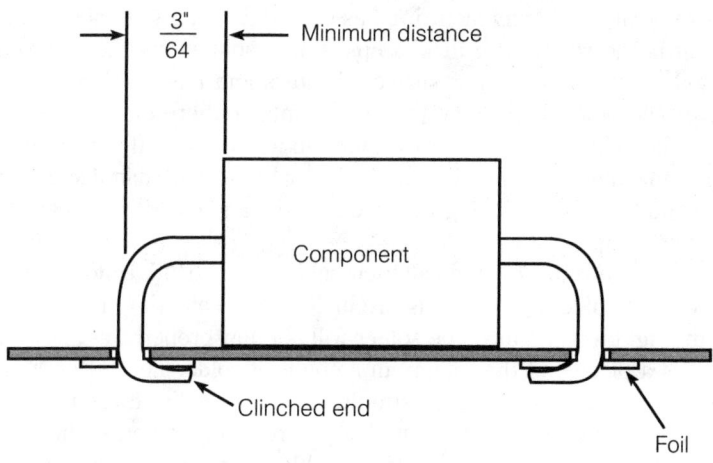

Fig. 5-5. Bend leads.

Most mounting problems occur when components are mounted by hand. Larger companies use automatic bending and inserting machines. Other insertion problems happen when integrated circuits (IC) are inserted into sockets by hand. It is very easy to bend a pin under without any outward indication. If a bent pin makes some contact, it might pass the manufacturer's test. Shipping, vibration, or environmental conditions can alter the contact and leave you with a defective board.

Other IC problems can result when an installer puts an IC into drilled holes in a board. The IC must be perfectly flat and not cocked as shown in FIG. 5-6. If it is cocked, the pins might not get a good solder flow and not pull up in plated-through holes. Also, be sure to check the capillary action of the holes at the corners of the IC. Ground pins are usually located at a corner position where they must have complete contact (i.e., inserted all the way, full capillary action, and no flux residue). Poor grounds cause intermittent troubles and are the bane of the troubleshooter.

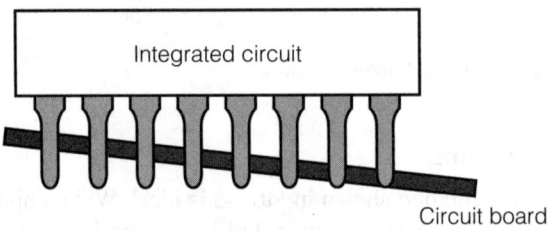

Circuit board

Fig. 5-6. Tilted integrated circuit.

Soldering

Up to this point, PCB manufacturing has passed through several critical steps. Soldering is the zenith of critical steps. When solder hits the right temperature and touches a prepared surface, it flows and has a shiny appearance. Whatever flux is used in the preparation, it must either boil off or flow to the edges of the solder where it gets cleaned in a later step. If a company has a soldering machine, the operator can make or break that manufacturer by the way they do the soldering. A good machine and a good operator can produce quality soldering.

Smaller companies often do all their soldering by hand. Unfortunately, this is where most soldering problems originate. If the soldering iron is not clean and at the right temperature, the solder will not flow properly, as shown in FIG. 5-7. This is a picture of the minimum amount of solder needed on a cinched connection and how the solder should flow. Normally, the entire oblong-shaped area where the hole is located is covered with solder. It should have a concave appearance and not be a blob of solder. Too much solder can result in bridging. Again, this will usually happen only with hand soldering instead of

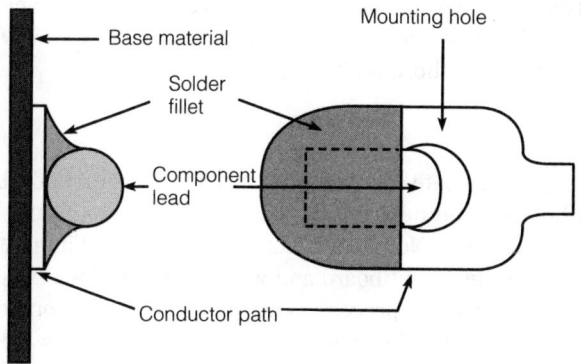

Fig. 5-7. Solder flow.

soldering machines. Always remember that the soldering should have a shiny appearance, not be excessive, and be clean of any flux residue. The following standards cover solderability of circuit boards:

ANSI/EIA 319-A, Printed Wiring Boards, Solderability
ANSI/Institute of Printed Circuits (IPC), S-804A, Solderability Tests
ANSI/IPC, S-805, Solderability Tests for Component Leads

Board defects

Printed circuit boards do not normally have cracks, chips, or flaws in the base material. If the board has a solder mask or protective coating applied after the plating, you will have a difficult time spotting cracks and flaws in the base material. Chips will be obvious because the coating cannot cover them up.

Quality-oriented companies will get rid of defective boards after the etching process. The company should have an inspection station that examines the etched and drilled boards before the PCBs are coated and components mounted. Companies working without good quality control will cover up the evidence. In the next part on selecting, we recommend visiting prospective vendors to see their level of quality. This becomes part of your risk analysis in reaching your final decision in selecting products or services. During that visit, you should make a point to look at etched and drilled circuit boards before they have a protective coating. If flaws exist, it is a sign that the manufacturer is purchasing the least expensive boards available and does not have a good quality program.

Cracks in the conducting pattern are not acceptable. If they go through the entire base material, they are not acceptable. Chips must not be greater than half the thickness of the board.

Coating

Coating unmounted circuit boards has two purposes. One provides a solder mask to prevent solder from bridging during the solder process. The other is to provide a protective coat to reduce problems caused by dust and humidity. ANSI/IPC SM-840B, *Permanent Polymer Coating (Solder Mask) for Printed Boards*, covers the subject thoroughly.

Flatness

Ground yourself to dissipate any static electricity on your body before you inspect circuit boards. The next thing is to grab the edges of the board and hold the board horizontally. Next, check for twist and warp. Figure 5-8 pictures twist from the end of the circuit board and warp from the side. Twist and warp happen just after the soldering process as the board cools and component parts contract. If there is more than just a minor amount of twist and warp, there will be problems with sliding or securing the circuit board into its mounting.

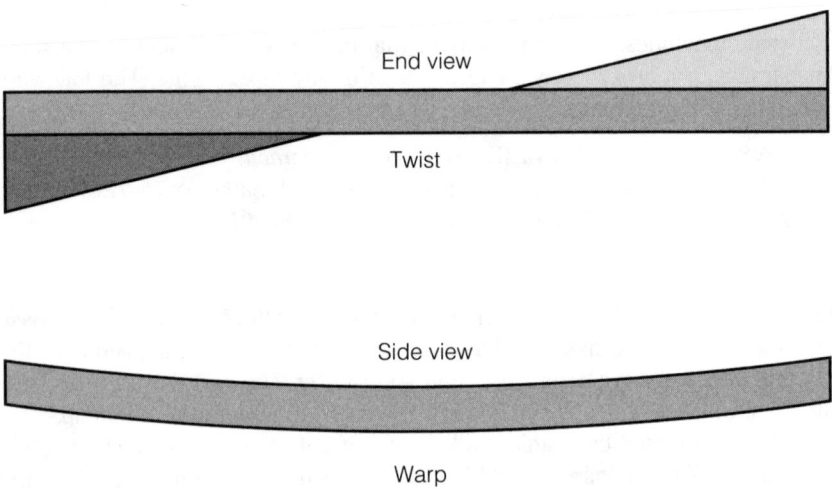

Fig. 5-8. Twist and warp.

While you have the circuit board in your hands, check component mountings and solder. Find a strong light and hold the board level with your eyes. Move the board around from end to side or side to end. Look for cocked components and integrated circuits. Now turn the board so you can view the large areas perpendicularly. You might need a magnifying glass or a very good light to inspect the soldering and plated-through holes. The last thing to look for is the contact fingers.

Contact fingers

Contact fingers are the edge connector of the circuit board. They are the interface points between the board and the other equipment. While it is hard to find manufacturers that do not plate these with a few microns of gold, there are some that do not know any better. Manufacturers bevel the very edges of the contact fingers to make it easier to push the board into its mounting. The one thing that you need to watch for is the length of the fingers. If they are too short, they won't provide enough wiping action, or contact with the mounting. A wiping action clears any contaminants that have accumulated on the fingers or on the contacts of the mounting.

Component quality levels

Component parts have three levels of quality. Quality-I Level parts are the lowest priced because they use the least expensive material and are shipped without any quality assurance testing. The vendor should have an incoming inspection of the parts to weed out defective units. Quality-II Level parts use better basic material and statistically inspect lot shipments. Quality-III Level parts use the best material and are 100 percent inspected before shipment.

Reliability

Reliability goes hand in hand with quality. If manufacturers maintain good quality, reliability is high. Using poor-quality products means reliability is risky at best. Reliability means the unit is dependable and provides the same results time after time. How does one make sure equipment is reliable?

To ensure reliability, a vendor must have a good quality program. Once a unit passes a quality program, it must undergo final testing. This usually consists of a burn-in test to ensure that the product will pass the infant mortality stage. Figure 5-9 illustrates just the left side of the typical reliability bathtub curve for a product's life. The right side is another curve going back up to complete the bathtub picture, which is the failure rate at the final life of the product.

Going back to the left side of the curve in FIG. 5-9, you see three different areas (i.e., A, B, C). Area A is the first 24 hours of a burn-in test. This test is under full power, in simulated normal use, and preferably in an enclosure to raise the temperature for stress. If the product makes it through this first stress-testing period, its chances of surviving improve. Using a burn-in test of several days or a week takes the product through the B Area. The product is now down to the knee of the curve where it then becomes an economical choice by the manufacturer of whether to continue the burn-in tests or shove the product out the door.

Ideally, the vendor will make burn-in tests that eliminate all infant mortality and supply only products that exhibit statistical failures. Economics will dictate just how long a vendor can perform burn-in tests. You can specify a desired level of confidence that the goods shipped exceed a 99 percent level. They might respond by saying their level is 95 percent and additional testing will increase the price charged. Of course, if they really wanted your business, they would do the extra testing free of charge.

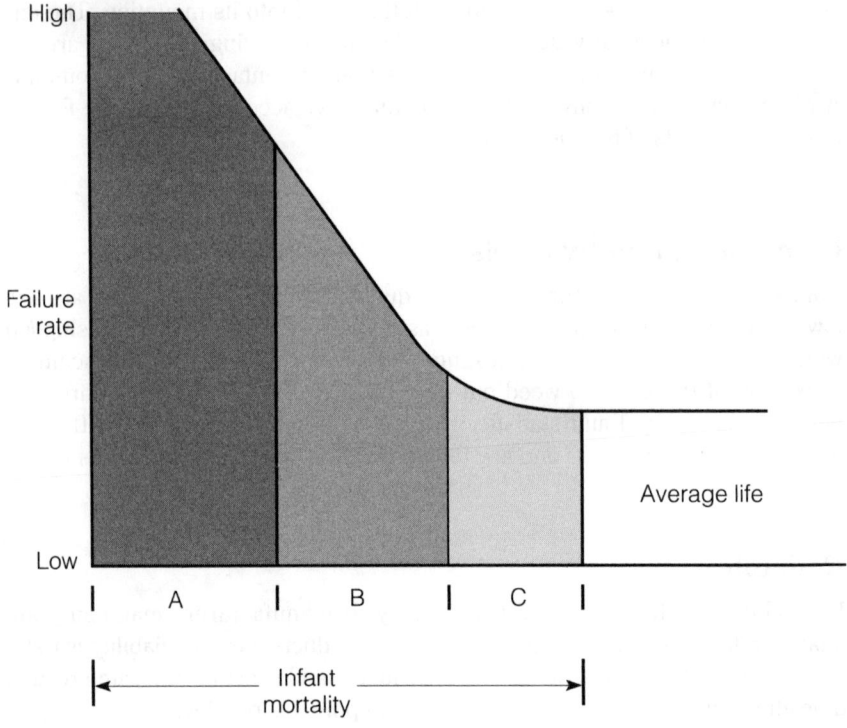

Fig. 5-9. Partial bathtub curve for reliability.

General quality standards

The following standards cover the general subject of quality. See appendix A for an address list of standard and technical reference suppliers.

—ISO 9000 Compendium. International specifications for quality assurance, testing, and auditing quality systems.

—Bellcore TR-TSY-000039 Quality Program Analysis. Bellcore's view of the basic elements of a quality program.

—AT&T 53250 Quality Program Evaluation - AT&T's view of the basic elements of a quality program.

—American Society of Quality Control (ASQC) Q90 (ISO 9000). Quality Management and Quality Assurance Standards.

—ANSI/ASQC Q90 (ISO 9001) Quality Systems. Model for Quality Assurance in Design/Development, Production, Installation, and Servicing.

—ASQC Q90 (ISO 9002) Quality Systems. Model for Quality Assurance in Production and Installation.

—ANSI/ASQC Q90 (ISO 9003) Quality Systems. Model for Quality Assurance in Final Inspection and Test.

—ANSI/ASQC Q90 (ISO 9004) Quality Management and Quality System Elements.

Summary

Quality is paramount. Without good quality, you have poorer reliability. Poorer reliability means you will spend more time trying to repair or fix your network. Consequently, your customers will not be happy because the system is down all the time for repair or troubleshooting.

You do not have to be an expert to judge quality. It is apparent after a few quality inspection trips. Neatness and cleanliness count a long way toward a quality manufacturer. Chapter 8 on dealing with vendors tells you how to go about making quality inspection trips. By combining some of the quality items covered in this chapter and using the Quality Evaluation Checklist in Appendix C, you will soon be that expert.

6

Writing
RFPs & RFQs

At this point, you should have completed your preliminary network plans. It is now time to write the request for proposal (RFP) or the request for quote (RFQ). I have treated these two requests differently because the RFP looks for assistance and the RFQ looks for money values. Most of the basic structure is the same, but the initial part of the RFP includes more information about your needs. The RFQ, on the other hand, details specific requirements, such as the type equipment.

Absolute needs

Absolute needs are your basic requirements. These cover safety, electrical, quality, and all your fundamental needs to operate. If a vendor cannot meet your absolute needs, you should eliminate them from consideration. If nobody can meet your basic needs, you need to review your network design. Do not stray from the basic safety, electrical, and quality specifications. These are unconditional needs.

When you write your absolute needs, it is imperative to use words like *shall* and *must* to describe various items. If possible, use bold print for these two words to emphasize the importance of the item. It will add strength to your writing and make it clear you consider the item very significant. Companies like Bellcore write many specifications and enhance line items with letter designations. Their approach uses **(R)** for required or absolute and **(O)** for objective or desired items. I use **(A)** for absolute needs and **(D)** for desired ones. The reason for this is that one synonym for absolute is unquestionable. Whereas, the word *required* has several archaic meanings that have less strength. Bellcore's use of objective is correct because they are in a planning stage and are open to suggestions. You have completed your planning stage, however, and now desire certain items.

The letter designation precedes the line or paragraph item to make it easier for the vendor to identify the requirements. You could lump all your absolute, desired, and extra features in individual areas, but it becomes disjointed. It is better to follow Bellcore's example, because there are times you will have absolute, desired, and extra values placed on a particular item. In the example below, we added the designation (E) for extra features.

Training Documentation: Training is an essential part of initializing the network and maintaining the total network. We place great emphasis on the value of clear and understandable documentation.

(A) The vendor shall provide operating manuals that are clearly written that fully describe the unit's functions, installation procedures, and maintenance requirements.

(D) The vendor should provide training sessions during the initial installation. These sessions can be located either at the vendor's building or on our sites.

(E) An extra feature is that all training is held at our locations.

(E) An extra feature is that the vendor will provide a videotape of their training instruction. This tape would assist training personnel after the initial turn-up period.

This example used several different levels of training documentation. The first one was the absolute need of good manuals, making this the bare bones. Good manuals and smart people can make a successful installation. The next item is the desire for formal training along with the basic manuals, and the last items cover good things that are not essential to the operation of your network—extras.

When it comes to your absolute network needs, you must have the capability to transmit all your normal data and voice communication. Telephone companies size their networks to meet the average needs during the year. This does not cover the additional traffic they get on Christmas, Mother's Day, or during emergencies. Nevertheless, the absolute network needs cover the typical or normal usage for your network as well as the telephone company.

In the case of the telephone company, they switch facilities from private line service to long-distance telephone usage during the holiday or peak periods. To meet your peak business periods, you need a way to provide alternative facilities. This is normally handled with PBX alternate routing or facility restoration. It is desirable that you include growth plans to reach a certain size in the discernible future. They are extra bonus items when you ask for a unit that expands easily even if you never plan to grow in size.

Desirable features

Desirable features are those items that would make you very happy if they were there, but you can live without them. If you went to purchase a new car, your absolute need is a set of brakes. It is desirable that the brakes are anti-lock to provide better control during emergencies. Another desirable feature is a duplication of the braking system. Both items would make your day a little better, but have nothing to do with the fundamental need of brakes.

There is a way of asking for the best product or service. Make the desired features a combination of the best features of all the competing products or services. There will not be any one unit that fully matches the criteria. The downside is that you have a little more analyzing to do to make your final selection. The good thing about it is that it doesn't look like your RFQ matched only one vendor. You do not want the proposal to sound like one company's specifications or brochure. When you get around to making your selections, you can reduce the number under consideration by the desired needs. The vendor that most closely meets these items has a better chance of coming out on top.

Use words like *should* and *may* when you write your desired features or needs. If possible, print these in bold to be consistent with the method used previously. Items that head your list of desirables can be modified with words like *highly* or *very desirable* to place a little weight to their value. Use the designations (B) for *highly desired*, (C) for sentences with the word *should*, and (D) when using the word *may* whenever there are several levels of desired features.

Extra features

Extra features are items used to provide material for a tie-breaker. If you find several similar products that meet both your absolute and desired needs, the extra features provide a way to decide which is best.

Usually, simple items like modems will meet all your basic and desired requirements. They also usually cost around the same amount of money. Now you can cut the field down with simple extra features such as color or size. It is enough to say you picked product A over product B because it was smaller or matched the decor of the office. You need some answer as to why you selected a particular vendor as the best product. Again, extra features can be the deciding factor when choosing between extremely similar products. When you reach a point where everything is similar, then you must assign values to the extra features and reevaluate the products. Equal products beyond this point require you to either accept all winners or select the best product by lottery.

Overview

Your RFP or RFQ needs an executive summary to precede the specifications. One reason is to provide a quick overview of the request; the other reason is possible reduction of detailed specifications needed for a general distribution. If you send only the summary with a cover letter requesting interested parties, you only have to send the entire package to those who want to bid on your request. This can take another week or two, but will reduce the expense of reproduction and delivery.

Figure 6-1 is an outline of the items to include in your summary. The mandate to provide a brief description means it should be as brief as possible and still give someone a general idea of the topic. The detailed specifications should include as much information as possible to make very intelligent responses.

Your Company Letterhead

Date Released:

Request-for-(Proposal)/(Quote)

Objective of the Request: Briefly describe the objective of the request. If it is an RFQ, then describe the generic equipment you need. An RFP's objective is looking for suggestions on how to meet your needs.

Overview of the Network: Briefly describe your proposed network in general terms. Specific voice and data traffic requirements are part of the detailed documentation.

Selection Process: A quick review of the selection process based on meeting specified **(A)**, **(D)**, and **(E)** features. Analysis is based on how well the individual product meet all items.

Schedules: List dates for the return of a response, when selection completes, and proposed installation dates.

Questions and Response: Provide the name, address, and phone number of the person to ask questions and where to send the response.

Fig. 6-1. Cover sheet for an RFP or RFQ.

Specifying details

When you select products or services, you will use a risk analysis process to improve your chances of selecting the best equipment. TABLE 6-1 is a list of those items considered under risk analysis, in their order of importance. Chapter 12 covers this process more thoroughly. Not all these items are obtainable through a request and response procedure. Some require visual inspection at a later date when making a final selection. The answers you get back for most items, however, will reduce the number of vendors under consideration.

Table 6-1. Items considered in risk analysis.

A. Meeting the absolute needs
B. Quality of the product or service
C. Meeting of the desired needs
D. Uniqueness of the product or service
E. Extra features
F. Safety certification
G. Availability of the product
H. Mean time to failure
I. Mean time to repair
J. In-house maintenance availability
K. Repair availability
L. Technical assistance or support
M. Training and operating manuals
N. Power and space considerations
O. Environmental considerations
P. Upgrade of operating hardware and software

The executive summary contains a brief description of the objective and the proposed network. Now you will expand both sections and be very specific about all details. The RFP requires both voice and data traffic requirements for the present and expected growth. Here you are looking for someone's answer to meet your needs. The RFQ need only cover the particular needs of individual units or how the units work in the network. This can take the form of listing the number of units needed with a particular capability (i.e., six 9600 b/s V.32 modems).

The rest of the specifications lists the absolute, desired, and extra features for the main topics in TABLE 6-1. It is not necessary to have all three needs for each item, but the more you can add, the easier to pick the best product or service later.

A. Meeting the absolute needs The biggest portion of the specifications covers the basic electrical and safety needs, basic operating needs, and required interfaces. All of these break down into absolute, desired, and extra features. When you make an analysis, you will divide these into separate groups because they have different values.

The biggest problem with a multi-vendor network is the interface. Manufacturers take liberties with unassigned pins or connectors. They also misinterpret the standards or use old documents. When the vendor states they have an EIA RS-232C interface, they are behind the times. The designation RS was dropped years ago, and the Electronic Industries Association has progressed to two newer interfaces. A suggested data interface specification is as follows:

> The manufacturer (vendor) shall specify all data interfaces as to the particular standard used (i.e., exact designation and gender of each interface). Further, the manufacturer shall identify the pins or contacts that do not specifically meet the said standard. This identification must specify voltages and functions that appear on all unassigned standard pins and the standard leads the manufacturer has reassigned to their own use (e.g., testing leads used during manufacture). The vendor shall identify all interface cables that are vendor specific (i.e., specially designed cables that are needed to make their unit function).

Another major problem with multi-vendor networks is the connection of different vendor's units that are supposedly compatible. The biggest trouble with compatible but different vendor products occurs during the handshaking or turnaround procedures. Finite timing differences between expected events are enough to prevent successful operation. It is not a wise choice to use compatible but different manufactured products unless you thoroughly test the operation.

B. Quality of the product or service   You can specify that the vendor must meet approved quality standards. Nevertheless, you still must make a visual inspection to verify that they do, indeed, follow good quality practices.

C. Meeting the desired needs   See A.

D. Uniqueness of the product or service   Uniqueness means the product or service is proprietary to the individual vendor and you can only get it from them. In risk analysis, this is a problem because there is not a second source in case the company goes out of business. It also means the vendor can charge you anything they want for repair or modifications throughout the life of the product or service. You should specify that the vendor (shall) identify the existence of all proprietary hardware and software. Also, specify that the vendor provide the proprietary information should the company go bankrupt or out of business. This can be done in advance through a lockbox arrangement. Finally, be sure that all updates and changes are in the lockbox.

E. Extra features   See A.

F. Safety certification   Safety certification is another risk analysis value. In your absolute needs, you specified the various safety requirements (i.e., power supply testing, etc.). The risk value depends on whether the vendor did the tests themselves, an outside testing laboratory made them, or no tests were made.

G. Availability of the product   Specify your installation schedule and the need for equipment availability. If a vendor builds products only when someone places an order, it puts you into a higher risk. Shelf availability is a lower risk. Also, you can have a lower spare ratio if the vendor can replace units in a day or two.

H. Mean Time to Failure   The vendor shall provide the Mean Time to Failure (MTTF) or Mean Time Before Failure (MTBF) figures for the product. Some people refer to MTTF and others use MTBF. Basically, it is a statistical figure that describes the average bell-shaped expected life curve. It does not indicate the life of an individual unit before it will fail. This says that out of every 100 units made, you can expect to see 63 (the mean) will fail in the MTTF period. You will use this figure later to compare competing units.

I. Mean Time to Repair Mean Time to Repair (MTTR) is another figure to use when comparing vendor's products or services. You should have some idea just how long it takes to repair a unit. If one product takes an hour to change circuit boards and another only takes 15 minutes, obviously, the latter one is less risky.

J. In-house maintenance availability Depending on the product or service, the vendor shall or should provide in-house maintenance. If a trouble is beyond the scope of your personnel, you want the vendor to provide trained maintenance personnel. Another point to specify is the maximum allowable response time to have the vendor's maintenance people at your location.

K. Repair availability Repair availability is different from MTTR and in-house maintenance availability. When you return a defective unit to the vendor for repair, they have several different choices to make. They might furnish a working unit to you before you return the defective one. The other choice is repairing the defective unit when it shows up at the plant. Specify that the vendor (shall) describe repair procedures and time frames. They should also describe the costs involved in returning the units for repair (i.e., who pays for shipment during and out of warranty periods). The shorter time a defective unit is away from your location, the less spare equipment needed.

L. Technical assistance or support The vendor shall specify the number of technical assistance or support personnel available, as well as how to reach them. Availability includes hours, days, and weekends or holidays. They should provide information as to the charges for technical support if it is not included with the product or service. They should separate charges for normal business hours and after-business hours technical support if they are different.

M. Training and operating manuals Training and operating manuals ranks very high, but is shown here because it is something that you can change. Your selection process needs to look at life cycle items to reduce competing products. If training is not available, it becomes your responsibility to originate some training program. The same thing is true with operating manuals. Poorly written manuals need revision before you can use them. Either you or the vendor—or a combination of both—must fix the problem.

Separate the training and operating manuals into two different specifications. Use something like the example given before for training. Operating and maintenance manuals need their own clarification. Here, the vendor shall provide a copy of the associated operating and maintenance manuals.

N. Power and space considerations Power Consumption and the size of the equipment can make a difference in your selection process. Power consumption and the power supply rating are two different things. A power supply with a 200-watt rating runs very well when the power consumption is only 100 watts. Increase the power consumption to 190 watts, however, and the power supply will run hot. This will not only shorten the power supply's life, but also produce more heat. Because this is vital information in your selection, the vendor shall provide the power supply rating and the actual power usage of the equipment.

Space in any building is expensive. The rationale here is that, the larger the equipment, the greater its life cycle cost to your company. Every square foot of space in your office has a dollar figure that includes the land and building expense. If one unit takes up 2 square feet of space and another uses only 1 square foot, the smaller one costs less to operate. Normally, product literature will specify the size of a piece of equipment. Nevertheless, the vendor should include the dimensions of any equipment installed in your location.

O. Environmental considerations   Environmental considerations would include such items as temperature, ventilation, and noise. These items figure into your life cycle selection process. Adding heat-producing equipment into an office will load the air-conditioning system down. Too much equipment, and you must add more air-conditioning equipment. While you can estimate the BTU output from the power usage, the vendor should provide the figure. It is a desired need because most vendors never made any temperature tests of their equipment.

Equipment ventilation needs usually means the equipment has an exhaust fan. Exhaust fans mean noise and additional space to vent the warm air. Noise will annoy personnel that must work near the unit. The vendor shall provide ventilation requirements, and should provide the noise rating. They know all about ventilation requirements, but probably never measured the noise generated.

P. Upgrade of operating hardware and software   The last item covers the policy of the vendor to initiate upgrades to the hardware and software. This touches on the uniqueness and availability of the equipment. Recently designed equipment will have the most changes or upgrades to overcome design flaws. There are many cases where the vendor has produced a second or "Series II" unit six months after producing the first or "Series I" unit. You can make the very best design, but it must see action in the real world to shake the bugs out.

Designers would like to believe they thought of everything, but it is inevitable that they'll find a new wrinkle in how people use things. One design was a synchronous multiplexer that the designer thought was one service using the same four-wire facilities. The second installation of the multiplexer found an end user that had two distinct services going in opposite directions. It required a design change to produce a true four-wire synchronous system.

The vendor shall provide information on their policy for upgrades. If the upgrade corrects a design flaw, the upgrade should be a no-cost item over the expected life cycle of the product. However, if it only adds features, you should have the option to upgrade. In any case, the vendor shall notify you when they make upgrades for features or design corrections.

Software quality assurance is an important item. If a software flaw appears during the installation or initial operating period, the vendor should correct it at no cost. You should specify that the vendor shall guarantee the quality of the software and agree to correcting problems free of any charge.

Summary

Most items in the detailed specifications are generic and cover all installed equipment at your location. The only difference is the operating features of a particular device. Generic requirements are written only once, and then particular operating features are added to the individual requests. Stress the value of the product or service meeting the standards in the previous chapters.

Part II

Selecting

7

Introduction
to selection

This part of the book deals with selecting products and services for a multi-vendor network. While selecting equipment and telephone services is an awesome responsibility, you'll learn how to make the very best choices and how to document what you have done. When you make that final selection, you'll have the evidence that you have made the best decision and the backup material to show your decision was based on a sound foundation.

The next chapter on dealing with vendors describes the best way to protect yourself. Just consider everyone you deal with will take you to court because they didn't like your decision. If you think this way from the start, you'll be sure to have all types of backup material. You need to show everybody you were right and they don't have a leg to stand on. This material can also prove to that skeptical boss that you really made the very best possible selection. It is important to retain all the documentation after your selection to protect yourself. Another reason is it is also very useful in the future for reference. For those companies that assign a file retention factor, you should hold onto all material for at least five years. In five years, someone will start a selection process for a new network to replace what you are completing now.

Searching for participants

Searching for participants is less of a challenge if you have studied the trade papers and magazines over the past year. There are several excellent sources of information that can reduce your task of finding the right organizations to send your request for proposal (RFP) or request for quote (RFQ). Trade magazines and newspapers abound with product information. If you spend some time in telecommunications, your name will seem to wind up on every mailing list so you can receive an avalanche of magazines or weekly newspapers. Although a number of publications are well-meaning, the major article contributors are product managers for individual vendors. Unfortunately, this type of magazine is too biased toward a particular piece of equipment and you will gain very little generic information.

Reduce the amount of trade magazines and papers you receive by concentrating on just a few of the better ones. The following seem to furnish the best information on networks and future directions:

NETWORK WORLD
161 Worcester Road
Framingham, MA 01701-9712

DATA COMMUNICATIONS
P.O. Box 477
Hightstown, NJ 08520-9362
Phone: 1-800-257-9402 (Outside U.S. 609-426-7070)

COMMUNICATIONS WEEK
Circulation Department
P.O. Box 2070
Manhasset, NY 11030

The following publication is directed toward engineers or technical management. While not network oriented, it has articles that are informative about future directions of products and services. Its information about changes often precedes articles in other trade papers by many months.

ENGINEERING TIMES
Circulation Department
Box 2010
Manhasset, NY 11030

Another place to look for prospective participants is at trade shows. Because trade shows are such a great expense to a vendor, they will limit the number of shows they attend. They have to expect a lot of return for the expense of the exhibit space and hospitality suites. Some large corporations expect to have expenses in the hundreds of thousands of dollars to exhibit at a major show.

As a consequence of a down-sized economy, many vendors have little choice but to further reduce the number of exhibits. If your company limits the number of trade shows you can go to, you should consider the three or four that have survived over the years. Several major trade shows have gone by the wayside in recent years because of poor attendance. Just because an exhibit or conference was good one year does not mean it will be as good the next. The following shows have lasted, even through poor economic times, and continue to attract major exhibits:

ComNet held in Washington, DC late January to early February. This show has greater emphasis on data networks than on voice networks.

ICA (International Communications Association) held in the later part of Spring in either Atlanta, Dallas, or Anaheim. The ICA leans more toward the voice segment.

TCA (Tele-Communications Association) held late September in San Diego. This show highlights data and telecommunication equipment.

CMA (Communications Managers Association) held in early October in New York City. A show that is oriented toward the voice segment.

INTEROP, held in the Spring (East Coast) and in Fall (West Coast). A newer show series geared toward the LAN segment.

Data Communications, McGraw-Hill's monthly magazine, lists these and smaller shows around the country. While the smaller shows might not exhibit as many vendors, they might be near your location and be less expensive to attend.

Reasonable search

What is a reasonable search for products or communications services? Just the word reasonable sends the message that you are not expected to locate everyone that makes a widget before you can make your selection. Also, you cannot be expected to review every modem manufacturer if you are trying to buy a 1200 bit per second (b/s) data set. There must be at least 50 to 75 different com panies that offer modems.

Being reasonable means that you made an effort to locate several different companies that either produce a product or offer a telecommunication service. Reasonable also means you have taken the time to locate more than one or two of your favorite vendors. You might have a passion for the color blue, but that shouldn't limit you to settling on IBM before you have looked elsewhere.

If for some reason you have not been able to locate several different vendors to study, you must be able to document why your study is limited. This can be a written statement describing where you have looked and the reason why some likely companies were not included. A possible reason for exclusion can be that your network was located entirely on the East Coast and that you excluded vendors that were located on the West Coast because of the distance for available maintenance.

Again, go back to your basic premise of protecting yourself and prove why you overlooked certain companies. You might want to limit your study of competing products to a reasonable number you can handle in the given time for the selection. In the case of a 1200 b/s modem, you probably would limit your study to 6 to 8 major providers. It would be impossible to look at every modem on the market, and you have made a reasonable attempt to give a number of vendors a shot at bidding for your business. Other vendors might be upset that they were not included, but they usually understand that you needed to keep your study within sensible limits.

Using consultants

If you feel you do not have enough expertise to implement a multi-vendor network, you could consider hiring a consultant. Consultants are used from a point of giving them full control, to hand-holding during planning, or to just verifying your results. Be aware that the caliber of the consultant's expertise ranges from very good to poor. When people use a consultant to verify what they have decided upon, they are usually looking for a third party to bless what they have done. The brave consultant will tell you the truth, even if it means not getting any more work. The uninformed consultant will probably not know the difference between right and wrong, and might readily concur with your work. If you are just looking for someone else to blame for any mistakes, just about any consultant will do.

How do you go about finding the right consultant? One place to look is the AT&T 800-Directory that resembles a yellow pages. The only drawback is that it only lists the AT&T 800-numbers. Nevertheless, you must weed out the communications consultants (public relations type) from the communications consultants that deal with telecommunications. The Society of Telecommunication Consultants (STC), headquartered in New York City, can direct you to a member near you. Looking at a list of the members shows they are heavily oriented toward voice communications and the PBX world.

Telecommunications consultants cover a variety of areas. Most consultants are voice and PBX-oriented. This is fine if all you need is someone to size the lines and trunks for a PBX or need to cost an alternative routing. In comparison, there are very few data telecommunications experts because they must have a better technical background. Data communications software solutions are better handled by computer consultants.

After you find a consultant, you should verify what their background is before you contract for their services. Let them tell you what they are capable of doing before you tell them why you need them. A consultant that needs work will tell you they are familiar with just about anything and then try to learn about the subject at your expense. Consultants that really know their subject can spout out answers without long study periods.

When you finally settle on a consultant that appears to fit your needs, you should write a simple contract. It should state exactly what the consultant will furnish, within what time frame, and how much they will charge. A closed-end contract is better than an open-ended one that charges by the hours worked. If, at the completion of the close-ended contract, you need additional work, it is simple enough to attach a rider to the contract. Be sure to check with your legal department on necessary clauses about nondisclosure of your plans and things like insurance or worker's compensation.

Issuing an RFP or RFQ

The next chapter on dealing with vendors explains how to locate the best person to send a copy of your RFP or RFQ, usually the product manager for the product or service. They, in turn, can assemble the best team to answer your request. If you send the RFP to a factory representative or some regional sales office, there will be a delay in response.

When you send the RFP or RFQ, provide a reasonable time frame for a response. Smart companies already have a good idea of your request. They are the ones that helped you in your planning stages and can turn around a response in a week. Those that are caught out in the cold, however, will require 30 to 90 days to respond, depending on the magnitude of the request. If you have a very large network that will require sizing and configuration studies, be sure to add in the extra time.

A reasonable time to you might be unreasonable for some vendors because of prior commitments or lack of understanding about the request. If a vendor requests more time, you have a choice to stick with your original schedule or give additional time to everyone. The decision will rest with the number of vendors already under study and your time frames for completion.

Verifying receipt

You should expect some verification from the vendor that they received your request. If you do not hear from vendors within a week, it is time to see if the request fell through the crack. Even if you sent the request by a delivery service or registered mail, there is a time delay to locate who accepted delivery. Don't assume a "no response" is a negative attitude. It could be that it just got lost in transit.

Dealing with participants

The next two chapters are about dealing with vendors and telephone companies (telcos). In this book, telcos is a generic term used to describe all companies that sell or lease communications facilities or services. There is no differentiation between regulated and unregulated telephone companies. While telcos are like vendors that sell or lease equipment, they are different in the way you must deal with them. In order to interface with upper management in many companies, vendors often create phony job titles. Telcos, on the other hand, have very structured job titles and tend to be very level conscious.

Some of the things in the vendor chapter are appropriate for the telephone chapter as well. It is recommended that you maintain a high ethical position at all times when dealing with vendors. It is a matter of dealing honestly and fairly with every vendor and not jeopardizing your decision by being unethical.

Clarifying responses

When you receive responses from your RFQ or RFP, you need to review them as quickly as possible to see if the vendor understood the request. If you receive five price quotes and one is very high or very low compared to the others, you need to go back to that vendor and go over the request. A wide variation such as this suggests the vendor did not understand what was being asked.

If you went ahead with the low bidder without verifying if they really understood your request, you run the risk of not obtaining your goal. Some vendors purposely exclude items or hide them in the fine print to appear being the lowest cost. This is especially true when you are requesting a quotation on some equipment. It is like buying a new car and the dealer quotes you the base price. Later, you find out that the wheels and the engine are extra options, and you have a whole different scenario. While this analogy is exaggerated, you might discover later that equipment providers did not include the needed optional parts in their bid. Find out exactly what is offered in the quote and check it against a price list, if possible. If the two do not agree, ask the vendor to explain the difference. They might have "inadvertently" left them off the quote.

Reducing risk

Risk analysis is an important part of the selection process. At first blush, it seems to be a lot of work to study each vendor. However, it can make your final selection take less time and give you vital information for your documentation. Appendix D contains a risk analysis worksheet that provides a format for studying vendors. Once you complete this analysis, your risk of making a poor decision and finding segments in the total system that need strengthening will be greatly reduced.

Making the big decision

After you have analyzed the various vendors, it is time to make that final choice. This is the place where you try to get the very best product or service for the least amount of money. It becomes a point of trade-offs of the better features or support against the bottom line. Another part of the final selection process is to look at the product or service over the life of the proposed network. Most networks have a life of only five years because of technological changes and tax depreciation schedules.

One should not make the mistake of opting for one vendor just because the product includes more (not better) features than other products. This is especially true when the extra features are of no value to the network now or in the future. When your basic requirement is buying a knife to cut string, you do not need the deluxe Swiss-army knife with 20 other features. It smacks of the pack rat mentality where the rodents store things away that they cannot use. If you cannot use a feature now or in the near future, don't judge the other products to be inferior because they do not have useless features.

Summary

Selection is the second step in implementing a multi-vendor network. Making the best selection possible improves your chances of having the network that is everything you planned on. This part of the book gives you the tools to make intelligent decisions and directs your study to cover the important points. It also includes unique features like risk analysis and a quality evaluation checklist.

8

Dealing with vendors

Dealing with vendors requires the highest level of ethics you can muster. Every vendor must receive the same treatment. You cannot show any favoritism toward any one vendor. It is much like how you are supposed to treat all your children with equal love and discipline.

Federal agencies probably go to the greatest length to distance themselves from accepting anything that might appear as a gift from a vendor. If a vendor serves a lunch of sandwiches and salads, they understand that the federal group will pay a nominal charge for what they eat. They are not allowed to accept even meals when dealing with outside contractors. Obviously, these rules have been designed to reduce any improper conduct or biased selection on the part of federal employees.

Everyday ethics

Ethics is a two-way street, and vendors are expected to exhibit the same high standards of ethics as the buyer. In fact, most sales personnel are very honest and ethical. Nevertheless, after knowing several used-car salespeople intimately, I can fully appreciate the other side of selling. The salespeople I know have a habit of making up so many stories that they sometimes didn't know the difference between fact and fiction. Unfortunately, there are some vendors that are unethical in their dealings and the line between fact and fiction also becomes blurred. Chapters 10 through 13 describe how to ascertain fact from fiction when dealing with vendors. A good method to protect yourself from vendors is to pretend that each vendor will not like your final decision and will take you to court over the matter. Your task is to adhere to the following ethical guidelines:

- Don't accept any gift with a value of more than a few dollars. Gifts of promotional material (i.e., the type they hand out at exhibitions) are acceptable to most companies. Dinners, theater tickets, or professional sports tickets, TVs, and other gifts of value are not acceptable. Check your company's guidelines on accepting any gift.
- Be truthful in all your dealings. Being truthful means not lying to the vendor, but it doesn't mean that you have to tell the vendor everything you know. Picture yourself on a witness stand and answer only the question asked; don't offer more information than necessary for the vendor to answer your proposal.
- Don't discuss the merits or shortcomings of any other product under consideration. In other words, don't tell the vendor who the competing vendors are—they'll probably guess who they are anyway.
- Treat everyone fairly. Don't extend special liberties to one vendor without offering the same to the other vendors under consideration. If you do make a concession to a vendor, you must contact the other competing vendors and offer the same opportunity. They may or may not take you up on the offer.
- Document any telephone conversation. Note the time, date, person calling, and what was said. If the information given could influence your final decision in any way, request that the vendor put it into writing. Signed letters have a certain permanency about them that memory often lacks. One only has to think about the number of trials in which someone has said "I don't remember." If they won't put it in writing, make a note of their reluctance to document what was discussed.
- Don't make any statements that the vendor could interpret as very positive input and construe as an almost certain order. Do not ask for changes in their design unless you are certain you will order their equipment after they go to the expense of changing to meet your needs. Do not suggest that certain changes would make their product more competitive.
- Repeatedly advise the vendor that any discussions that occur between the two of you are strictly exploratory and that the decision to buy or not buy will be made later.
- Make sure the vendor understands that any information provided by him must be public knowledge. You should not accept any document marked proprietary at this point. When you get closer to a decision, you might sign a nondisclosure statement to see their proprietary information.

Again, the best way to protect yourself is to assume the vendor will probably sue you in the end. If you have documented every dealing with the vendor, you have the basis to clear yourself and your company of any alleged wrongdoing. Making sure you do everything ethically will prevent the vendor from assuming you are going to buy their product. Lawsuits have been generated because a vendor assumed they would get a large order and then spent money to get things rolling. Keep it ethical and you won't have any problems.

Vendors vs. factory representatives

It is best to deal only with vendors. They fully understand their product and have the technical expertise to answer your questions. Most factory representatives sell a large cross section of products from different manufacturers. As a result, they are usually jack-of-all-trades and master of none. While factory representatives make some effort to know the product line, they are not as well versed as the actual vendor or manufacturer.

If the first response back about a particular product comes from a factory representative, you should request contacts at the manufacturing plant. Two contacts are the product manager (first choice) and the engineer who designed the product (second choice). The factory representative will usually be glad to hand you off to someone else as long as they end up with the commission.

Factory representatives normally receive a commission for products sold in their territory. When your network is national in scope or crosses over territories, things get a little murky as to who gets the commission. If your network is large and spans many states, you should insist on dealing only with the manufacturer. The major reason a manufacturer would not deal directly with a customer is when they do not have any personnel to handle the matter. You should then consider this a high-risk factor in your selection process. Risk analysis is covered in chapter 12.

Requesting presentations

Making presentations is a business expense for the vendor. If your prospective network looks like a promising place to sell their product, they will be very happy to go anywhere to make sure you know about their equipment. If they received a copy of your request for proposal or quote, they already know the value of your network. Again, an RFP, in this book, refers to the buyer who is looking for some guidance from the vendor. An RFQ, on the other hand, is a buyer looking for a hard dollar figure for specific items back from the vendor.

If your proposal or quote is for a limited amount or value, the vendor might opt for a presentation at their place. It will reduce their business costs, and it will let you see their manufacturing plant. There are pros and cons for the location of a presentation:

- If you have a large committee making the final decision, it is better to have the vendor come to your place. Large committees usually denote a large network and a valued prospect.
- If you have a very small group of decision makers, it is better to go to the vendor's plant for a presentation. You can then combine the trip with an inspection of their plant for quality, repair, and technical capabilities.

- If you are still not sure about the proposed network, you will want more people around to hear the vendor's input, and the vendor should make an effort to visit the buyer. When you get down to selection and risk analysis, you will then want to see their manufacturing plant.

Sending an RFP or RFQ to a vendor's main mailing address and not addressed to an individual will eventually find its way to the product manager. This source will be your main contact for future interfacing with the vendor. Instead of mailing a blind drop to a vendor's address, call the main number and request their marketing department. They, in turn, can advise you as to the proper person to deal with. More than likely, the product manager for the particular equipment will be your contact. Requests for a presentation or information on the product are addressed to that person.

Chapter 10 thoroughly covers how to manage meetings and presentations. While this chapter's thrust is a presentation in your building, your planning and control remain the same for both locations. Your objective is to make the very best use of your time and give the vendor a chance to present their product in a meaningful manner.

The hierarchy

One thing you will notice about vendors is that many Indians have chief titles. Financial institutions are the most notorious when it comes to titles. It often appears that everyone above a clerk level is at least an assistant vice president. Vendors of electronic equipment do not go to the same lengths, but they do dish out important-sounding job titles. This serves two purposes: one, the employee likes the sound of being a director or assistant vice president; second, it provides the mechanism to meet with the upper management of your company.

If the vendor feels your proposal will mean a large order for their company, they will bring out the heavies. Don't be surprised to see the president or chairman of the board, if they think it will sway the sale. While it is flattering to draw that much attention, it is also overwhelming for personnel that are normally isolated from their own upper management. Presidents of privately owned companies usually like to get involved with any major project. It is hard to let people bring someone into your sandbox and not want to check them out.

Checking quality

Quality is a mind-set of any company. Many vendors claim they are quality minded because that is the popular thing to say. However, quality must start at the very top of the company and trickle down to the lowest employee. It does not work if the quality talk is only from the promotional staff or just the quality control team in the plant. One recent example comes from a well-known American automobile manufacturer that advertises their quality to be near perfection. A worker spotted a major quality problem on the production line and was told to forget what he saw. A true quality program would have pulled that car out of the line and corrected the original quality problem before building more cars.

Appendix C contains a quality evaluation checklist that serves as a reminder of the things to look for when visiting a vendor's plant. It is divided into four sections—administrative policy, manufacturing controls, collection and analysis of field performance, and corrective action. Don't read the questions directly to the vendor, because you'll just get answers they think you want to hear. Instead of asking "Does the quality consciousness stem from the vendor's top management?," ask "Who is the head of quality control around here?". Companies that are strong in quality control will tell you the president is a bear about quality and everyone else follows his direction.

Section B under administration policy stresses that documentation of the quality system is critical. If the quality control manuals are not in sight around the floor of the manufacturing plant, it is a sign that quality control might only be lip service from the vendor. Companies with the best quality control document everything from incoming parts to failures during manufacture and failures during actual use. Inspection stations around the plant should have a set of manuals to clarify and instruct as to quality levels.

If a vendor's manufacturing plant lacks quality direction from the top and there isn't evidence of quality documentation around the plant, you must assign a high-risk factor to that product. One memorable manufacturer fitted the high-risk factor. There wasn't a shred of documentation in the plant. They used different types of capacitors (i.e., disk, electrolytic, ceramic, etc.) in the same location in their power supply. To someone's thinking, all types of capacitors exhibited the same characteristics and were all right as long as the unit rating was the same. A little farther down the production line, there were finished products waiting for their enclosures. One unit had a pair of half-hidden, long-nose pliers resting on one of the circuit boards inside. Had they put the enclosure on without double checking, they or the buyer would have gotten a surprise. In other parts of the plant, defective circuit board blanks were stacked alongside good units without any distinction, perhaps later finding their way into production. At that plant, it was almost a sure bet the defective boards would have found their way into the finished product. That visit was enough to stop a telephone company's product team from entering into a contract to purchase the product.

What to look for

When you narrow down a few vendors of competing products, you'll want to check the quality of their manufacturing plant. It doesn't make sense to visit everyone before this time because some vendors will be eliminated during the initial evaluation process. Those vendors that meet most of your needs are the ones you should request a visit with to see how the product is made. A tour should start at the point where component parts enter the plant and continue along the manufacturing path to the shipping of the finished product.

First, you don't have to know anything about quality to look for it. In, fact, it is better to appear unfamiliar and ask many dumb questions. Ask many questions about why they do things a certain way. Why did they choose to use a certain soldering machine instead of another? How often do they have to clean the solder machine? What does the operator of the machine look for in the soldering operation? Isn't there something about flux they must take care of during and after soldering? As you might guess from the line of questions, the soldering stage is very critical to good quality.

At the very next quality check, you will be well on your way to knowing all about quality. It is still a good idea to appear unknowledgeable at subsequent quality checks. People have a tendency to say more to a person who seems to lack understanding than to someone they feel is smarter than they are. Just absorb what they say even if they make that used-car salesperson seem like a saint. If they try to pull the wool over your eyes, you will soon see the difference between what is said and what is reality.

A quality manufacturing plant will be neat and clean. Circuit boards will be stacked in holders to prevent them from touching other boards, not lying on top of each other in a pile. Soldering machines have ventilation problems and are usually contained in a special room. While there are chemicals associated with soldering, the room should be very clean to prevent contaminants from getting into the soldering process.

Before you go on a quality check, review chapter 5 on quality. When you tour a plant, use the Quality Evaluation Checklist in appendix C as a guide. A quality company will have very few, if any, negative answers to the items. You now have a basis to evaluate one vendor over another. A high number of negative responses means there is a high-risk factor when selecting that product.

Training and operating manuals

Training and operating manuals are essential during the initial phases of the network but become a lifesaver later. They should be clearly written at an eighth-grade reading level. That doesn't mean you expect to have a batch of dummies trying to operate the system, although many network managers might feel that way. An eighth-grade reading level means sentences are short and multiple syllabicated words are not used. Another phrase meaning the same thing is KISS, or keep it short and simple. Some of the worst manuals are written by engineering staff or interpreted from the original Japanese version via a computer program or someone who isn't sure of the English language.

You should review all manuals and operating instructions to see if you have any trouble reading and understanding them. A better test is to have someone you consider a novice read the manuals and then operate the equipment. If the manuals are hard to read and understand, you have two choices. You can try and persuade the vendor to improve their manuals or you can rewrite them yourself. Either way, you should add a few more points to your risk analysis. Having a vendor rewrite their manuals will entail another expense they might not want to take on. The expense might not be the only reason. They might still have the same source to rewrite the manual as they had for the first one. If you really like the product over the other competition, you are better off writing your own manuals. Another possibility is to collaborate with the vendor to produce a document that serves both you and the vendor.

One last bone of contention with vendor's manuals is the use of their service or trade name in great profusion throughout the document. One manual used a trade name 23 times on just one page. You had to take the P6 Kumquat cord and plug it into the N43-Kumquat jack, and then operate the Kumquat switch to the on position. It was like reading a grade-school child's report about a little kitten that went meow, meow, meow, meow, etc.

Returns and repairs

A portion of the Quality Evaluation Checklist in appendix C deals with collecting field performance data and the corrective action taken. The usual point to find this information is where the vendor handles the return and repair of their products. In addition to looking at the repair records and other data, find out what the repair and return process is all about. See if they have a guaranteed turnaround time for repair and return. What you must determine is the length of time you would be without a spare for emergency restoration. Some companies will immediately replace units in the field before receiving the defective one. If this is the case, you should find out the following:

- What guarantees do you have that the unit you receive is the latest version and not one that is about to reach the end of its life cycle?
- Does the vendor's original warranty period apply to the replacement?
- Is the unit considered a direct replacement or just a loaner until your unit is repaired? A loaner might require taking part of the system down to reinstall the repaired unit.
- If the defective unit has a questionable component that caused its failure, does the vendor plan to exchange the other units you purchased?
- Who pays for shipping the units in each direction? Because the vendor sent a unit first, the defective unit uses the same shipping box for return and reduces your expenses. Nevertheless, if the defective unit is still under the warranty period, the vendor should also assume the shipping expense in both directions. If the defective unit is outside the warranty period, you probably will find you have the expense for shipping.

Technical assistance

A cartoon in *Network World* depicted what network managers always suspected about the people answering the technical assistance hotline. The scene showed a telephone answering device sitting on one small desk in an otherwise empty back room. The caption said something like "I am sorry, but all our technicians are busy on other calls, but if you would leave your name and number, we will try to get back to you as soon as possible." When you need assistance to solve your problems, you want it in the shortest amount of time. This is another item to check when you make a quality evaluation. Try to meet the people that you might have to deal with if you select that vendor. You should learn the following:

- What type of information will they need to help you with your problem? Do they need serial and model numbers? Is there a particular format they use, like a printed form? Can you use the form and fax them the information?
- How is technical assistance handled out of normal business hours? Is there an extra charge for technical assistance during out of normal business hours?
- What is the expected time interval to get in touch with a technician who is on call but is out?
- If you had a minor technical question, what is the best time in the week or day to call? Like most businesses, there are slack periods during the week that provide a greater chance to talk to a technician.

Summary

Remember to bend over backwards to be ethical in all your dealings with vendors. If you accept gifts from a vendor, it places your decision in jeopardy. Pretend all vendors that do not get a piece of the action will sue to recover damages. Document all verbal conversations. Keep extensive files that include all documents between your company and the vendor. Verify the vendor's quality, manuals, manufacturing processes, and technical support. By following just a few simple rules, you can make intelligent decisions that are supported by facts.

9

Dealing with telephone companies

When I use the term *telcos*, I am referring to all telephone companies that sell or lease communication facilities or services. While many countries still have a central or government-run telephone company (telco), the United States has gone from one near-monopoly to many smaller units. So, for the purposes of this book, a telco is any business that provides telecommunications or carrier services to other businesses. This book also considers that a telco is a vendor if they sell the equipment to you and you are going to maintain it yourself.

One advantage of government-run or near-monopoly telcos is the tight control they have over what is connected to it. While this seems heavy-handed, the networks they offer will work from end-to-end. Everything connected to the network has gone through exhaustive testing and was made to the telephone company's specifications. It was also usually made by a unit of the telco. Today, all this has changed because of the many companies competing for the telecommunication business. In a sense, a telco is a vendor of communication services. Nevertheless, they react differently than vendors of electronic equipment, and therefore, I have put this information in its own chapter.

Vendors vs. telephone companies

The one major thing that separates the vendors of equipment from the vendors of telecommunications is their approach. Most equipment vendors wait for some contact from a prospective buyer to make a sale. The opposite is true of vendors the size of IBM or Siemens. Most telcos have large marketing teams to go after buyers. In fact, very large vendors and telcos even have account teams dedicated to just one customer.

Account teams can contain the whole gambit of talents, from pure marketing to pure technical assistance. On the other hand, smaller business ac-

counts might have only one person dedicated to one company or several in-
dustry-specific companies share the individual. Unfortunately, there isn't a
general description for the type of salesperson you will deal with. You will meet
varying levels of expertise when dealing with telephone companies. They can
have a technical background or be people with their Master of Business
Administration without any technical ability.

At one time, account team members spent time in the operations and
engineering departments before they went into sales. Of course, that was when
the telco was engineering-oriented instead of market-directed. Telcos then
started the practice of using the generalist instead of the specialist in most
departments. A generalist doesn't have to know anything about the service to
sell it. Conversely, the specialist knows everything about the service, but
doesn't know anything about how to sell it.

The last item in each column in TABLE 9-1 shows the major difference
between most telcos and vendors. Of course, there are exceptions, but the
sales effort is more active under the telco. Back in the days when telcos were
led by engineers, there was an attitude that the service or product would sell
itself. Most engineer-oriented vendors also have this same pride that the
product will sell itself without a lot of effort from the sales force. If the
president of a vendor company also designed the first unit made, you will find
that he still leans towards the engineering philosophy.

Another thing you can gather from TABLE 9-1 is that telcos typically have a
larger marketing staff than vendors. Being larger means they can devote people
to an active role and pursue sales instead of waiting for someone to call. Because
telcos make 80 to 90 percent of their revenue from 10 to 20 percent of the very
large businesses, they devote a great amount of time with them. Companies with
smaller revenue potential get less support. This continues down the line to a
point where they rely on the customer to call just like many vendors.

Company hierarchy

The thing that sets telcos apart from smaller companies is the hierarchical
system of management. It varies slightly from company to company, but is

Table 9-1. Telephone companies vs. vendors.

Telephone companies	Vendors
Marketing vice-presidents	Market vice-president
Industry managers	Sales staff
Product managers	Product manager
Account managers	Factory representatives
Account executives	Passive sales effort
Product support teams	
Active sales effort	

based on the premise that you didn't talk or write letters to anyone that is two levels above or below you. There were cases of telco personnel asking what level you were before they talked to you. If they found out you were beyond one layer in the structure, you could expect them to hang up the phone.

Telco employees located away from headquarters rarely saw third-level managers. Even rarer were visits from fourth level and above managers. Other than the annual Christmas walk through the office, one seldom knew who was who in their own upper management. TABLE 9-2 lists a typical telco's hierarchy. The names change as companies change their structure, and there can be half-level positions between the main levels.

Table 9-2. Telco hierarchy.

Title	Grade level
Supervisor	1st
Manager	2nd
District manager	3rd
Division manager	4th
Director	5th
Vice-president	6th
Executive vice-president	7th
President	8th
CEO	9th

There is another level under the first level of management. The U.S. Army has a level called Warrant Officer. It isn't a full officer level, nor is it a non-commissioned officer level. Instead, it offers some benefits of both worlds. In a telco, there are staff assistants that are paid somewhere between first level and nonmanagement. They can get overtime payment for extra work that the first level manager can't get.

Your dealing with a telco will normally put you in touch with someone that starts at this staff assistant level up through the second management level. If your network promises a large revenue base, they might bring out the heavies, as any vendor would. However, now the heavies will only talk to heavies. It all goes back to the philosophy of interfacing on a one-up or one-down level. Your best prospect of meeting upper-level telco people is to create a title for yourself like Director of Telecommunications before dealing with them. And if you have several people working with you on the project, make sure they all have great-sounding titles. Again, telcos are title-conscious people and tend to be condescending to people they consider well below their level.

Pushing the level awareness one step further, you can use your created title to ring the chimes of the telco's upper level when you have a major maintenance problem. Talking on the same level as a telephone director will make things happen very quickly—a lot quicker than dealing with lower levels. They usually do not hear complaints directly and respond as if it was a major catastrophe. Of course, you cannot over-abuse this ploy, because it will be like crying wolf too often. It won't be long before you will end up talking to some underling when they or their secretary hears your name. The other brush-off tactic is the telephone tag game where you never get to talk to anyone.

Brochures, presentations, and seminars

Brochures, presentations, and seminars are three different levels of information provided by telcos. Unfortunately, brochures usually contain little or no information about the service or product. They are marketing pictures painted with very wide brushes and do not get into specifics. What starts out as a thing meant to wet the appetite will often turn the readers off because it does not tell them anything. The lack of information can lead to the wrong conclusion about the product. Product or service names is another area that can be misleading. In attempting to derive a unique name, the marketing department can create a name that doesn't provide a clue as to its function. It is like calling a garbage collector an environmental control specialist. If you needed a garbage collector, you would never look for them under the other title.

Presentations are a little better, but they often fail because the person giving them has the stock slides and speech provided by the product manager. Giving presentations can be a challenge to some people, but it is compounded when you have to use someone else's slides and speech. The presenter does not know the material as well as the originator and often lacks the understanding of what the originator had in mind. Consequently, the message gets lost. When a telco puts on a group presentation for many companies, the person who originated the slides and speech is usually the presenter.

If you request a presentation about a service from a telco, be sure to follow the instructions in chapter 10 on managing meetings and presentations. This chapter explains how to plan and control a presentation to fit your needs and make the best use of your time.

Occasionally, some telcos will conduct seminars on several associated services at their own presentation center. This is beneficial because you have a chance to meet other network management people and learn what they are doing. The downside is that the seminar cannot be adjusted to meet your specific needs and remains generic in scope. While it might have been more appropriate to attend one of these seminars during the planning phase of your network, it might still be valuable in finding something that you haven't overlooked.

Training and operating manuals

Quite often, the only instruction a telco provides is how to operate their service or product. Maintenance of the network or equipment is usually the responsibility of the telco. Your only role might be replacing equipment at your sites, and then you wouldn't need maintenance manuals.

During your discussions with telcos, learn about the different levels of training they will provide. This can go from having a telco instructor providing on-the-job training (OJT) to how-to-operate manuals. Even if they will provide OJT, you should ask to see their operating manuals to see if you can understand them. Very large telcos will use writers that assemble a manual out of bits and pieces of engineering documents. While their writing skills are great, they lack any comprehension about the subject. How good the manual is depends on the time they had to develop it. If they were rushed to meet a deadline, the manual will probably have flaws that might never be corrected. In one sense, the manual writer and product manager met a commitment to produce a manual and received high praise at rating time. The manual will not be revised for flaws until there comes time to reprint more manuals. Major flaws would require a revision, which would, without a doubt, upset the product manager's budget.

In chapter 12, risk analysis is covered, and you'll learn how to assign a value to the manuals and training a telco provides. If you have to rewrite the manuals so your people can understand how to operate the service or product, you must give that company a higher risk rating.

Questions to ask the telco

Unless you ask a telco many questions, they will not offer much information as to what they really are providing. You need to know exactly how they plan to handle your network. This is especially true if you haven't used a particular telco before. If you have experience with a telco, you might only need to be concerned if you plan to use a new or different service. The following are some examples of things to ask telcos:

- What are their maintenance and repair guarantees? While their systems might have a stated failure rate of say 99.5 percent up-time, find out what that really means. The practice is to average the failure events over a long period that tends to obscure the actual performance.
- Do they provide priority restoration of services if your network has critical service?
- If your network has duplicate services to provide greater reliability, how can they guarantee the services do not go through the same office, master nodal clocking source, or cable system? How can they guarantee the duplicate services will not inadvertently be put back together again?
- What are the limits of the services or products? Every piece of equipment has a design limit. Switching machines can handle just so many calls simultaneously. Fast-packet multiplexers, or for that matter, all multiplexers, have a physical limitation as to the amount of digital bits they can cram onto a telephone line.

- What is the gross delay you could expect on your network? What is the delay on the segments between nodes?

This last question tries to get the telco to tell you something they are reluctant to tell you. They like to quote a figure that equals the delay of a 4,000-mile-long circuit. Nevertheless, 90 percent of the high-speed digital circuits are less than 450 miles in length. There is a vast difference in the delay of the two lines. While you can fine-tune your system later to get the optimum performance, the question delves into the actual mileage of the parts and the total system. If you have two nodal points 100 miles apart, you do not want to end up with a circuit that is routed all over the place because the telco didn't have facilities. Some telcos have greater cross sections than others and can offer a shorter distance than others. Shorter lines mean greater reliability because there is less equipment and sources of transmission impairments.

Maintenance

Telco maintenance provisions vary from the very sophisticated to the very rudimentary. This is directly expressed in the rates charged. If you want a highly maintained network with a quick response to troubles, you can expect a higher charge than services with little or no maintenance. Therefore, how a telco provides maintenance becomes a risk factor.

Telco maintenance provisions are much like the maintenance contract on a new appliance—and they only come into your area on Thursdays. Too bad the appliance went on the fritz on Friday and you have to wait. The local oil burner-repair company offers two types of maintenance contracts. On the first one, they will come out anytime of the day or night—including weekends. The other contract only covers normal business hours and you are second in line to the premium service. Figuring which contract costs more is a real snap.

Before you make your final decision on which telco or combinations of telcos to use, you should fully understand exactly what type of maintenance you will receive for your dollar. You need to know:

- Where are the maintenance centers located in respect to your locations? You do not want to find out the nearest center is a three-hour drive away. Just because they guaranteed a two-hour restoration doesn't mean they will fix it in two hours. It just means you do not have to pay for it after the two hours.
- What are the normal maintenance hours? Are there additional charges for maintenance beyond the normal Monday-to-Friday business hours?
- Does their network management system generate automatic trouble reports to the appropriate test center or are there several layers of testing and referrals before the trouble report gets to right person?
- If the network doesn't generate automatic trouble reports, what are the telco's trouble-reporting procedures? Do they use a toll-free number?

Do they use a dispatcher arrangement where you talk to a clerk and the maintenance personnel call you back later?

- Does the trouble-reporting center prioritize working on troubles according to amount of circuits involved or is it first in first out? If you have a line carrying an equivalent of 50 circuits, you do not want to wait in line until someone fixes a trouble affecting only one circuit.
- What are their escalation procedures? If a test center or maintenance group can't fix the trouble in a short time, do they bring in the experts that can solve the problem?

The last question addresses what happens if the test center or maintenance people find themselves in over their technical heads. For example, the old Bell System had a nationwide group of data experts (DATEC) that had the test equipment that could locate obscure problems. After a few hours of outage, the trouble was referred to these regional experts. If they had difficulty in diagnosing the problem, they contacted headquarters where there were even more highly trained technical experts. In just a few hours after the trouble started, the technical people could involve scientists or technical staff at Bell Labs.

The trouble-reporting center

Visiting the actual trouble-reporting center makes good sense. It lets you meet the people that would work on your lines if they are selected. You can also see the extent of their operations. Again, a telco's maintenance can range from very imposing to the ridiculous, and seeing is believing. Ask if they can show you exactly how an actual trouble report is handled. In chapter 8 where checking on quality is discussed, you read about not appearing to know much and to ask many questions. Personnel in the operations side of a telco are usually very talkative, and you can learn a lot about their maintenance operations. Ask questions similar to the following:

- What is the hardest thing to troubleshoot? Is one carrier facility better than another?
- What types of tests can you make from here? Are there some tests you would like to make but need a new test set to do it? Operations personnel normally think they should have the latest whiz-bang test equipment that another office has. They will normally respond to this type of question, telling you information you would never get otherwise.
- How do you restore service if a facility goes out? Do you set priorities on how circuits are restored? How do you decide who is first?
- Do you call the customer to tell them they are going to be without service for a particular time frame?
- What happens if you have problems trying to locate the problem—do you just call your supervisor?

Technical assistance

Technical assistance varies from telco to telco. Unfortunately, telcos have downsized their companies by offering early retirement to people who have taken years to become technical experts. Companies that once had technical experts on hand did away with them entirely or substituted them with a lower level of expertise.

If you are relying on the telco's networking specialists to size your circuit requirements, they should be able to tell you what system they use and who is going to make the calculations. A very large telco will probably use a computer system they developed. Smaller telcos do not have the personnel to develop their own system and will use a commercially available one. Even smaller telcos do not have the personnel to make any network sizing.

Try to locate just where the technical experts are located in the telco. What you are trying to learn is just how long it will take to have a true technical expert on your site to correct a difficult problem. You also do not want to find out that good old Ace is the only one who knows about the equipment and he won't get back from Timbuktu until next week sometime—they think.

Summary

Telephone companies are different from vendors in many respects. Many are level conscious about who they deal with, and you need to play the game of creative titles. Many telcos are very large businesses, and their marketing departments are very active in sales. Telcos also vary in their level of maintenance and support. A greater level of support is reflected in the rates charged. If you assume the total maintenance responsibility, then you must include your labor costs and expenses in the risk analysis. In this case, the labor costs include the loading of all the fringe benefits and the prorated operation of the building.

10

Managing meetings & presentations

Managing meetings and presentations seems to be a lost art. Meetings, as well as presentations, are time-consuming and, thereby, too expensive to be done without forethought. If it is a vendor presentation, it is a business expense incurred in anticipation that they will sell their product, but the company that is getting the presentation also incurs an expense—the added cost of all the personnel attending the presentation. Neither party can spend their money on fruitless adventures. If you had the opportunity to work on both sides of the presentation (i.e. the giver and the receiver), you quickly learned the right way to get the most for your dollar. Take heed vendors, and you might increase your sales potential.

Meetings

Meetings are a part of everyday business. Those that run effectively reach their goals in the shortest amount of time. They are a joy to go to because they don't take long and they accomplish the most. When meetings grind on for hours, they are boring and never seem to result in much. At times, you can accomplish more by leaving a meeting partway through rather than sitting to the bitter end. At least you can finish some other work.

Why do some meetings wander? Well, maybe wander isn't the right word. Wander suggests you have strayed off the main subject. In some meetings, it is difficult just recognizing the main subject. Therefore, before arranging a meeting, the first thing you should do is create an agenda that lists all the items for discussion. This is true for internal meetings as well as meetings with vendors.

The agenda

An agenda takes the guesswork out of what will be discussed at a meeting. It is a road map to keep everyone focused on the goals of the meeting. One of the main goals of a properly run meeting is to prevent hidden agendas, or someone else's agenda, from popping up and disrupting the meeting. The agenda doesn't have to be detailed. It can be just a few words that everyone can recognize. If there is a new topic that is foreign to most people, then include an attachment that covers the subject in greater detail.

After you lay out the agenda, you need to prepare a meeting notice. A meeting notice is important even if you already scheduled established dates and times in advance. It serves as a reminder and spells out the topics for discussion. Needless to say, the notice should be sent with enough lead time that participants can schedule their time.

In the sample meeting notice in FIG. 10-1, there are four main sections. Section A lists the time, the day of the week, and the calendar date. Just the simple inclusion of the day of the week relieves everyone from checking the calendar to see which day it is.

Network Evaluation Committee

Meeting Notice

A Time: 9 am Tuesday Sept 15th

B Place: Conference Room 401; Phone: X6845

C Topics for Discussion:

1. Open items from last meeting.

2. Review multiplexer Request for Proposal (see attached)

3. Verify additional data bandwidth requirements

4. Schedule adjustments

D Attendees: Bob White, Communications, Chairperson
Jim Brown, Engineering
Mary Astor, Accounting
Ossie Byter, MIS
Ben Hurdle, Operations

Fig. 10-1. Meeting notice.

Section B gives the location. If the conference room is in a new or strange location, include directions on how to get there. One very large corporation had conference rooms spread all over a sprawling complex. Several conference rooms were located in portions of the building that were inaccessible from normal corridors. To get to the conference room, you had to use a particular elevator or staircase. People that didn't know of the special access were either very late or never found the room.

Be sure to include the telephone number of the phone located in the conference room. This serves two purposes. If a person is late or cannot find the room, they can phone (presuming they still have the meeting notice in hand). Second, the attendees can readily leave a number with their support staff for emergency contact. The only drawback about the telephone number is when the support group gives the number out in nonemergency situations.

Section C lists the agenda topics. Again, if the topic is new or requires additional information, be sure to attach it to the meeting notice. Item 2 makes note of the particular attachment for this notice. Section D includes the attendees' names and organization. In the example, the chairperson or controller for the meeting was noted to tell everyone who was leading the meeting. The name and organizations of the other people tell who and what group is expected.

Meeting rooms and power seats

When you see the term *power seats*, you might think about the six-way power seat in your car. In a meeting room, however, there are seats of power that influence the outcome of a meeting. Figure 10-2 shows a conference room with eight chairs and a long table. The seats are shaded from very dark to white. Sitting in one of the shaded seats, designated as a power seat, puts you in a

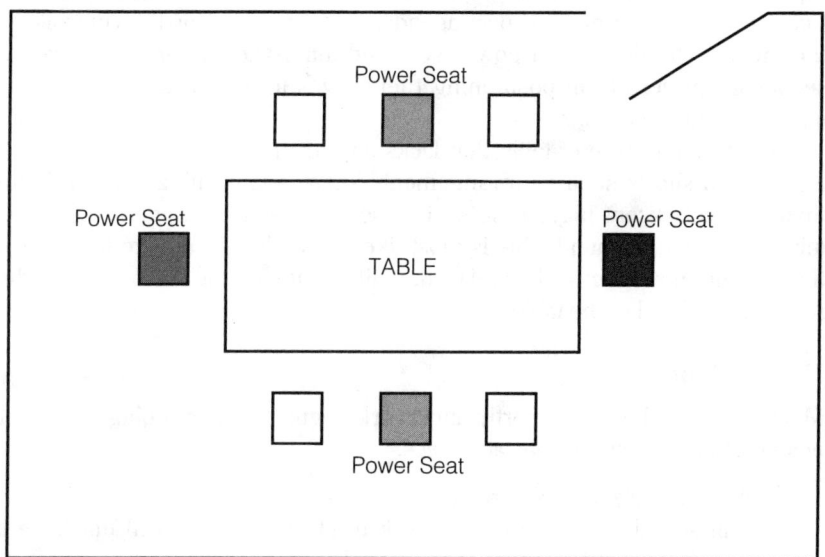

Fig. 10-2. Power seats in conference room.

position of strength. As the shading gets lighter, the seats become progressively subservient. The one with the darkest shading has the greatest strength.

People who know about power seats usually get to a meeting ahead of time to stake out their position. Being the controller of the meeting, it is imperative that you beat everyone else to the meeting so you can grab the best power seat. In the case of FIG. 10-2, the seat at the end nearest the door is the ultimate power seat because it is on the end and it is near the door. How the power seat came about is not obvious. Nevertheless, all you have to do is think back to other meetings, and the person with the highest position in the company usually found a way to get that seat.

The next power seat is at the other end of the table. This is similar to the old family tradition where the authority figures of the household sit at the ends of the table. Father sits at the head of the table, and the children sit in the non-power seats. Whichever end father sits on is the head of the table. Another sign of authority at the dinner table is a chair that is different from the others. Dining room furniture usually has at least one chair that is set apart from the others, such as one with arms. In some meeting rooms, the head of the table also has a chair that is different from the others. This is especially true if the room is a conference room for upper management. The one high-backed chair establishes the head power seat.

While the best position might be at the end of the table near the door, a blackboard or other audio-visual aids always seem to be located at the other end. That end is still better than any other location. Remember, you cannot run an effective meeting from a non-power seat. If you sit in a non-power seat, someone that is in a power seat can turn your meeting into theirs. This is especially true if the other person has a domineering personality, and wants to assert their position or their own agenda. It is important for the controller of the meeting to get a good power seat and almost as important to prevent secondary players from positioning themselves in one. You need your key players in those positions.

There is one type of table that lacks any real power seats—a round one. Figure 10-3 shows such an arrangement. There really isn't a position better than the rest except maybe the seat closest to the door. Then it only has a minor influence. A round table is most like the kitchen or dinette table where the morning meal is casual or relaxed, unlike in the dining room where father reigns at the head of the table.

Meeting times

Meetings that take place shortly after work begins in the morning reap many benefits. Starting early means attendees:

- Are relatively fresh and rested.
- Can schedule their normal work to start later and will not have to interrupt what they are doing to attend.
- Will not be worrying about how soon it is to lunch.

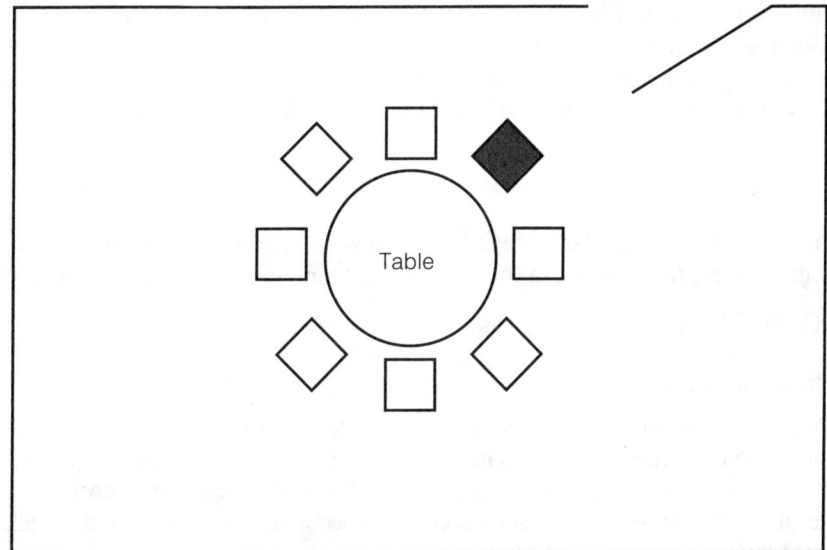

Fig. 10-3. Round table vs. power seats in conference room.

Running a meeting too close to a lunch period is foolhardy. If the company has staggered lunch periods, you will find individuals who take the earliest time available will lose interest to everything else as soon as their stomach starts to rumble. Holding a meeting right after lunch is also foolhardy if there is a possibility anybody attending would eat a large lunch. A large lunch will put them into a semi-stupor. This factor is very evident with presentations.

Controlling meetings

Over the years, the name for the person that controlled the meeting went by the name of gatekeeper or facilitator. What you should be is the conductor of the band of participants. You pick the music (agenda) that everyone will play. You get to select where the band will play (location), and if you are very smart, you will even designate where people will sit (power seats).

Controlling a meeting means the whole orchestrated affair. If you think back to meetings that went quickly, a strong leader had things under control from the very beginning. The meeting went quickly and it had positive results. Conversely, the meeting that meandered had little or no leadership. It doesn't take a hard-nosed drill sergeant to run a meeting. Nevertheless, the individual cannot be timid and let individual attendees take over. When they do, they introduce their own agenda that differs from the original goals. Planning, setting goals, and controlling the meeting lead to a productive time spent by everyone.

Ending meetings

After the main topics have been covered, it is time to review the open items and assign responsibility. Everyone should leave the meeting with no doubt in their mind as to exactly who was going to do what in a particular time frame. As an added reminder, you should send a copy of the open items and their due dates to the responsible people. If additional meetings are necessary, this is a good time to set a mutually agreeable date to assure the best attendance.

Presentations

Presentations are similar to meetings in several respects. They require your control to get the best out of them. Also, they must be orchestrated to achieve your goals.

Preparation

Preparing for a presentation is as much the responsibility of the presenter as the presentee. The presenter is happy to get a chance to hawk his/her product if there is a possible sale. The presenter will usually have a few stock slides he/she uses for generic presentations. The problem is the presentation lacks direction. Another goal-setting opportunity is in the making.

One of the first things a vendor and a prospective buyer need to agree on is what the presentation should include. The makeup of the intended audience is a major concern. If the audience is interested in technical issues, a marketing presentation will fall flat. When the nontechnical marketing or factory representatives are asked technical questions, the usual response is "I'll have to get back to you on that." What happens now is that the technical types are turned off completely by the presentation because they believe the presenter doesn't know anything about his product. The presenter, in turn, has just blown his/her time making a fool of himself/herself.

If you enter a presentation without any idea what the backgrounds of the audience will be, then the presenter should include an engineering representative from the factory. Most marketing types are appalled at the thought of including engineering personnel because they usually lack the talent to skirt issues that marketing would rather see hidden. If you asked a marketing person what would make the product better, they will tell you it is already the best in the world. Ask the engineer who designed the equipment if he or she would do things differently if there was more time and money, and go through a list of items. The list not only tells you what the shortcomings are, but what they found wrong with the unit after turn-up.

Some of the best presentations are made when the presenter has a knowledgeable technical type on hand that can answer all the technical questions without having to get back to the group later. It not only makes the presentation complete, but also shows the vendor appears to know their product. To appease the marketing types, the technical person stays on the sidelines until asked a specific question. He is instructed to answer only the question and not take over the presentation.

Therefore, the first thing that needs to be settled between the vendor and the people getting the presentation is the type of material. This responsibility is shared between the vendor and the controller of the presentation. Oh yes, there has to be a controller of the presentation too. Prior to the presentation, the controller should know the following.

- A close approximation of the number of people that will attend. An open invitation could attract people with no specific need to be involved. Also, the vendor usually likes to bring brochures or other material to the presentation and a head count helps.

- The makeup of the personnel attending. You should be able to tell the presenter the approximate mix of technical and nontechnical people attending. A possible decision would be to hold two separate but concurrent presentations. One part would discuss features; the other would delve into technical issues.

- What are your goals for the presentation? You should direct the vendor to tailor their presentation to fit your needs. An open presentation with no direction is of little value to you or the vendor.

Now that you know these three things, the vendor can gear the presentation to meet specific needs. They can bring an approximate number of brochures or other material. There is nothing worse for a vendor than to prepare for too many or too few people. When they expect to see only 5 people and 20 show up, they end up sending additional material at a later date. It is also unsettling to the presenter to see a very large crowd when he or she expected only a very few. The presentation for a large crowd is entirely different than one for just a few. When this happens, the presenter has to readjust their presentation on the fly. A presenter might have opted for a small, contained display unit for a small crowd but would need an overhead projector and transparencies for a large group. The opposite happens when the presenter expects a large crowd and only a few show up.

Keeping track of the number of people attending is the responsibility of the controller. You should check the probable attendees a day or two before the presentation to verify the number of people. After the final number is given to the vendor, don't accept additional attendees. Gate crashers can be turned down. What you are trying to accomplish is making sure the vendor will get an even break to give the very best presentation.

The next thing to agree on is the length of the presentation. Most sales pitches are not very long and rely on questions from the audience to prolong them. The vendor knows how long his normal spiel takes, so it is prudent to agree on the additional time you will allow for questions. Once this is known, a meeting notice like FIG. 10-4 is sent to key players.

Section A lists the length of the presentation, the starting time, the day, and the date. Section B tells which conference room and the phone number of the room. Remember to include directions if the room is in a new or strange

---

Network Evaluation Committee

Presentation Notice

Date of Notice:

A Time: 9:30 to 10:30 am Tuesday November 17th

B Place: Conference Room 200; Phone: X6830

C Presentation By: The Amalgamated Widget Company, LTD

D The Amalgamated Widget Co. will make a presentation of their Model 201 Network Controller. This device is designed to manage and report troubles on data networks.

E Please contact Bob White on X5858 or use electronic mail address BOWHITE to indicate if you will or will not attend. A head count is needed by Nov 13th.

F List names of people invited to attend.

Fig. 10-4. Presentation notice.

location. In Section C, name the company, and in Section D, tell what device is being shown. Also include enough information about the product to clarify what the presentation is about.

The next section, Section E, gives the contact or the controller's name and how to acknowledge if the person will or will not attend. Section F lists the names of the principal people (the decision makers for the committee) invited. A second group of invitees might be workers under the principals (secondary people) who could have a large influence over the final outcome. The last group of people that could attend are the interested others who heard about the presentation.

Finally, you need to arrange for any audio-visual equipment that might be needed for the presentation. Vendors usually have a trusty slide projector or other device to demonstrate their product, but the logistics in checking one through your company's security system or transporting it might be a hassle. If the presenter is going to use the audio-visual equipment already in the building, make sure of the following beforehand:

- Spare bulbs for the various projectors are readily available in the room. The only spare should not be locked up in some cabinet in another part of the building.
- The vendor knows what type of slide projector tray is used (i.e. round, long, or cube).

- If a VCR is available, make sure it is the right type. Some machines use a wider tape (i.e. 1-inch vs. 3/4-inch tape; Beta vs. VHS).

Presentations fizzle when the slide or overhead projector's light bulb burns out and a replacement isn't available. One very important presentation went to extremes for backup equipment. It had two movie projectors aimed at the same screen with duplicate films. Both were turned on at the same time with one lit and the other dark. If a bulb blew during the showing, the other projector's light would be turned on and the audience would only see a momentary flash. Everything used in the presentation was duplicated and, in some instances, triplicated.

Scheduling

The same scheduling sense applies to presentations as for meetings. The biggest problem for a presentation right after the start of work in the morning is logistics. Travel time and time to set up audio-visual equipment might preclude an early morning start. Steer clear of holding presentations after lunch, however. They are worse than holding meetings after lunch because the presentation might use a slide projector, which usually requires the lights to be dimmed. A full stomach and low lights are the greatest sleep catalyst known to the human race.

One large vendor had a great presentation center. The downfall was the center was located near a lot of restaurants and the center had a complete ice cream fountain. People would have a large lunch and then top it off with an equally large sundae with all the trimmings. A few minutes later, they were in a room with almost no lighting save the light from the slide projector. Within five minutes, 90 percent of the attendees were asleep or in a comatose state.

You can have a presentation right after lunch if you control the eating habits of the attendees. This is possible if you cater a lunch with sandwiches, salads, or some other low-calorie meal. People will come early to eat the food, and they will not be stuffed.

Opening a presentation

As the controller for the presentation, it is your responsibility to open the meeting with introductions. This only entails presenting the principals involved. You can mention the secondary personnel to identify they are not principals.

NOTE: Japanese and other foreign companies usually exchange business cards between individuals at the very beginning of the presentation. Be sure all the principal players have, and bring, their business cards to the presentation.

It is a lot easier for the presenter to have the principals seated next to each other. They are the ones that should have the undivided attention of the presenters, and the presenter should not have to search around the audience to look for responsive signs from the important listeners. A suggested layout for a presentation is shown in FIG. 10-5. You can position the principal players in front

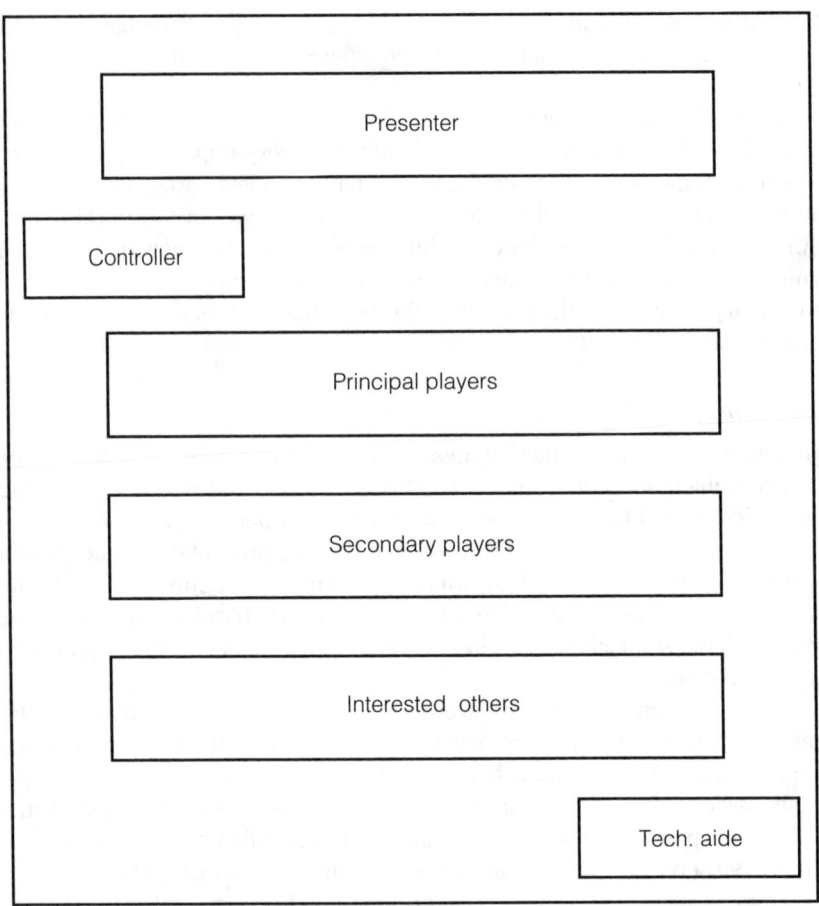

Fig. 10-5. Presentation location in conference room.

by making name signs. It positions the secondary people and the interested others to the rear. When you use name signs, the presenters will have a reminder of the principal's names and be able to address them personally.

Good presenters can look at the eyes of the audience to see if the message is getting across. The better ones can adjust the presentation to make it clearer and remove the glazed look. As one presenter put it, "They just saw God" as their eyes lit up.

During the introductions, you should also point out the job associated with each person. Another way to do this is to have each principal introduce themselves and indicate what they wanted from the presentation. This can be as simple as "I am Jim Brown from engineering and my special interest is in your interfaces." The presenter or controller can make a list of the interests to make sure everything was covered by the end of the presentation.

Controlling presentations

As controller, you should set the tone of the presentation from the very beginning. You and the vendor have the choice to field questions during or after the presentation. Waiting until the actual presentation is over to pose questions is better because most questions will be answered during the presentation. Allowing questions during the presentation is disruptive and throws the flow off. The presentation becomes jumbled unless the presenter puts the question off by saying it will be covered later. It is far better for the attendees to make notes of their questions to be answered after the presentation.

When it comes time for a question and answer period, the controller should take an active part to screen the questions. Large audiences are divided between principal personnel that are the decision makers, a secondary group, and interested viewers. The principal members of the audience should have first access to the question period. Secondary members should not have access to a question period until after the principals are through asking questions. You might even schedule a special time for the secondary people. This way, the principals can go back to their own work. You, as controller, must make sure the secondary people or interested others do not prolong the vendor's time any more than you are willing to spend. Your own work takes priority over their needs.

Ending presentations

Most questions should be answered during the meeting. Nevertheless, a few questions usually remain unanswered. Make note of any question that wasn't answered during or after the presentation. At the very end of the presentation and question period, review the open questions and the names of the people that asked them. First, make sure the vendor understands the question thoroughly. As an added check, write the question out so the vendor can get the right answer. Getting the right answer to a question requires that someone fully understands what was asked. Set a reasonable time period for the vendor to return with a written reply. Answers to most open questions usually interest only a few people in the audience. Therefore, a copy of the answer is then distributed only to people who indicate at the meeting they are interested in receiving the information.

Summary

Managing meetings and presentations require some of the same tactics to make them effective. They both require planning, control, and follow up. The two most important items are the planning and control. Without either item, your chances of success are between slim and none. Both meetings and presentations are expensive to your own company. If they are not effective, you have not spent your time wisely.

11

Vendor responses

When you get a response back from a vendor, you must review it to see if the answers seem to fit the questions or requests. Don't wait until all the responses are back before beginning your selection process. This review is a scan of key items and not an in-depth study of their answers to your request. The objective is to catch glaring omissions and unusual answers.

Oral and written communications is an art form. It takes skill to ask the right questions and receive an answer that meets the question. Politicians consider themselves great communicators, but they normally give answers that do not address the original question. Congressional hearings are noted for this type of communication. Ask a simple question and get a very complex answer that does not come close to the original question. Vendors also revert to smoke and fairy dust to cover the fact that their unit is not capable of doing something.

You need to review vendor responses to make sure your original request was understood. This is done for several reasons. One is to check that your written requirements were not vague and that the responder provided an answer that fit your original request. The second is to ensure that nothing was left out of the response that could make their pricing look better than others. Third, you need to determine if they discovered items that you overlooked or were missing in your original thinking.

When you wrote your request, you hoped there was no doubt as to exactly what you wanted. Writing technical papers is a challenge to many people, and chances are, something got left out. The mind often skips over what seems to be obvious and we fail to put it into words. Even after reviewing the document, you can sometimes fail to see the trees for the forest. We even fail to read what is written because the mind converts things the eyes see. An example of this comes from an unknown source that goes back at least 20 years. Individuals were directed to read the sentence like the one shown in FIG. 11-1 and count the number of F's they saw.

"FINISHED FILES ARE THE RE-

SULT OF YEARS OF SCIENTIF-

IC STUDY COMBINED WITH THE

EXPERIENCE OF MANY YEARS"

Fig. 11-1. What you see is not what you read sentence.

If you said there was a total of six, you were right. Most people will count three. The mind makes the word (of) sound like (ov), letting you skip past the letter because it appears to have a *vah* sound instead of an *eff* sound. You were instructed to count all the *eff* letters, and your mind eliminated everything else.

What you are looking for as you scan the responses are the glaring differences. If you spot a major omission or confusion by the vendor, you must contact them at once. Any further delay to clarify the response will either delay your selection process or cause the vendor to be eliminated from consideration. One way forces you to adjust; the other hurts the chances of the vendor. Just remember, even a well-written document can be interpreted to mean several things. The U.S. Constitution and the various bibles are prime examples of documents having different meanings for people.

Clarifying a response

There are two times to clarify a vendor's response. One is during the initial period and the vendor has questions. If one vendor had trouble understanding your request, it might mean others are also having trouble. When this happens, you must contact the competing vendors and make sure they do not have similar problems. This will help make all the competing responses answer the same interpretation of your request. It might take some unscheduled time to do this, but you at least have everybody reacting to the same thing.

The other time to clarify is when you do not understand the vendor's response. Even the vaguest point should be clear in your mind before you enter your selection process. Some vendors have a habit of low-balling their bid by overlooking necessary optional equipment. It is optional because of their pricing structure, but necessary because it will not work without it. An example of this is the need for a specially wired interface cable that is necessary to let the unit function, but is listed as an optional item. If you requested a quote for so many multiplexers without specifying all necessary optional equipment, you will get a price for what you asked for.

Very high or very low quotes suggests the responder did not understand your request. You must quickly get back to the vendors with extreme price disparities. Even if you only have two responses that have widely divergent prices, you need to check with both parties to verify they knew what you were asking for. Be sure to document all phone calls you make about the pricing.

If the vendor or telco responded with a very high bid and no backup material, it is highly probable they do not want to win the bid. This is often done to show you they want to be considered for future RFPs or RFQs, but they really do not want to join this particular project. You should call the person that sent the response, and ask them if this is the case. It is a direct question, and they will normally tell you the truth.

Reviewing a response

Reviewing a response is slightly different from trying to clarify the document after a quick review. So far, you have reviewed the responses for glaring differences. Now is the time to take the vendor's response and go over each section so that you fully understand their response. Assuming at this point will get you into trouble. If you received just a letter quote, it probably does not tell you the vital information you need to make a correct selection. While the letter can state they meet all the safety, electric, and operational needs of your request, it might not cover other critical items.

Some things are completely obvious to the vendor or telco, but they never spell out what is or is not provided. The vendor or telco's response should include specifications as to things like installation, maintenance, manuals, and especially the interfaces. Experience has shown that about 80 percent of all equipment compatibility tests are delayed because of an interface problem. This happens less if the interfaces are discussed before the tests, but it still occurs because of a misunderstanding between parties.

Determining the exact interfaces

Interfaces are the most troublesome things when it comes time to tie different units together. Simple things like the gender of the connector will delay initial testing or the actual installation. If you used the suggested interface requirement statement in chapter 6, you should review the response to see if they answered the following questions:

- Did the vendor specify all data interfaces as to the particular standard used (i.e., exact designation and gender of each interface)?
- Did the vendor identify the pins or contacts that do not specifically meet the said standard?
- Did they list the specific voltages and functions that appear on all standard unassigned pins and the standard leads the manufacturer has reassigned to their own use?
- Are there any interface cables that are vendor-specific (i.e., specially designed cables that are needed to make their unit function)?

Be certain that the vendor has fully answered the interface request. Vague or half-answered requests will cause delays and trouble later in the selection or installation process. References to old terminology like EIA-RS-232 are vague. Other than telling you it is probably a data interface, it is not specific enough to tell you what it is. If they said it was an EIA-232D, you have the problem of not knowing if they meant the old nine-pin connector or if they thought it was a direct replacement for the EIA-RS-232C. Referring to the interface as a DB-25 connector tells you only that the connector has 25 pins. It does not tell what functions are on the pins nor the electrical characteristics. Similarly, stating they have a nine-pin D-connector does not tell if it is the older EIA-232D or the new EIA-574 interface.

Don't assume that you know what the vendor meant. If it is not eminently clear as to the entire interface question, call the vendor and request clarification. The design engineer knows the interface best and can supply information the product manager might not have. Often, your main vendor contact is a product manager or a marketing person. In this case, insist on talking to the engineer or their technical support group. This serves two purposes. One is getting the best answer, and two, you can get a feel about their technical support.

Missing parts

Figure 11-1 is a checklist of the main categories used in your request and in the risk analysis. You will check off whether they were either provided, missing, or that the particular item was not needed. If you were reviewing a telephone service, there are some items that have little or no meaning. They all have meaning when it involves equipment located on your premise.

Response Items	Provided	Missing	No Need
A. Meeting the Absolute Needs			
B. Quality of the Product or Service			
C. Meeting the Desired Needs			
D. Uniqueness of the Product or Service			
E. Extra Features			
F. Safety Certification			
G. Availability of the Product			
H. Mean Time to Failure			
I. Mean Time to Repair			
J. In-house Maintenance Availability			
K. Repair Availability			
L. Technical Assistance or Support			
M. Training and Operating Manuals			
N. Power and Space Considerations			
O. Environmental Considerations			
P. Upgrade of Operating Hardware and Software			

Figure 11-2. Checklist.

110   Vendor responses

Guarantees or warranties

Reading that an item is fully guaranteed sounds so much better than seeing a limited warranty statement. By the time you get through reading all the caveats with a limited warranty, you get a feeling you're in trouble if you turn it on.

When you get around to your final selection, you need to know exactly what is backed and for how long. A fully backed product has a greater advantage over one with a limited warranty. Also, a two-year guarantee is better than a one-year guarantee. If you are not sure what is backed, ask for a simpler written explanation. All this becomes apparent when you read about life cycle studies in chapter 13 on selecting equipment.

Summary

The object of reviewing a response is to make sure the vendor understood your original request. It also reduces delays in your real selection process by making sure you have all the necessary information. One sign that the vendor did not understand the request is a widely divergent price quote from other quotes. Don't assume the vendor understood your request, and don't assume you understand the response. Clarify everything that appears to be vague.

12

Risk analysis

Risk analysis improves your odds of making the correct decision. By using this process, you will often be able to eliminate vendors from your selection list because of a high risk number. The best choice will almost spring out at you when you complete the analysis. Products or services with a very low risk number will have very few problems.

You will note the thing that separates this chapter from the next one on selection is that the cost of the product or service is not addressed. At this point, you are looking strictly at the merits of the vendor under study. After making the risk analysis, you will use those values to make the best selection of the individual parts of your system for the least amount of money. Initially, some products or services might seem inexpensive until you complete the risk analysis. Then, those with a higher risk number require a greater spare allocation than the ones with low-risk values. This, in turn, drives the low cost up until it is no longer inexpensive.

Appendix D is a risk analysis worksheet that contains the tables used in this chapter. You need a separate worksheet for each vendor. There is space at the top to include the vendor's name, their product model, its generic description (e.g., modem), and the reviewer's name. As you go through this worksheet, circle the risk points that apply to each category. Then, total the number of risk points for each vendor and enter that number on top of the first page.

The risk points assigned are suggested values of the risk for each category. You might adjust these to meet your needs either in an upward or downward direction. Once you have assigned risk factors to each competing vendor for a particular part of your system, it will become evident that the vendor with the least number of points is the best.

Another advantage of going through a risk analysis is to learn if there is a weak link in the total system. A weak link is the best possible product or service that also carries a high risk number. You made that reasonable search for products, but all the responses showed a high risk. Compounding this problem, your schedule does not let you go back and start a new study. When there is an apparent risky area in the system, it requires additional equipment to provide a higher level of maintenance spares. It might even require duplicate or diverse parts of the system to prevent failures from taking the system down.

Absolute needs

If the product or service doesn't meet all the absolute needs, it will be very difficult to include it into your system. A lot of these requirements deal with standards and basic safety specifications. Not meeting a safety or electrical need is a major deterrent. You could change the type of interfaces or provide interface adapters for a product that didn't meet your original absolute requirements, but there is no way you can adjust for deficient safety and electrical items.

TABLE 12-1 assigns risk points for missing items from your list of absolute requirements. If competing products have the same number of missing items, you could go over the items and assign different factors to various missing absolute requirements. These factors should follow the same pattern, where a missing item that is very critical for the operation has the most points. The least critical missing absolute item has the lowest factor. Go back over the responses to see if one product stands out.

Table 12-1. Risk points for
missing absolute requirements.

Missing items	0	1	2	3
Risk points	0	25	50	100

Your other choice is to see how the products shake out after the complete analysis. It is unlikely that there is not at least one product or service that meets at least some of the absolute requirements. If all competing products fail to meet any absolute needs, you must stop and change your proposed network and find a replacement method. It is far better to have a fresh start instead of driving ahead with a known mistake. There is no reward for people that have forged ahead with bad plans just to meet a time commitment.

Quality

The quality of a product or service plays a dominant part in your decision process. Not paying attention to quality will get you into a heap of trouble. A product or service might meet your basic or absolute needs, but have quality problems. While the unit might function within the system, it is a very weak link. What you hope to reach is a network that meets all your customer's needs and has the least amount of downtime.

If you find that a vendor has major quality problems, you should disqualify them from further review. Chapter 8 on dealing with vendors described a poor-quality product under review by a telephone company. Had they gone ahead and offered the product, they would have had many customers complaining about the failures. There also would have been an unplanned increase in maintenance expenses that would have negated any profit.

TABLE 12-2 lists the risk points for quality. Unfortunately, there isn't any way to determine a vendor's quality other than visually looking at their equipment and manufacturing plant. It would be great if some enterprising group would rate the quality of all telecommunications vendors and telephone companies. Not only would you be able to readily find the quality outfits, but it would compel the poor-quality companies to improve.

Table 12-2. Risk points for quality.

Quality	Excellent	Good	Minor problems	Major problems
Risk points	0	10	50	100

One other point about quality. Don't judge a company as having good quality because they are very large and, as a result, they are probably a good quality risk. They might have selected another manufacturer's product and put it out under their own name. This is called *original equipment manufacture* (OEM) products. The company buying the OEM gear will usually check the equipment just as you are doing now. This doesn't say the group doing the selection made a good choice. Be like that person from Missouri, and say, "Show me."

Desired needs

Desired needs are those items that are prefaced with words like *should* and *may* to differentiate them from the absolute. They are usually the features you would like to see in a product or service but if one or two are missing, you can still operate. This is like that vanity mirror in the car. It is nice, but if it's missing, you can cope by looking in the rearview mirror instead.

How vendors answer this section will depend on the method used in your original proposal or quote. One method covered in chapter 6 pointed out a way of asking for the very best. This was done by combining the best features of several competing products or services. There will not be any one unit that fully matches the criteria. It is a little more work when you make your final selection, but it doesn't look as if your RFP or RFQ matched only one vendor. You do not want the proposal to sound like one company's specifications.

TABLE 12-3 lists risk points for only three missing items. If competing products have more missing items, you can do several things. One is to reevaluate the desired needs to see if you have requested the impossible. Two, expand the risk table to include more missing items and adjust the risk

Table 12-3. Risk points for missing desired needs.

Missing items	0	1	2	3
Risk points	0	15	25	50

points. You would do this if you had a large list of combined features from many products.

The other thing you can do is rate the list of desired features in a scale from highly desired to least desired. Next, draw a line somewhere in the middle and then judge the vendors on the upper side of the desired features. This should separate the better units from the rest of the pack.

Uniqueness

Uniqueness of a product or types of service presents problems when you have a need to replace that part of the network with another product. If you lived in a development controlled by an association, you might find out that they do not allow outside TV antennas. The only way you can see any television is to pay the cable-TV provider whatever they want to charge. You would like to have an alternative at the next price increase, but are stuck with the only game in town. Buying a one-of-a-kind product or service puts you into a poor bargaining position. You have no other choice if the pricing of the service goes up or the vendor becomes unresponsive.

TABLE 12-4 lists the risk points to assign uniqueness. Products that have a proprietary operating system or method are one-of-a-kind, and you will have substitution problems. If you are dead set on buying something like this, be sure to consider contingency plans to replace this portion. Ask yourself, what if the vendor goes out of business or the product is a bomb, what do I do then? A beta test is the first installation of a production model to see if it really works in the real world. The beta test product is worse than the one-of-a-kind because it is an unknown entity. Some network managers like the feeling of being on the cutting edge of the industry, and take a chance with new technology. Nevertheless, it is risky to include a product or service that doesn't have any track record.

Table 12-4. Risk points for uniqueness.

Uniqueness	Multi-source	One-of-a-kind	Beta test
Risk points	0	50	75

Extra features

Listing extra features gives you the freedom to decide between very close competing products or services. They only come into play when you cannot find any major differences between the competing products. You could desire visual displays to be a certain color or height. When it came down to the final decision of several equal products, you can use this section to break the deadlock.

TABLE 12-5 lists the risk points for extra features. Note that they do not carry much weight. At this point, they just add to the overall risk analysis and are not an ultimate deciding point.

Table 12-5. Risk points for extra features.

Missing items	0	1	2	3
Risk points	0	5	10	15

Safety certification

Safety certification is a serious subject in some cities. It should be a serious concern for the people in the locations where it will be used. Do not be fooled by the vendor claiming they have the Underwriters Laboratories (UL) approval when they are just referring to the power supply. It should have passed tests, similar to the ones listed in appendix E—FCC-Part 68, that check for many safety considerations.

Several large cities have fire codes that require a UL-type test of the entire equipment before you can install the device in your building. The other required independent laboratory testing is for equipment that falls into FCC Class B certification. Class B testing specifies that electromagnetic interference levels must be made by an independent testing laboratory and have an FCC identification number.

When you wrote your RFP, you should have included safety criteria in the absolute needs. The risk points in TABLE 12-6 considered the vendor claimed to meet all the absolute needs. Now you need to determine who tested the unit or product. Vendor certification is better than no testing at all, but it is not as good as having an independent testing laboratory test it. They have a better handle on the necessary tests.

Table 12-6. Risk points for safety certification.

Safety certification	Indep. lab tested	Vendor tested	No tests made
Risk points	0	25	75

Availability

Availability is a risk factor because it will influence your implementation. Products that are readily available off the shelf present few problems, and you can expect quick delivery. Also, if you receive a dead-on-arrival (DOA) unit, they can easily replace the bad unit and your installation schedule will still be on time. Custom-built equipment suggests risk in that it is a special or unique unit. If that type of unit was DOA or died shortly after, it would cause unplanned delays. It will also require a higher maintenance spare ratio to provide backup equipment.

The last item in TABLE 12-7 lists a product that is still undergoing prototype testing. The difference between a prototype test and a beta test is a matter of stages. A prototype unit is a vendor's first working model and not the production version. A beta test is the first installation of a production unit in a customer's network. Vendors have a habit of announcing a new product to the world before it has been fully tested in anticipation of getting market share. Believing that a new product will fit your network well before it is even in a production stage can put you in a deep scheduling problem. There have been many announced products that suddenly disappeared from view before reaching production. There also have been many networks that were delayed because they had to revamp their plans. Try explaining why your company has spent a lot of money buying other parts of the network, and now they can't use any of it because a critical part is missing.

Table 12-7. Risk points for availability.

Availability	Stock item	Special order	Prototype test
Risk points	0	20	50

Mean time to failure

Mean time to failure (MTTF) or mean time before failure (MTBF) are factors that manufacturers calculate by adding the failure rate of all the components. Each component of the product has a standard failure in time (FIT) factor that is expressed in some many failures in 100,000,000 hours. Using that many hours might seem unwieldy until you add up several hundred or thousand parts. A high-speed modem might have an MTTF of 87,600 hours. This does not mean the equipment will last 87,600 hours before it will fail. Dividing a year of hours (8760) into that MTTF, you see that approximately 63 percent of the units will fail in 10 years. If you could spread your failures evenly over those 10 years, you can figure out how many will fail each year.

To use TABLE 12-8, you need to know the MTTF of all the competing products and then rank-order them. The product with the highest MTTF is first. If the particular product under risk analysis had the third highest MTTF, you would assign 20 risk points. Again, the risk points are suggested. You might want to change these depending on the number of products under consideration. Just remember that a very high MTTF means the number of failures is spread over a longer period. Statistically, the failures will still occur, but it means fewer interruptions to your network in a given year.

Table 12-8. Risk points for MTTF.

Rank order	1st	2nd	3rd	4th	5th
Risk points	0	10	20	40	80

Mean time to repair

Mean time to repair (MTTR) is the average time it takes to make an actual repair on equipment. In this case, MTTR does not include response time for a repair person to reach your location. The actual repair might require an inordinate amount of time just to open an enclosure so you can get at the parts of the equipment. An earlier Bell System microwave generator unit had all but one vacuum tube accessible from the front. One tube was located inside. You would change everything you could on the front before venturing on to replace the one on the inside. It meant busting your knuckles to get the unit out of the relay rack. Then there were 23 screws holding the cover in place. This one tube took a better part of an hour to replace.

TABLE 12-9 lists the risk points on a rank-order just like you did with the MTTF. Only this time the vendor with the lowest MTTR has the number one position. A high MTTF and a low MTTR are desirable.

Table 12-9. Risk points for MTTR.

Rank order	1st	2nd	3rd	4th	5th
Risk points	0	10	20	40	80

If a vendor can't give or predict the MTTR, then you must visually inspect the unit and estimate a time to repair. Any time you must dismantle the enclosure to get at the circuit boards means a long MTTR.

On-site maintenance

How long will it take a vendor's maintenance personnel to get to your locations? Because you are looking at a network spread out over many locations, you would like to make a risk analysis of the system. You can either average the maintenance availability times for the entire system, or look at several key locations. TABLE 12-10 lists the risk points for on-site maintenance availability. Some vendors use repair services like TRW or GE as a maintenance force. While these services might be familiar with the equipment, the vendor's own

Table 12-10. Risk points for on-site maintenance availability.

On-site maintenance	<2 hours	<4 hours	<8 hours	<24 hours	>24 hours
Risk points	0	10	20	40	80

maintenance force should have a better handle on how to repair. There is nothing worse than to see repair service spend the first couple of hours reading the maintenance manual to figure out what is wrong. The person who shows up and immediately understands the problem is who you want.

Repair time

Repair time is different from MTTR and maintenance availability. TABLE 12-11 lists the risk points for the length of time it normally takes a vendor to make a repair on equipment sent back to their factory. The interval reflects actual time in the repair shop and does not include shipping time. While the vendor will probably tell you they turn them around immediately, the best place to look is at their repair records. What you need to consider is the amount of time a unit will not be available to you as a working part of the system or as spare equipment. Long delays in actual repair will dictate whether you need to provide more maintenance spare equipment.

Table 12-11. Risk points for repair time.

Factory repair	<3 days	<1 week	<2 weeks	<2 weeks
Risk points	0	10	20	30

Technical assistance or support

Technical assistance or support is different from having on-site maintenance. It is the ease of obtaining expert technical advice over the telephone. A very recent encounter with one of the major software houses did nothing for the ease of getting to speak to someone. It took a while to reach an 800 number and then listen to a recording explaining many different non-free phone numbers to call. After punching a number according to the recording, there was another recording listing more telephone numbers. Calling one number took more tries to reach that line only to be greeted by another recording. Again, you were instructed to punch a number to get whom you wanted, and then get a recording to say hang on because everyone was busy. After a short wait of listening to music, a person came on to check to see if the caller indeed had privy to counsel. This took some time to go through serial numbers, phone numbers, etc. Upon completion of the inspection, they transferred the call to another individual. What started out as a need to talk to someone turned out to be a giant hassle. Had they furnished the last telephone number in the operating manual, it would have saved a lot of time and telephone expense.

When you have a problem and there does not seem to be an answer in the manuals, you want to talk to someone for guidance in a short amount of time. You have spent a certain amount of frustrating time trying to figure out what is wrong and you do not need more stress trying to get to the right person.

TABLE 12-12 lists the risk points for technical assistance. Again, this is a

Table 12-12. Risk points for
technical assistance or support.

Rank order	1st	2nd	3rd	4th	5th
Risk points	0	10	20	40	80

rank-order of the vendors of competing products. You should be able to estimate a rank-order for the amount and level of technical assistance that is available. The analysis should consider times and ease of reaching a technician (i.e., out-of-business hours). Usually, a large company will also have a larger and higher technical level available. Gaining accesss to them is another thing. Just trying to reach the technical group on the phone might give you an idea of how hard it is to reach them. They might have the technicians or they might just have a recording that tells you they are all busy.

Training and operating manuals

Training and operating manuals are important at start-up and later when new personnel are introduced to the network. As you read previously, you should read manuals to ensure they are clear. The best way to check a manual is to give it to a person that might not know anything about the system, and get their opinion on whether it seems clear. If the manuals are not clear, you have two choices: get the vendor to rewrite it or write your own. TABLE 12-13 rank-orders the competing vendor's manuals.

Table 12-13. Risk points for
training and operating manuals.

Rank order	1st	2nd	3rd	4th	5th
Risk points	0	10	20	40	80

Power and space considerations

Competing products often have different power requirements and come in many sizes. Power and space are two cost items that figure into life cycle studies in the next chapter on selection. Their study here is to find large-scale differences between products. If the unit under study requires 220 volts instead of 110 volts, it might mean a change in power provisions. Providing direct-current power instead of using available alternating-current outlets is another consideration. Power requirements might also mean changing the power distribution to obtain the required wattage rating.

The size of equipment or its enclosure can also cause problems. One multiplexer manufacturer housed their unit within an enclosure that looked like the size of a telephone booth. Most other competitors had units that were very small in comparison. TABLE 12-14 lists the risk points for making changes

Table 12-14. Risk points for power and space considerations.

Changes needed	Minimal	Some	Major
Risk points	0	10	25

to power and space considerations. Finding the product will not fit in a planned location requires you to make some changes. Making a power change really becomes major in scope.

Environmental considerations

TABLE 12-15 lists the risk points for environmental considerations. This is similar to the previous category on power and space. Here, the changes have to do with ventilation and temperature. If the product has little tolerance to temperature change, you might have to locate it in an expensive computer room. The role this risk analysis plays is to look at the problems you might have with heating, cooling, or ventilation. A temperature and humidity-tolerant unit could be located outside a computer room in less expensive space.

Table 12-15. Risk points for environmental considerations.

Changes needed	Minimal	Some	Major
Risk points	0	10	25

Another thing to consider is the amount of noise the unit might generate. If it has noisy ventilation fans, you will not want to place the unit next to personnel. The noise will get them stressed out and it is very difficult to talk over.

Upgrades

The last item in the suggested list of risk analysis is upgrades in operating hardware and software. A pet peeve is buying a piece of equipment and finding out the vendor is going to grandfather that design and introduce a much better unit. To grandfather a piece of equipment, the manufacturer agrees to maintain the older equipment, but does not plan to make any more equipment like it. Computer manufacturers are answering this by introducing the upgradable computer. Instead of changing complete units or motherboards, the speed and the type of processing unit is on a circuit board that plugs into the mother-board. When your computing needs require a faster computer, it is readily adjusted by a new chip or board instead of a new computer.

If there is an improvement in the software or hardware, you usually want to upgrade your system. There are a few things you want to know about the vendor and the product:

- What procedures has the vendor used in the past to upgrade their equipment?
- If they haven't upgraded in the past, what do they guarantee to do if there is a need for a change?
- Most vendors build a Series II unit in a short time after their Series I box to correct omissions or unforeseen quirks. Will the vendor upgrade the hardware of the initial units at no charge?

TABLE 12-16 lists the risk points for upgrades. The points here reflect whether you will have minimal or major problems getting or making upgrades.

Table 12-16. Risk points for upgrades.

Changes needed	Minimal	Some	Major
Risk points	0	10	25

Summary

Risk analysis is an investigative tool. It lets you find the best products or services, and lets you make intelligent decisions. After you have made all individual risk analysis, it is time to look at the big picture and see how it all fits in. As you read before, the weak links in the total system will show up during the risk analysis. When you spot these, it is time to make contingency plans.

It is one thing to realize one weak link, but it is almost impossible to complete a workable network with two or more weak links. Two or more weak links add exponentially to your problems instead of on a linear basis. If you arrive at this conclusion, it is time to rethink your original network plan to eliminate the desired generic equipment. If you continue in your original plans, then you must include a greater maintenance spare ratio to compensate for the apparent high-failure location.

13

Selecting equipment

After completing the risk analysis portion, your next step is to select the very best remaining products or services with the lowest price. You can compare equal alternatives with the equal operating expenses over their life based only on the initial cost and any salvage at the end of its life. However, it becomes a cloudy issue when the alternatives are not equal or have different operating expenses.

This is not a cut and dry operation of just finding which vendor bid the lowest. You must use the mathematics of money, and find the real costs for the product or service. If you can bring every issue back to one point in time, you have a basis to make comparisons. Just comparing the first cost of several vendors gives you the wrong conclusion. It is the proverbial case of comparing apples and oranges.

The time-value of money

One way to think about the mathematics of money is that it is the earning power of your company's funds. All money has earning power. A sum of money can grow over time with interest. Money spent in the future has a lesser equivalent value today. This says there is a time-value to money, and with a few equations, you can find the value at any particular period. Another way to look at this is to recognize the difference between equivalent and equal.

That $100 in your bureau drawer is equal to five $20 bills. It also is equivalent to five $20 payments at zero interest. Had you put that same $100 in the bank for a year at 5 percent interest, the value is equivalent to five payments of $21. This implies the term *equivalent* as a time-value concept using some interest rate.

When you invest your money in a savings account or the money market, you expect it to draw interest. There is a nominal interest rate and an effective interest rate. How the bank compounds your interest makes a difference in the final amount at the end of the year. Equation (13-1) is a way to change a nominal interest (i) rate into an effective one (E) in a compounding time (N). If you compounded interest on an annual basis, the interval is one and a nominal interest of 8 percent is also an 8 percent effective interest. Compound on a monthly basis and the same nominal interest is now 8.2999 percent. Because the equation has an exponent, there is a limit in the number of compound intervals that has any appreciable effect. Daily compounding is about the best you can get without getting unreasonable.

$$E = \left(1 + \frac{i}{N}\right)^N - 1$$

$$E = \left(1 + \frac{.08}{1}\right)^1 - 1 = 8\% \qquad (13\text{-}1)$$

$$E = \left(1 + \frac{.08}{12}\right)^{12} - 1 = 8.2999\%$$

The present worth (P) of a future amount (F)

The present worth of a future amount (P/F) says that, if you wanted to see $10,000 in the bank at the end of one year, you needed to know how much to invest today. Equation (13-2) for P/F at an interest rate (i) over a compounding period (N) provides the time-value factor to multiply against the expected future amount.

$$(P/F, i, N) = \frac{1}{(1+i)^N}$$

$$(P/F, 5\%, 1) = \frac{1}{(1+.05)^1} = 0.9524 \qquad (13\text{-}2)$$

Present Worth = Future Amount × Factor
Present Worth = $10,000 (0.9524) = $9,524

The $9,524 (is equivalent to $10,000 after a time of one year invested at 5 percent interest. When you buy a car, you always hope it will have some value in the future and plan to use it to reduce the cost of the next car. Its trade-in or salvage value in five years is $1,000. Usually, we consider that $1,000 trade-in at the end of five years as a reduction in the next loan. If you considered the present worth of that salvage in today's loan, it is not that pretty. The true value of your future trade-in uses a higher interest rate in the following example because it is debt capital or the money you borrowed.

$$(P/F, 8\%, 5) = \frac{1}{(1+.08)^5} = 0.6806 \qquad (13\text{-}3)$$

Present Worth = $1,000 (0.6806) = $680.60

When considering salvage at the end of your network's life, you must bring all these values back in time to understand their impact. Salvage is a reduction in the initial money needed, and not in the money for your next network. Nevertheless, the previous time-value example says that $1,000 salvage is really only worth $680.06 with today's money.

The future worth (F) of a present amount (P)

The time-value of money also goes the other way. Equation (13-3) is the future worth of a present amount (F/P) using an interest rate (i) over an annual compounding period (N). In this and the following examples, use a capital debt interest rate of 8 percent spread over a five-year period. This time, you just invested $10,000 in a bond at 8 percent interest with a maturity date five years from now. The equation (13-4) lets you find out the amount of money you will get back at maturity.

$$(F/P, i, N) = (1+i)^N$$

$$(F/P,\ 8\%, 5) = (1+.08)^5 = 1.469 \tag{13-4}$$

Future Worth = Present Amount × Factor
Future Worth = $10,000(1.469) = $14,690

The present worth (P) of an annuity (A)

An annuity is some type of payment made on a regular interval. While the word is derived from the Latin word *annus*, meaning yearly, it also represents monthly lease payments. Because lease payments for most companies are on a monthly basis, you must use the equivalent interest rate (E) and the number (N) of monthly payments over the five year life. Equation (13-5) gives the present worth of an annuity (P/A). In the following example, the monthly lease for one modem is $210 for the next 60 months. The nominal interest rate of debt capital is 8 percent, which means the effective rate is 8.299 percent.

$$(P/A, E, N) = \frac{(1+E)^N - 1}{E\,(1+E)^N}$$

$$(P/A, 8.299\%, 60) = \frac{\left(1 + \frac{.08}{12}\right)^{60} - 1}{\frac{.08}{12}\left(1 + \frac{.08}{12}\right)^{60}} = 49.318 \tag{13-5}$$

Present Worth = Monthly Annuity × Factor
Present Worth = $210(49.318) = $10,357

Over the life of the five-year contract, the present worth of that one modem is $10,357. That is the amount of money you need in an annuity account at a nominal 8 percent interest to make payments of $210 for 60 months. It is the equivalent time-value of your money. Had you persuaded the vendor to bill you yearly versus monthly, you could have saved almost $300 as the difference between equivalent and nominal interest rates. The following example lumps 12 monthly charges into one yearly payment of $2,520 and uses the nominal interest of 8 percent.

$$(P/A, 8\%, 5) = \frac{(1+.08)^5 - 1}{.08\,(1+.08)^5} = 3.993 \tag{13-6}$$

Present Worth = Yearly Annuity × Factor
Present Worth = $2,520(3.993) = $10,062

Most of your calculations will only use the *P/F* (13-2) and *P/A* (13-5) equations. There are other formulas that appear in most engineering economic books but have little value other than moving money around in different ways. Other equations that might be useful are the present worth (*P*) of a linear gradient (*G*), and annuity from a present amount (*A/P*).

The present worth (P) of a linear gradient (G)

If you expect a changing progression of payments over a period of time, use the present worth of a linear gradient (*P/G*) equation (13-7). Figure 13-1 pictures the changing gradient over a five-year period. A changing gradient is either a positive or negative in direction. When the vendor increases the amount of the lease each year, the gradient will add to the annuity. I depicted a negative gradient to the annuity in FIG. 13-1 as if the vendor cut their price a fixed amount each year after the first year.

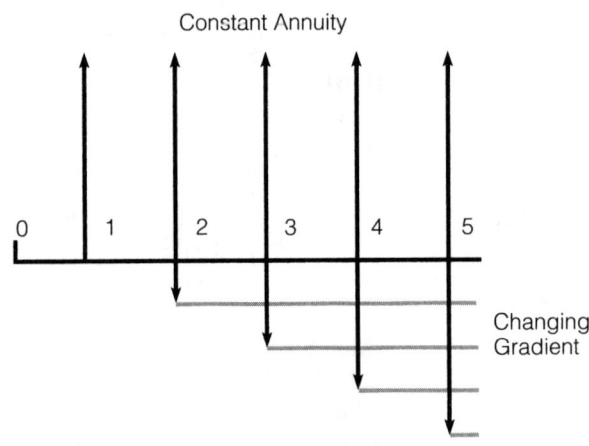

Fig. 13-1. Present worth of a linear gradient.

$$(P/G) = \frac{1}{i} \left(\frac{(1+i)^N}{i(1+i)^N} - \frac{N}{(1+i)^N} \right)$$ (13-7)

A vendor is trying to entice you into leasing their product over a five-year span and offers you a deal to reduce the annual \$1,000 payment (P/A) by \$100 each year (P/G). The example uses a nominal interest of 8 percent with annual payments to simplify the following:

Present Worth (P) = Annuity (/A) – Progression (P/G)

P = \$1,000 (P/A, 8%, 5) – \$100 (P/G), 8%, 5)

P = \$1,000 (3.993) – \$100 (7.372)

P = \$3,993 – \$737.20 = \$3,255.80 (13-8)

Lease vs. purchase

The major economic difference between owning and leasing is the relative financing cost your company would pay for debt or lease financing. Owning requires a lump-sum payment up front, while a lease spreads its payments over time. The interest rate at which the two payment schedules are equivalent is the implicit financing rate of the lease. If there is an expected salvage value at the end of the life of the product or service, the implicit financing rate equals the present worth of the initial cost minus the present value of the future salvage. Incremental financing rate is your company's difference between the "buy" cash flow and the "lease" cash flow. The main goal is to have the cash flow equal zero.

When you make economic studies, you must bring the different costs (over time) back to the present to make a comparison. There are a couple of ways to show you when a lease might be more economical. Our examples will use a hypothetical LAN router that costs \$10,000. Because electronic equipment is outdated so quickly by new technology, I will use only a five-year life span for capital depreciation and our lease. While most five-year-old electronic equipment is nearly worthless, give it the benefit of the doubt and assign a 5 percent salvage value. The lease for the same router will cost \$2,520 annually. Most leases are on a monthly basis, but for simplicity, the example is using annual interest compounding.

One method is to find the implicit financing rate (r) interest rate that causes the present worth of the cash flow to equal zero. If there is some salvage or the lease payments are unequal, you must use a trial and error method with equation (13-6).

First Cost – Salvage = Annual Lease Payments

First Cost = Annual Lease Payments + Salvage

\$10,000 = \$2,520 (P/A, r%, 5) + \$500 (P/F, r%, 5)

Try r = 9%: \$2,520 (3.890) + \$500 (.6449) = \$10,128

Try r = 10%: \$2,520 (3.791) + \$500 (.6209) = \$9,864 (13-9)

The zero cash-flow value is somewhere between 9 and 10 percent. To find the rate, use equation (13-10) to interpolate the difference.

$$r = i + \frac{\text{(high value − first cost)}}{\text{(high value − low value)}} \times 1\% = \text{implicit rate}$$

$$r = 9\% + \frac{(\$10,128 − \$10,000)}{(\$10,128 − \$9,864)} \times 1\% = 9.48\% \qquad (13\text{-}10)$$

The implicit financing rate is then 9.48 percent. You should not use the lease method if debt-type capital costs less than 9.48 percent. If the debt capital costs more, then the lease may be economically sound. There are other factors like income tax benefits by capital investments that you cannot get with a lease. Check with your accounting department for assistance.

A quick way to find the break-even lease payment is to use equation (13-11). In this example, we knew the debt capital (9%) and want to find the break-even point for an annual lease payment. If the lease payment was below $2,487, the lease is a viable alternative. In the previous example, the lease payments were $2,520, and owning is the better way to go.

$$\text{PW (first cost) − PW (net salvage) = PW (lease payments)}$$

$$\$10,000 − \$5,000 \ (P/F, 9\%, 5) = \text{(lease payment)} \ (P/A, 9\%, 5)$$

$$\$10,000 − \$500 \ (.6499) = \text{(lease payment)} \ (3.890)$$

$$\text{Lease Payment} = \frac{(\$10,000 − \$500 \ (0.6499)}{(3.890)}$$

$$\text{Break-even lease payment} = \$2,487 \qquad (13\text{-}11)$$

Using spreadsheet programs

Lotus 1–2–3 spreadsheets or comparable programs provide an easy way to calculate the different factors. TABLE 13-1 is a Lotus 1–2–3 setup to find the different factors discussed in the previous section. Comparable programs usually use the same basic format. Cells A12 and B12 calculate $i(1 + i)N$, and Cells D9 and E9 calculate $(1 + i)^N$ for a reduction in annual and monthly formula input elsewhere.

Figure 13-2 is an example of the economic study spreadsheet with an 8 percent interest rate, five years for an annual study, and 60 months for the monthly lease. Because it is highly unlikely that anyone would have a monthly gradient, it is not recommended to include the formula in the spreadsheet. You could include a location to input other data like the first cost, salvage, and monthly costs. Input simple multiplication formulas in other cells to complete

Table 13-1. Spreadsheet input for economic factors.

Cell	Input
A1	Economic studies
C1	^Factor
D1	^Annual
E1	^Monthly
A3	Interest =
B3	[insert interest as a whole integer (e.g., 8) for study]
C3	P/A =
D3	(D9–1)/(D9) * (B3/100)
E3	(E9–1)/(E9) * (B3/1200)
A5	Years =
B5	(insert years for study)
C5	P/F =
D5	1/D9
E5	1/E9
A7	Months =
B7	(insert months for study)
C7	P/G =
D7	(1/(B3/100)) * (((D9-1)/A12) – B5/D9
E7	(Not recommended to run on monthly basis)
C9	F/P =
D9	(1 + (B3/100)) ^B5
E9	(1 + (B3/1200)) ^B7
C11	^A/P =
D11	((B3/100) * (D9))/(D9–1)
E11	((B3/1200) * (E9))/(E9–1)
A12	(1 + (B3/100) ^B5 (Hide cell A12 and B12 after entry)
B12	(1 + (B3/1200)) ^B7

the spreadsheet. The one difference between the values in the spreadsheet and economic study books is that the books normally truncate to four decimal places and the spreadsheet carries the values out further. It will result in a few dollar's difference if someone compares the two ways.

Economic studies

There is no other way to show the true costs of a project or the differences between alternatives without some type of economic study. It is simple as that. When it comes to buying that new car, most people shop around for the best price on a particular brand and model. Their economical study stops there because the operating expenses are the same over the life of the car. Had they narrowed the selection down to two different cars, it would be time to study the economics. In our example, we'll look at two cars that cost approximately the same and use a five-year loan at 11 percent. Our first cost is the price of the car

ROW	A	B	C	D	E
1	ECONOMIC STUDIES		FACTORS	ANNUAL	MONTHLY
2					
3	INTEREST=	8	P/A=	3.9927	49.3184
4					
5	YEARS =	5	P/F=	0.6806	0.6712
6					
7	MONTHS =	60	P/G=	7.3724	
8					
9			F/P=	1.4693	1.4898
10					
11			A/P=	0.2505	0.0203
12	HIDDEN CELLS				

Fig. 13-2. Economic study spreadsheet.

minus any trade-in or factory rebate. The mileage for the year is the same for both cars. Other than that, the operating costs are different. Car A requires routine maintenance at the dealer, gets 20 miles to the gallon, and burns only the super-premium-grade gasoline. Car B has minor maintenance, gets 25 miles to the gallon, and uses regular gasoline.

	Car A	Car B
First cost	$20,500	$21,000
Operating expenses		
Insurance	$850	$860
Maintenance	$250	$100
Fuel	$710	$448
	$1,810	$1,408

Our model buyer does not have the money on hand to pay for the first cost, but instead takes out a loan. You can figure the monthly payments for the loan by using equation (13-9) for an annuity (A) from a present amount (P). This equation is included in the spreadsheet information in TABLE 13-1 and is in the example FIG. 13-2. The interest used below is an effective 11 percent interest generated by the spreadsheet.

$$(A/P, i, N) = \frac{i\,(1+i)^N}{(1+i)^N - 1}$$

$$(A/P, 11\%, 60) = \frac{.11\,(1+.11)^{60}}{(1+.11)^{60} - 1} = 0.0217425 \tag{13-12}$$

Car A monthly payments = $20,500 (A/P) = $445.72
Car B monthly payments = $21,000 (A/P) = $456.59

How much money should the buyer set aside at the first day to pay for all this? The thing to remember is that money has earning power. If it was not invested, you would lose that earning power. Take the lump sum out of the bank to buy the car, without a loan, and immediately lose that earning power. Unfortunately, this buyer does not know about good investments and is going to get only 5 percent from a bank account. First, find out the money needed to pay the 11 percent car loan from both cars, and then calculate the operating costs:

$(P/A, 5\%, 60)$ = monthly loan payments × (52.9907)
Car A = $445.72 (52.9907) = $23,620
Car B = $456.59 (52.9907) = $24,195

$(P/A, 5\%, 5)$ = yearly operating expenses × (4.329)
Car A = $1,810 (4.329) = $7,835
Car B = $1,408 (4.329) = $6,095

Money needed for Car A = $23,620 + $7,835 = $31,455
Money needed for Car B = $24,195 + $6,095 = $30,290

In this example, the more expensive car to buy was the most economical because of the operating expenses. This leads us back to the premise that the lowest initial price is not always the best. You need to know all of the costs over the life of the network.

Life-cycle studies

Life-cycle studies include every known item that will cost money over the life of the product or service. Some items you need to include are:

- Maintenance spare equipment needed to maintain the network.
- Power usage in kilowatt hours.
- Special environment considerations.
- Maintenance labor.
- Floor space allocation.
- Guarantee or warranty stipulations.

- Upgrades.
- Training personnel.
- Survivability and restoration requirements.
- Capacity (i.e., number of bits or CCS per dollar)
- Taxes
- Insurance

The first item is based on the MTTF, quality, and location. A low MTTF figure means a higher spare ratio must be kept on hand. Poor quality means even more spares because there will be a higher failure rate no matter how they calculated the MTTF. Last, the location plays a big part. Sites spread out in many areas might require several storage centers or at least one spare at every site. If the service is critical, then there must be at least one spare unit or a percentage if there are many units at that site. Sometimes, a vendor can recommend a spare ratio based on past performance of their equipment. This, of course, is part of your first costs and is not an operating expense.

The next item, power usage, is an operating expense that is best handled on an annual basis to find significant numbers. How significant the figures are depends on the hours of usage. Remember, the wattage rating of the power supply is not an indication of the usage. It is hoped that the vendor used an overrated power supply that will prolong the life of the equipment. When the usage and the rating are almost the same, you should expect a higher failure rate of the equipment and add more spares.

If the equipment is turned on and never turned off, the annual usage is 8760 hours. Using the equipment only during normal business days (five days per week, eight hours a day, with eight holidays) will lower the figure to 2016 hours. The other part of how significant the power question is rests on the total number of units. In the following example, we'll use 100 units of equipment. One unit under study uses 150 watts and the other 200 watts. Another assumption is that the price of electricity cost 15 cents per kilowatt-hour.

$$200w \times 8760 \text{ hours} \times 100 \text{ units} \times 15¢ = \$26,280$$
$$200w \times 2016 \text{ hours} \times 100 \text{ units} \times 15¢ = \$6,045$$
$$150w \times 8760 \text{ hours} \times 100 \text{ units} \times 15¢ = \$19,710$$
$$150w \times 2016 \text{ hours} \times 100 \text{ units} \times 15¢ = \$4,530$$

Even if you decided to instruct everyone to turn the equipment off each night, there is still a significant difference between the two units. Before you run off to write a decree to save electricity, electronic equipment will age quicker and fail sooner if you turn it on and off. It likes to be turned on once, and kept on always. Besides, you will need a higher spare ratio to cover the higher number of expected failures, and that will add to your first cost.

Labor costs are most of your operating budget. There are certain functions within a network that must be handled by someone. If one vendor or telephone company (telco) relies on you to do things that are included in other proposals, you must add in your loaded maintenance or operating cost to that particular alternative. You must judge everyone on the actual operating maintenance and who is providing the labor.

Continue down the list and find or assign an operating price to each. Add any additional items that are particular to your network. When you have completed the list of operating expenses, make a present worth of an annuity *(P/A)* calculation for each product or service under the selection study. This assumes you have eliminated products or services under risk analysis and are studying the remaining ones.

One other comparison to make is the amount of data and voice you are getting for your dollar. This is figured in kilobytes per dollar for data and in hundred-calling-seconds (CCS) per dollar for voice.

Final selection

Your final selection is based on the best possible product with the least present worth costs. Between risk analysis and economic studies, you should be so confident with your final selection that you will be glad to put your name on the final document. You should have no doubts at this time that the product or service you selected is the very best.

The final competing vendors are probably aware that you are in the later stages of your selection phase. You have gone back to them for clarification and visited their manufacturing plant since the response phase. At this point, the hungrier vendor might approach you to see if they can sweeten the deal. If sweetening involves reducing the price, you might want to listen. Ethics plays a big role when dealing with vendors at this time. Don't get involved with accepting any gift, even if it appears harmless. Vendors at trade shows often give away great prizes to some lucky person who dropped their business card in a hopper. Often, they will never draw a name out of the hat, but instead, make the "lucky" winner a person on the verge of making a big decision. Even in this type of situation, it is still unethical if you accept the prize. You were not lucky, you were set up.

If a vendor lowers their bid at the last moment, you must choose between accepting or not accepting. Accept that lower bid from one vendor, and you have to offer the opportunity to the competing vendors. You must then go back and redo your economic studies. It could add more time to your study, but it might not be that difficult if you used a spreadsheet program.

Documentation

The documentation of all the events up to this point is the thing that closes the case on selection. It is vital that the information about competing vendors ends up in an individual file on the various selected products or services. All the information leading up to the selection of a particular unit is in one place. This will help other people making future network studies, and it serves to show everyone that your decision was based on sound judgment.

Your final document is organized a little like the request. The front sheet is a summary of the selection so someone can look at the file later and know what the contents are about. It should include a brief description about the product or service under study. Next, list the vendors and their products or services under study. Briefly list the reasons why one was selected and the others were not. The rest of the file should be partitioned into individual vendor sections for the economic studies, risk analysis, responses, and other pertinent documents.

Unless you have carte blanche from upper management to spend whatever money is needed for a multi-vendor network, it is likely you will need their approval before ordering the parts. Going before upper management means orchestrating a well-planned presentation. You can draw on some of the information mentioned in chapter 10 on managing meetings and presentations, but this presentation is different. It requires you to be the controller and the presenter. At this point, you become the salesperson that asks for the order.

Executives do not have the time to sit and read volumes of material. They can easily become overwhelmed by too much material and draw the wrong conclusions. Your first page on any documentation is an executive summary. It

---

EXECUTIVE SUMMARY

Date:

Subject: Include just enough information to let the executive focus on the subject. They may know that you were looking at a network, and just need soething to remind them what the material is about.

Fig. 13-3. Executive summary.

Overview: Include items that executives understand. Tell about the benefits they will get for the dollars spent. They want to know the three big questions. Why do it? Why do it now? Why do it this way?

Index: List the other items in the presentation package. Do not include the total cost to the company at this point. Again you are now a salesperson and are trying to convince the executives they really must have the thing you are selling.

---

is as brief as possible while still informing them what the subject is about. *How to Get Your Point Across in 30 Seconds or Less,* Milo O. Frank, Simon and Schuster, New York made a good point. Frank pointed out that communications must get across within 30 seconds or the reader's mind starts to wander. Whether it is an advertisement or a letter to someone, you will not get your point across if it drags on. Two and three-page job resumes are thrown in the trash without anyone reading them. You need to keep it short, simple, and to the point. This is what an executive summary is all about. You must get your message over within that 30-second period. Most executives have learned to read quickly and should cover an organized single page within the time. Figure 13-3 is a suggested format for an executive summary.

The rest of the presentation package should include your economic studies and the reasons for selecting certain vendors. Do not follow the practice that a thick package shows how diligent you were. Most of the material should be back in the files. You should include enough information that will answer most questions. Give the executive a concise and informative package. It should be something he could easily throw into a briefcase and review later. Put tons of material in a big binder and it will never be opened. Remember, you are the salesperson and you want to get your point across quickly to make that sale.

Presentation skills

In addition to a presentation package, you will want key points on slides or transparencies. If you want to show your network, make sure it is as simple as possible. Showing every line or connection is too busy and it loses all meaning. One way to show how the network will look is to take just one cross section of your network. Using transparencies, you can build layers of data, voice, and other networks on top of each other.

Your key points are simple bulleted items. Don't put too many words on them or the audience will tune you out and what you are saying to read the slide. Only put a few bulleted items on a slide (i.e., no more than four); that serves more as a reminder to you than to inform the viewer.

If you are not an accomplished presenter, make several rehearsals in front of people until you are confident. Have the people watching your rehearsal pop questions in the middle of your talk to learn how you will get back into the flow of your presentation. You should expect someone asking questions at the most inopportune time. Should the answer to the question appear later in the presentation, you can politely put the executive off until later. It might not always work because some people have a low retention span and need an answer before they forget the question.

The final portion of any salesperson's presentation is to ask for the sale. After the questioning has slowed to a dribble, it is time to ask for their concurrence. It is better to ask than just let it hang in the air. They at least know you are looking for an answer. If they are not ready to answer that day, they will be in the near future.

Summary

The final selection phase after risk analysis is the economic study. This puts all cost information back to one time frame. Other than the first cost information, the life cycle operating data is often a deciding factor. After you have made your final selection, it is then time to get the concurrence of upper management and make that sale.

Part III

Implementing
&
maintenance

14

Introduction to implementing & maintenance

Implementing a multi-vendor network is the moment of truth for those who planned and selected the equipment or services. Will it get off the ground and fly or be like Howard Hughes' famous "Spruce Goose" that barely made it into the air only to flop back to the water.

Networks are like snowflakes. There are no two alike in the world. Even if you copied the exact layout of a similar industry, there are small nuances that make your network unique. Some of the things that make your network different are:

- Traffic loading.
- Network distances and delays.
- Possible variations in generic programs.
- Timing.
- Possible revisions or updates to the equipment.

To ensure that your final selections will work in your network, you must make compatibility tests of the component parts. It is extremely important to make these tests if it is the first time the equipment was used in a particular configuration. If it already works in a similar environment, then it is necessary to verify that it works in your network.

This type of testing is done after you have selected the parts of the network but before you have committed to a large contract. It becomes your final test drive around the block before buying. While you will probably stick with your selection, you will learn if some changes or additions are necessary. Prototype equipment will almost certainly require some fine-tuning by the vendor to make it work properly in your network.

Real-time testing

Real-time testing means connecting equipment and services together and testing them with your own telecommunications. It also means trying to stress the equipment under a full traffic load. This is important because the equipment is stressed only under a full load and might exhibit problems not seen under a light load. If you cannot get actual traffic, you should simulate traffic by gang feeding every port or connection.

When the service is a 1.5 Mb or higher digital service, it is difficult to arrange tests before installation. In this case, you delay equipment tests until they install the service or you use a line simulator. Another testing possibility is using an existing line in the off-hours when the line is available for other things. Also, some carriers have test lines at their disposal and can provide a test bed for equipment tests.

Actual services are better than line simulators on a workbench. Nevertheless, some form of testing is better than no testing. In this case, you should rent a transmission-impairment simulator. This can provide some insight as to the tolerance level of the equipment by adjusting various levels of impairments. It still cannot duplicate the real-world environment, however.

Types of tests

You should test any new network or additions to an old network with actual voice or data traffic. This is accomplished by either cutting a few circuits over to the new section, double-feeding circuits, or using taped recordings. Cutting a few circuits over to the new section allows you to compare the new way of communicating against the old way. Although double-feeding has some limitations, it lets you see how actual traffic passes through the equipment.

If you have analog circuits, you should make and record various transmission tests. These can serve as benchmarks for future testing on whether they are deteriorating. Any circuit that goes from 4-wire to 2-wire has a hybrid and the balance of the hybrid must be tested. This calls for echo return loss (ERL) and singing point (SP) tests. These tests are usually required only at installation. Once the correct balance is found, the values rarely ever change significantly enough to disturb ERL or SP.

Digital circuits and data communications equipment should have tests that stress the communication stream. Normal data test sets use pseudo-random bit generators that provide an even distribution of one and zero bits. Real-life data often presents something different from a steady stream of pulses. It might have long strings of either one or zero bits. There can be little packets of data that turn on and off. If you cannot use real data, then get a data generator where you can select and send similar data patterns. Abrupt changes in the data stream have always played havoc with data communications. You will find that repetitive patterns find problem areas that the pseudo-random signal never finds.

One test that most people overlook is to see what happens when a part of a system fails. If you have a section that looks like FIG. 14-1, you can have a ripple

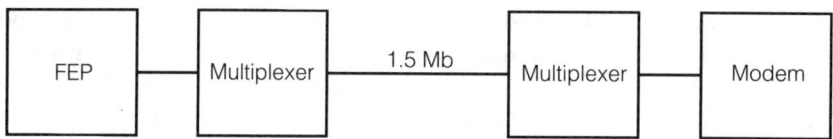

Fig. 14-1. Ripple effect.

effect. First, the 1.5 Mb facility takes a three-second hit and goes into an alarm condition. The multiplexers on both ends fall out of synchronization and turn their clear-to-send leads off on all interfaces. They also start a retrain sequence. At this point, the FEP recognizes the modem is no longer communicating and terminates the transaction. If the modem on the right side was on a switched line, the call holding would drop and cut the connection. This creates a ripple effect much like throwing a stone into a calm pond.

As soon as the 1.5 Mb facility is restored, the multiplexers start their resynchronization process. After that, the control leads on the multiplexer's interface tell the modem and that FEP is ready to communicate. Although the end user sees a 30-second or better outage, the problem was a three-second hit on the 1.5 Mb line.

Arranging system tests

It is very important that new products in any network are tested for compatibility with services before large-scale implementation. Also, it is wise to see if new services are compatible with existing products. The word *new* means both uniquely designed products (i.e., first of a kind) and prototype copies of old designs (i.e., the vendor is just entering into an established market).

Some companies like AT&T have developmental relations programs where the vendor can request compatibility testing. This allows the vendor to see if their equipment is compatible to AT&T services or equipment. The advantage is that the vendor can state that they were compatible with AT&T. If your vendor is not already aware of AT&T's Vendor Liaison Program, have them contact 1-800-225-5856 for information.

There are other testing entities around the country. Some Regional Bell Operating Companies (RBOC) provide similar services, and there are a few independent testing organizations. The economical way to ensure that tests are made is to ask the vendor or telco to make them for you. Stress that the tests are very important and that the implementation of their product or service rests with a successful demonstration.

The people at the test site include both parties concerned with compatibility and a technical representative from your organization. Your person can make sure your questions are answered and that there are no technical problems. At this point, you are the controller of the tests. Do not get into testing unless it is clear to the vendors or telco that you are in charge.

You should host a meeting that specifies the tests, procedures, and schedules. Each party involved in the test should agree on the objectives and have a full understanding of the interfaces and what equipment is involved. There should be no doubt as to how the products and service will interface with each other. More time is wasted by testers fabricating special cords to connect the equipment together than it takes to make the tests.

Identifying problems

If you discover a problem during the test, you must press for an identification of where the fault lies. The vendor might be reluctant to admit they are at fault and start finger-pointing to the other side. As the controller of the test, you should have an impromptu meeting on the spot. You must first clear the air by reminding the various groups that you are not trying to place blame but are trying to find a way to make the system work. There should be a review of the events leading up to the problem. After this, assign responsibilities to the various vendors and establish a time frame for finding an answer to the problem. These intervals should not drag on for more than a week. If they do not have an answer by then, you should start to look for alternatives.

Correcting design problems usually can be accomplished in a few days. One company was having a compatibility test made on the East Coast of the United States on a Friday afternoon. There was a design problem that prevented the products from operating. Three technicians flew back to Japan that night, corrected a design of an integrated circuit (IC), and were back on the East Coast again for testing on Monday morning. They identified the problem, redesigned the IC, and were able to fabricate a new IC in a couple of days. Not every company is prepared to correct a problem over the weekend, but they should have an answer within a week's time.

Nevertheless, most equipment designers can arrive at a solution if given the right facts. If the vendor's engineer did not participate in the actual test, make sure the vendor's representative fully understands the problem. The problem should be written out right on the spot while everything is fresh in the minds of everyone. It should have as much detail as possible leading up to the time of failure or malfunction. Include test voltages, frequencies, or whatever was linked to the equipment at the time.

Dealing with conflicts

Implementing your network requires a revised project schedule. Ideally, equipment will arrive on the site the day before you want to connect it to a facility or another piece of equipment. In real life, that rarely happens unless the products are off-the-shelf items and the facilities are readily available. Controlling the arrival of newly designed equipment is even a greater rarity. Managers have ordered other equipment for their network to work in conjunction with the brand new unit. All the other equipment arrives, but there is an unexpected delay due to a manufacturing or design problem of the new unit. Sometimes, these delays last for months. Meanwhile, you have bills to pay for the other equipment that now sits idle.

Dealing with implementation or operational conflicts requires a get-tough attitude. While you can make a lot of telephone calls, you need to write letters to the upper management of the vendor or telco. Phone calls that tell you things are just about fixed can put you off for a few days, but a letter to a high-level corporate manager that requests an immediate answer will get results. One method that gets quick results is a simplified style letter that is similar to the one approved by the Administrative Management Society (FIG. 14-2). It is short, it gets to the point, and simplifies the typist's work.

Date

(4 Spaces)

Name, Title
Company
Address
City, State Zip Code

(Triple Space)

CONFLICT OR PROBLEM

(Triple Space)

This letter is in block form with no indentation. There is no opening (e.g., Dear ____), or a closing statement (e.g., Sincerely). It gets right to the point by stating what the letter is all about (do not include the word SUBJECT: or RE: in front of the subject line).

(Double Space)

State as briefly as possible what the conflict is, who in their company is responsible. Request an answer in a reasonable time after their receipt of the letter.

(Double Space)

Your name and title are all upper case, and the typist initials are lower case.

(5 Spaces)

YOUR NAME
TITLE

(Double Space)

typist initials

Fig. 14-2. Simplified letter about conflicts or problems.

The beauty of this type of letter is that it shows you are concerned without having to address the person as dear so-and-so and close with an inappropriate "sincerely" or "yours truly." It always seemed odd to be upset about something and then close with a traditional phrase. This is like being angry with someone and then wishing them to "have a nice day!" Your company's letter-writing guidelines might require the traditional salutations and closings, and of course, this will rule how you will address other companies.

Maintaining the network

How you maintain your network depends on a number of factors, primarily the complexity of the network and how automated your system is to manage the complexity. Unlike the supervisor in a telco, there is no set table to find the number of personnel needed to maintain a network. Telcos assign factors to every segment of a test room and the supervisor then just calculates how many people are needed. Install 100 new circuits, and that equals so many hours of work. Get enough hours together and you can add another person to handle the work load.

Most industries are reluctant to add more personnel unless there is solid proof they are needed. When you planned the network, you probably assigned maintenance time factors to all the circuits and equipment. The best way to do this is to rely on historical data about maintenance times on previous networks. Next, find out what individual vendors recommend as routine maintenance and the expected mean time between failure rate of the individual equipment. You now have a base to estimate the hours needed to maintain the new network. Be sure to include an administrative time factor to update records and fill in trouble reports.

Adding new personnel gets everybody in a turmoil. You have to write a job description, the human resource department has to assign a job level, and upper management has to agree to the addition to the corporate budget. If you can show a need for personnel, you can also show that automating testing and trouble reporting reduces the need for additional people.

Trouble reporting

Trouble reporting takes on two roles. One is how to report the trouble to the responsible group; the other is what to do with the information after the trouble is fixed. Some of the newer network management systems (NMS) have the capability to automatically initiate a trouble report to the responsible group. This is beneficial if the responsible group acknowledges they received the report and is working to fix the problem. It would be even better if the report flagged the next level of management if the trouble was not fixed in an hour or so. Then, to top it all off, the responsible group would report back as to the actual trouble found.

People are normally reluctant to tell you what the problem was, preferring to just tell you it is fixed. You should have a better explanation than everything is OK now. Knowing where and what the troubles are is essential to managing your network. If problems keep cropping up in one segment, you have a choice to bypass that area in the future or get the responsible group to make major changes. Put trouble report information into some sort of database going back to the last 12 months. Information past that point is not that meaningful.

The rationale for a year's worth of historical data is to locate circuits affected by seasonal impairments. Twice a year (March and October), satellites line up with the Sun and the receive dish for several days. Around noon each day, the noise generated by the Sun wipes out communication. Another recurring transmission impairment occurs with microwave radio systems. In certain parts of the country, microwave radio transmission suffers from fading (transmission power diminishes due to signal cancellation) between 2:00 AM and 10:00 AM from April to October. Both these transmission impairments are somewhat predictable but require extraordinary reconfigurations to prevent transmission loss. The other reason for historical data is to locate repeat offenders that the responsible group is putting Band-Aids on instead of curing.

Trends in network maintenance

Companies like AT&T and IBM were at odds about how to manage your network. AT&T introduced Accumaster Integrator and IBM brought out NetView; two network management systems that approach network management differently. One is based more on the equipment and the facilities. The other is geared for the computer and its peripheral equipment. Fortunately, the two companies are working together to find ways to combine the two systems because both parties benefit from receiving information about the other system.

The benefit of competition from the various NMS units or software on the market is that they feed on each other. If one vendor brings out a "probable cause option" that helps identify the problem, the others must follow suit. As new features are added, the NMS equipment must have faster processors and larger memory storage. Nevertheless, faster processing and larger memories increase the cost, which reduces the market. On one hand, the added features improve what an NMS can do. However, raising the cost of the NMS because of the additional features requires greater justification to purchase.

At this point, there is not a standard protocol that you can specify. Things should improve when there is a final agreement as to an international network management protocol. Until then, vendors will either have to use their own proprietary code, use a de facto standard, or provide the software to work with different protocols. Your best bet is to specify software that will work with different protocols with the stipulation that the software be upgraded to the standard at no cost at a later date.

Summary

Implementing a network is the time to iron out the problems found during initial testing and installation. Here, you use some of the same techniques learned in chapter 10 to control the testing and eliminate problems or conflicts. Later, maintaining the network will depend a lot on what you and your personnel learn during the installation. Start building a historical database to track trouble reports for a maximum of 12 months.

15

Turning up
the system

Turning up the system is full of frustration, anxiety, and problems. It is, however, one of the best training spots for staff to learn about the parts of the network. Doing the actual installation and acceptance testing provides the best hands-on education you can get. If the vendor installs the equipment, you should have people assigned full-time to be with them during the installation. Either way, the technicians are learning as much as possible about the device. If your staff attended training classes before installation, you'll find the actual installing of equipment is reinforcement.

The frustration comes from unforeseen problems either not picked up during testing trials before installation, or because it was not possible to make prior tests. It is almost a certainty that you will have some type of problem during turn-up. Dealing with the problems requires your organization to be in full control to identify and assign responsibility to correct. This has a dual purpose. One is to make sure someone is working to fix the problem, and the other is to provide proof to your upper management that the problem is not yours. If you followed the planning and selection guidelines in the previous parts of this book, you would have the documentation to show you took every available step to have a successful installation.

Scheduling implementation

During your planning and selection process, you asked about the availability of the product or service. Take this information and start to lay out your implementation schedule. Find the item with the longest lead time, the next longest time, and so forth, listing lead times in a descending order. This project schedule is the reverse of the one you made in your planning stage. There, your start date was at the beginning of the planning period. Here, you know the probable completion date of the last segment of the network and work backwards.

Facilities, special construction, and custom-manufactured products usually have the longest lead times. Facility planning is normally a five-year process for telcos. Future growth and telecommunication trends revolve around a rolling five-year planning period. This spreads capital investment as evenly as possible over the years. When you request a service that is not in the telco's five-year facility installation plans, they might offer special construction at a price. This price is either a bill for labor and material, or a long-term contract to ensure they get their investment back.

Custom-manufactured products are similar to other custom-made items. Vendors start building only after a firm order, usually with some portion of the price up front. If they do not require a down payment, the contract will normally contain an escape clause that compensates the manufacturer for work performed should you cancel the order.

Once you know about the lead time, work backwards from the longest interval. Block out sections of the network by what is affected by the longest interval. Figure 15-1 is an example segment. The 1.5 Mb facility in our example is going to take six months to complete. The FEP takes three months after order; the multiplexers arrive in two months; and the modems can ship in two weeks.

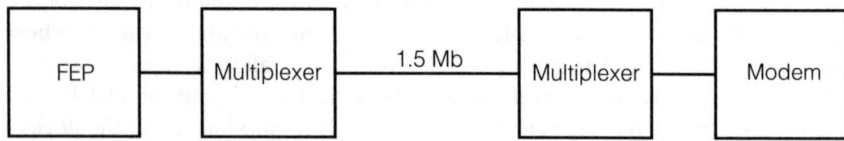

Fig. 15-1. Network segment.

The date the 1.5 Mb facility is turned up for service is the point of reference. This date is the promised due date furnished by the telco after you place the order. At this time, both directions are worked from the reference point shown in FIG. 15-2 as "Acceptance Testing." The left-hand side lays out when you must place an order. The right-hand side indicates a period for acceptance testing and final problem solving. If you cannot get firm commitments from vendors for a date that equipment will be at your sites, you should include an additional safety factor for the ordering and delivery period.

Next, the various segment schedules are folded into one chart that covers the entire network. It is easier to cut over segments to a network instead of one massive cut-over. While the whole network cut-over is dramatic if everything works, it is a disaster if it does not.

Acceptance testing

As soon as equipment arrives, it is wise to turn it on and keep it on. Keeping the equipment at operating temperature until you are ready to start acceptance testing allows the unit to complete its infant mortality period. Some equipment

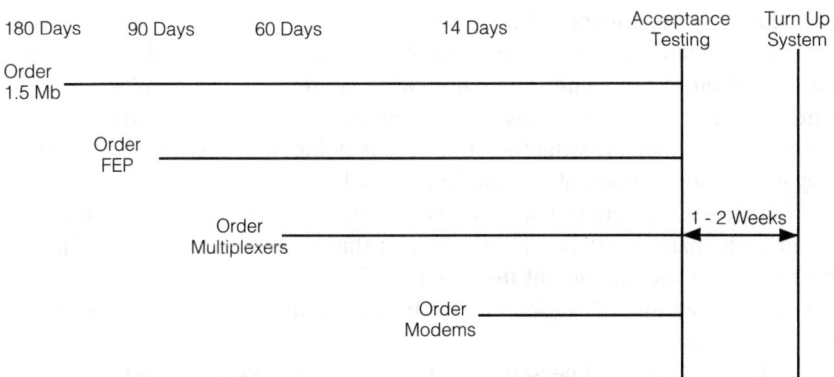

Fig. 15-2. Segment implementation schedule.

can be put into a looped mode with internal testing capability. This checks the unit out, keeps all alarms quiet, and ensures that one works.

Acceptance testing is different from maintenance testing. Acceptance testing tests everything provided by the vendor and the facilities for the stated performance criteria. Maintenance testing, on the other hand, entails trouble sectionalizing and some routine analysis. When you accept equipment, you should check every function to see if it performs properly. Equipment like large matrix switches might have too many combinations to test everything. In that case, you must make a reasonable sample. If there are failures within the sample, then increase the sample size to see if other failures show. All failures should have the immediate attention of the vendor.

Data communication tests should use real-life patterns instead of pseudo-random data generators, as well as sending repetitive patterns that include long strings of one or zero bits and an occasional reverse bit. Try different combinations to see if the system is upset by any pattern. All data tests should be end-to-end instead of remotely looping the circuit back on itself. That does not mean you should not make remote loop-back tests because they serve to isolate troubles in the future.

Switched-voice communication tests include dialing, level, and noise trials. At this point, you should sample some of the circuits. The real trial comes when the network is loaded down with traffic. That is when you will learn if the network switches properly or develops noise problems. You should test and then busy-out circuits to verify the number. Level and noise tests check the quality of the trunks (circuits between switches) provided. Verifying each line (circuits to the end user) off the switch is not realistic if you have a large system, and you must rely on trouble reports back from the end user to locate defective lines.

Escalating problem solving

You need commitments from the various parties to solve any problem that might be discovered during acceptance testing. When compatibility is in question, you need technical people from both organizations. While it is often difficult to arrange for an agreeable joint testing, those involved need to be at your location at the same time. Otherwise, finger-pointing results instead of finding the solution. Usually, finger-pointing is a result of the technical personnel not knowing what the other unit is doing. It is easy to point the other way when your equipment functions properly by itself.

Notify the vendors of your problem by escalating the issue to their middle or upper management. You want it known that you are unhappy and that you cannot accept the equipment the way it is. They understand that they will not see any money until it works and are in a position to make commitments for their company.

When the technical personnel arrive, you should handle everything similar to holding a meeting. You are in control, and you establish the agenda for their actions. Describe the problem and events leading up to it. They probably already know something about the trouble, but this clears any prior misunderstandings. If the technical personnel have not checked their own equipment beforehand, make them verify it is operating properly. As soon as everyone agrees their unit is functioning, demonstrate the incompatibility between the units. There should be a feeling of agreement between parties as to who should fix the problem. If there is not any agreement, then you should move the problem solving up another management level at each vendor's headquarters. Closing your joint testing is like closing a meeting. Everyone should know exactly what items are still open and then assign responsibilities to complete in a time frame. Also, remember to write a simplified letter (see FIG. 14-2) to record the vendor's commitment to fixing your problem. This type of letter is quick to put together and has a lasting effect.

Training by installation

As mentioned before, installing equipment is one of the best training areas you can find. Several years ago, Heathkit sold components and plans to build television sets as well as other products. Other than the satisfaction of putting a television set together all by yourself, you knew everything about the set. Building the set gave you the confidence to adjust or fix any problems in the future.

Learning about equipment is best done during installation. The amount of training you receive will depend on the amount of installation work and the complexity. It also depends on whether you do the entire installation or if the vendor is responsible. Of course, the other possibility is that your personnel do part of the installation and other parties complete outlying locations. You want your people involved in the installation for their own first-hand knowledge. This involvement might only mean watching or assisting the vendor's personnel install the equipment. Factors like vendor guarantees and union restrictions can also govern the amount of involvement.

Old-time telco supervisors would assign new personnel to watch and accept any new installation made by the Western Electric Company. Sometimes, it meant crawling around cable racks overhead to verify the installer ran the cabling on the right cable rack. In a very short time, the new person was an expert on all aspects of the equipment.

Installation is also the time to check the manuals provided by the vendor. Installation and operating manuals should be judged for clarity and completeness. The trouble with writing good manuals is that what seems perfectly obvious to the writer is not always clear to the reader. It is like someone writing out their favorite recipe for someone else. Little things like not writing directions to grease the baking pan first leads to the other person's culinary disaster. Missing items in the manuals should be corrected by the vendor as quickly as possible, but, in the meantime, write addendums to the manuals to clarify sections or add the missing pieces.

Training the end user

If your new network causes the end user to operate in a different manner, you must plan to train them. Training must be built into your implementation schedule prior to turn-up. Often, change in the workplace is the hardest thing to accomplish. People get set in their ways and forcing a change is upsetting. Getting people into the paperless office where all internal correspondence is electronic is a good example. The first obstacle is the keyboard. It either presents a problem of dexterity or it is a symbol of an underling's function. Some people adapt readily, and others will stack papers on top of the keyboard.

People adapt to change better if they think they are part of the change. For the most part, they are brought in on the change only after all the decisions are made. Being after the fact, they normally do not feel they are a part of the change. In the next section, you'll learn about getting feedback from the end user after the system is up and running. When end user training is started, you should explain the reasons and advantages for the change. You can then explain how they are now a part of this change because they will provide the feedback about the new system. This is vital to overall communications—to know if you reached your original goals. Once personnel are part of the change, go through a step-by-step explanation of the new process.

To ease apprehensions, you can establish several addresses that the end user can practice dialing or sending data. In the case of electronic mail, the practice number can include instructional documents on how to edit or send to multiple addresses. The whole object of training is to make the transition as easy as possible and have the system accepted by the end user.

Getting feedback

End users

Part of the turn-up procedure is to find out how well the system is working. A lot of data is derived from traffic analysis, but other information is an evaluation from the end user. Traffic analysis can show changes in how long it takes to access databases, complete transactions, and any improvements in the way of doing business. It does not, however, show how the changes are perceived by the end user. To complete your final implementation period, you must survey the end users for their opinions.

Surveys take several forms. One method is to have one-on-one interviews with people from different groups around the company. Another is a one-page questionnaire with simple ways to answer the questions. The questions should only take a few moments to answer to get the largest response. When questionnaires ask too many questions, people tend to see it as an infringement on their time and become uncooperative. Be sure to leave an area where the end user can write comments. There will always be someone who wants to give you additional words.

The thing about surveys is that the results follow the typical statistical curve. You will have people that will hate the change and others that love everything about it. The comments you are looking for are the ones from the majority of the people in the middle. They are the ones that offer constructive criticism that helps shape modifications to the network. A survey response summary becomes part of your final documentation or report.

Network management

Those who were involved in the planning, selecting, and implementing of the network need to sit down and critique what went on during the process. Before meeting to discuss the process, have each person write down a bulleted list of things they would do differently, things that went very well, and suggest modifications to the new network. Compile the lists and make that the agenda for the meeting. Take the feedback from the end user, and then modify the agenda to key in on the items that both sides perceive.

At the meeting with the network people, go over the feedback from the end users first, then go over the compiled list to see how to improve the network as the end user sees it. Other items concerning planning and selection should become part of your final selection documentation to help network planners in the future. Without historical information, new people will make the same mistakes for the next network.

Final report

The last thing to complete is a final report on the planning, selection, and implementation process. How you word this report depends on the outcome of everything that happened. Pratt's Rules says that, if you bring the project in on time and within the budget, people will feel the job was not that hard in the first place. Run the project past the due date and way over budget and people have the notion that the project must have been harder than they originally thought. Either way, you can be blessed or damned for your performance by how upper management perceives the deed.

Your message to upper management should be contained in an executive summary similar to the one described in chapter 13. It must get the point across in less than 30 seconds. You can attach other pertinent material to the executive summary as long as it pertains to the executive summary. Don't add documents to balloon the size of the report as if your salary increases depended on its weight. If they want additional information, they'll ask for it.

When the project goes very well, you want people to know who was responsible for pulling it off. The project leader should recognize their personnel in their own organization and other groups by writing a short digest of what the individual did to make the project a success. This serves as a reminder for merit review at a later date. If you are not sure what the person actually did, you should sit down and ask what they thought was their greatest contribution. In both cases, do not wait until the end of the year to remember what happened. The written digest or the interview needs the benefit of fresh memories.

If the project had some problems, you want to tell people how the project team solved the problems in a timely manner. The message here is to briefly describe the problem and how it was solved. Adversity appeared on the scene and was quickly dispatched by some action. Getting back to Pratt's Rules on how people perceive how difficult a task was if it was on time and under budget, it is always wise to add some problem solving. It gives the impression that it really was not easier than it seems and that it was a job well done.

Projects that had problems that could not be solved need a final report that describes the actions taken to correct and where the responsibility rests. If the correction is beyond your control, you need to show why it is really beyond yours or the company's power to correct. Include suggested alternatives to the projects original plans to circumvent the problem area.

Summary

Implementing a multi-vendor network is an optimum time to train maintenance personnel and end users. Personnel can better understand the system and provide better feedback to fine-tune the network as well. It is also the time to fully test the complete operation of the equipment and facilities. Testing becomes a benchmark for future maintenance or troubleshooting. While testing looks at the operation, simulated failures to the total system provide insight as to how the network reacts. Small failures often have a ripple effect that could cause large outages.

16

Test equipment & network management

Testing requires different skill levels. The person with the lowest level of technical skills usually does not know one test set from another and cannot operate any. Then there is the highest-trained technician who can operate complex test equipment, but usually only needs to listen to a circuit to tell you what is wrong. This person is much like the expert mechanic that can tune your car just by listening to the sound of the engine.

Test equipment

Before you go out and buy a lot of test equipment, it is better to start with just a few essentials. If it appears you need more complex test sets, it is best to rent the test equipment. This provides a couple of advantages. One, you can "test drive" the set for a month to see if it really does the job you thought it would. If it does what you want and there is an obvious need for extensive use, you can then purchase the unit. The alternative to renting is to locate a test equipment vendor that will loan a demonstration unit for a week or two. You should know the worth of the test set in a short time.

The second advantage of a trial is finding out if the equipment is too complex for the technical level of your personnel. There is nothing worse than to open up a cabinet and find expensive test equipment stored because nobody knows how to use it or there really is not any need.

In order to test, you need some type of access point between interfaces. Two- and four-wire transmission systems normally provide jack appearances between interfaces to aid in sectionalizing troubles or aligning the circuit. Most large networks find some way to have a patch panel at the central location so circuits can be accessed. You should follow the example of the telephone company that almost has an overkill of access points. Upper management might not understand the need for rows of patch panels for voice and data circuits, but they are necessary for quick trouble sectionalizing and restoration. Disconnecting wires and jerry-built interfaces is not the best way to make tests.

The tests and equipment described in the rest of this chapter assume there is some easy access point. In most descriptions, you will see the following references to the technical level needed to operate the test equipment or make specialized tests:

Level I: Lower skill levels—results do not need interpretation.
Level II: Medium skill levels—moderate interpretation needed.
Level III: Highest skill levels—analytical qualities needed.

Analog voice-grade transmission test equipment

Analog private-line circuits have three major trouble areas. One is the open circuit where there is no continuity, as if someone cut the wire. Second is the long or high-loss circuit that has continuity but the level is below operating ranges. The third is noise on the circuit that prevents data transmission. These three troubles account for 95 percent of all analog private-line problems.

The simplest test set (Level I) is a headset to listen to the circuit. If the circuit does not have any continuity, it is usually dead quiet. If there is high loss, the volume is very low compared to good circuits. White noise has a frying or sizzling sound, while static has a crackling sound. Impulse noise is a very short-lived spritz or zap sounds.

A basic Level II test set combines at least a tone generator that covers the 300 to 3400 Hz voice range and a level-measuring section. The most important tone for voice-band analog circuits is 1004 Hz. It is the reference frequency for all measurements. This testing tone is offset by 4 Hz to eliminate problems with the digital carrier systems that use an 8000 Hz sampling frequency. A Level III test set will also include a noise-measuring section. North American tests require a noise-measuring set that has a C-Message notch-measuring capability. The notch is a high-Q filter that eliminates a 1004-Hz tone that operates companders during the measurement. European measurements use the psophometric weighting that is slightly different from C-Message.

Wandel-Goltermann is a leading test set manufacturer of test equipment for the international arena. Most of their sets are built for telephone companies around the world. However, one test set visually depicts the entire frequency spectrum and is handy when equalizing circuits. It can also spot frequency dropouts that occasionally appear. Using this type of test set requires one to send and another to receive and is useful only when you have many circuits.

Getting into the other 5 percent of the troubles requires a Level-III-type test set. The best single instrument to diagnose many different transmission impairments is a vector scope. It gives a visual display of all the possible impairments at one time, and with a little training, a good technician can quickly sectionalize the trouble. There is little need for expensive test sets that measure every possible transmission impairment. If you cannot sectionalize the trouble using simpler methods, you can always rent an all-purpose test set. Just remember that it takes time to learn how to operate this level of test equipment, and you must use it often. Otherwise, you'll be unfamiliar with it every time you turn it on.

Test level points (TLP)

All tests must have some reference point to judge the value of the circuit. The standard reference for frequency gain on analog voice-grade circuits is the milliwatt. This is a 1004 Hz tone across a 600 Ω resistance such as to produce 1 mW of power. When you have a reference level, the other readings are logarithmic ratios designated as decibels (dB). Because the milliwatt is not the only reference point, you will see a tag added to the dB unit to name which reference. The other designations are as follows:

dBm   Referenced to the milliwatt.
dB0   Referenced to a zero test-level point.
dBrnC0   Referenced noise with a C-Message filter at a zero test level.
dBm0p   Referenced psophometric noise.

Figure 16-1 pictures the difference between the signal power level and test level points for a private-line data circuit. The first thing to look at is the left-hand modem's transmit (T) point. Here, the TLP reference to a zero level is +13 dB0, and the output of the modem is 0 dBm. There is a designed loss (-29 dB) on the circuit between your location and the carrier's office. At the carrier's receive (R) point, the TLP is -16 dB0 and the data power level is -29 dBm. The carrier amplifies the signal by +23 dB to output at a +7 dB0 TLP. In the last section, the designed loss is -10 dB to reduce the data signal to the -16 dB required receive signal level of the right-hand modem. Only the left to right direction values for TLP and signal power appear in the figure.

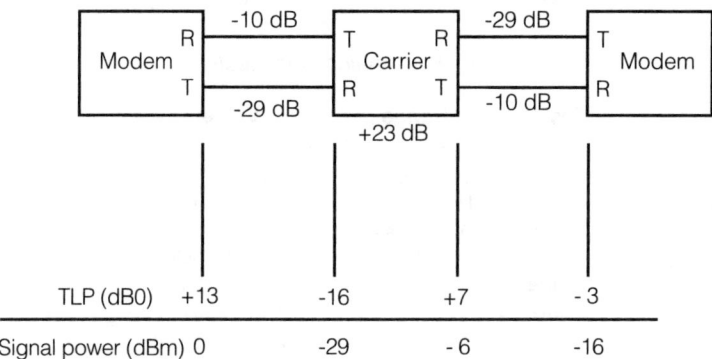

Fig. 16-1. Signal power vs. TLP.

Analog tests

A basic analog test is checking for continuity with a frequency generator and a measuring device. Figure 16-2 shows a generator connected to a line going to a remote location. At the remote location, the circuit loops back to the other side of the four-wire circuit. This side of the circuit then connects to a measuring test set. Normally, both functions are in one test set. Unfortunately, this is about all a loop-back test is good for. If there is loss or some transmission impairment on the circuit, you will not know which direction has the fault. The other thing is that certain impairments mask themselves when the circuit loops back on itself. A frequency shift in one direction will shift back in the opposite direction. Ideally, the combined test set will have a speaker so you can listen for noise.

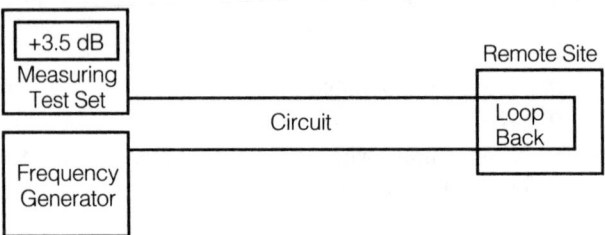

Fig. 16-2. Loop-back tests.

Dedicated analog voice circuits have a few requirements. TABLE 16-1 lists the values for level, noise, slope, echo return loss (ERL), and singing point (SP). Level is the power at the 1004 Hz reference point. Noise is shown for just two ranges. As the circuit gets longer, the noise level will increase. The confusion occurs when you learn that dBrn is a positive reading in respect to the -88 dBm point where noise begins. A dBrn reading means the noise level is going more positive in respect to the -88 dBm point. The upper line in FIG. 16-3 depicts various noise measurements in dBrnC0. The lower line is the difference between the -88 dBm noise reference point and the noise measure-

Table 16-1. Analog voice tests.

Test	Range	Value
Loss	Transmit	0 to +4 dB
	Receive	−4 to −10 dB
Noise	0-50 miles	> 38 dBrnCO
	51-100 miles	>39 dBrnCO
Slope	304 - 3400 Hz	+3 to −12 dB
Echo		5 to 11 dB
Singing		2 to 6 dB

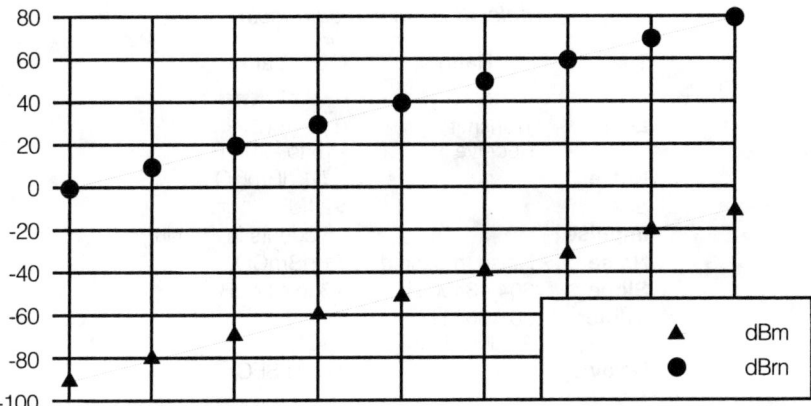

Fig. 16-3. Relationship between noise reference and noise measurement.

ment. There is another modification to this chart and that is a reference to the TLP.

Slope is the variation of the complete frequency spectrum to the reference 1004 Hz level. There are many different values for the various types of circuits. AT&T PUB 43202 & 43202A1—AT&T Analog Voice is a good reference that lists just about every type of circuit and its values.

One way of checking switched-service circuits is to dial off-net into the local telephone company's milliwatt supply for level and their quiet termination for noise measurements. You can locate the right telephone number either by asking or experimenting. Usually, the tone and quiet termination are in the very last numbers of each exchange (e.g., 123-9992). You learn whether the dialing works and you can check the quality of the return circuit.

Analog data circuits are different from analog voice circuits. Voice can tolerate several transmission impairments that will stop data. As modem technology improves, some of the impairments are meaningless. Envelope delay was a big thing at one time, but today, all high-speed modems have automatic equalizers, which eliminates the problem. These same equalizers also correct the majority of slope problems. There is not much you can do to correct jitter and noise problems other than provide forward error correction. Most high-speed modems also include trellis coding to improve the performance.

TABLE 16-2 lists the requirements for an unconditioned data line. Conditioning has tighter requirements to permit certain modems to function. A signal-to-noise factor of only 24 dB would restrict the line to lower speed modems.Some 9600-bps modems have a hard time functioning with a 27 dB S/N reading. The thing to note is that impulse noise measurements are made over a 15-minute period and that there is a threshold where impulse noise records. Noise below the threshold is recorded in the general noise measurement. Jitter is not a common occurrence, but if it occurs, it will disrupt your data. A vector scope visually pictures jitter as the name implies. The last item, envelop delay, is

Table 16-2. Analog data tests.

Test	Range	Value
Loss	Transmit	0 to −4 dB
	Receive	−16 to −20 dB
Noise		< 51 dBrnC0
S/N		≥24 dB
Impulse		15 counts in 15 min.
Noise	Noise threshold	71 dBrnC0
Slope	304 - 3400 Hz	+3 to −12 dB
φ **Jitter**	20 - 300 Hz	≤10°
	4 - 300 Hz	≤15°
Delay		1750 µSEC

not part of the normal installation anymore, although they might test for it after everything else is tested. This type of test set is not recommended.

Digital circuit tests and test equipment

Making tests over digital circuits or testing analog modems requires a data pattern generator and checker. A common variety test set has a pseudo-random data generator and maybe a dotting pattern. It is pseudo because the same pattern of evenly distributed one and zero bits repeats after so many bits sent. Some sets allow you to change the length of the pattern. Nevertheless, the best data generators will let you create specific patterns.

While the random patterns will provide normal data testing, a repetitive pattern with strings of one or zero bits and an occasional opposite bit will give your system a workout. Abrupt change from a steady stream of similar bits seems to play havoc with some communications systems. One digital transmission system built up a charge on a bypass capacitor when a long string of one-bits went through one circuit board. Along came a zero-bit, and the capacitor discharged to create a one-bit in its place. Normal data transmission would have requested a resend of the data. This particular repetitive pattern happened to be a resynchronization code necessary to restore transmission.

When it comes to data checkers or detectors, the favorite of most is the bit-error mode. Other units can test block-error or error-free-seconds. While different transmission rates and methods use one of the three methods, it is not necessary to have all three methods on hand. Digital data services use the error-free-second mode, but make tests using bit-error checkers. Block-error rate says no more than one block in error out of 100, 1000-bit blocks sent. If you normally send 1000-bit blocks, you might find this type of error-checking method has some importance. A bit-error rate easily converts into a close approximation of an error-free-second percentage by the following formula. It is close because random errors do not occur in digital systems, and therefore, the formula is not scientifically valid. Nevertheless, it is accurate enough for almost everyone except the purist.

$$\%P_{EFS} = (1 - P_{RE})^{BIT\ RATE} \times 100$$

$$\%P_{EFS} = (1 - 10^{-7})^{56,000} \times 100 = 99.44\%$$

Where: $\%P_{EFS}$ = Percent Error-Free Seconds

$\qquad\ P_{RE}$ = Probability of Random Errors $\qquad\qquad$ (16-1)

Trying to equate block-error to bit-error is not an easy thing to do. Equation 16-2 first shows that 100 blocks of 1000-bit blocks equals 100,000 or 105 bits. If you only had one bit in error, the error rate equals the normal bit-error rate of 10^{-5}. However, you could also have one block or 1000 bits in error and still meet the block-error performance. This says you can meet the block-error performance, but have an atrocious bit-error performance. The original block-error rate came at a time when synchronous data waited for an acknowledgment after each block sent. Now strings of blocks travel in one direction before an acknowledgment is sent back. It looks like very long blocks of data that do not fit the criteria of 1000-bit blocks. While the supported error rate for analog modems over 2400 b/s is the block-error, the bit-error rate is the better indication of performance. The relationship between bit-errors and error-free-seconds can be seen in FIG. 2-4

$$100\ Blocks \times 1000\ \frac{Bits}{Block} = 10^5\ Bits$$

$$\frac{1\ Error\ Bit}{10^5\ Bits} = 10^{-5}\ Bit\ Error\ Rate$$

$$\frac{1000\ Error\ Bits}{10^5\ Bits} = 10^{-2}\ Bit\ Error\ Rate \qquad\qquad (16-2)$$

Minor data errors are masked by the newer high-speed modems with error-correction coding. A circuit could start to deteriorate and you would not know about it until the modem dropped its operating speed.

A Level-I test set for data is the trusty breakout box that is highly recommended for everyone. It is a relatively low-cost device and is coveted by the people that use them. People that have a breakout box usually lock them up so they don't wander off. Their size makes them very convenient to carry in a pocket or briefcase.

Protocol analyzers were strictly Level-III-type test equipment for many years. Even knowledgeable people felt like the piano player that was asked to play the cathedral's pipe organ for the first time. There were so many switches and options to set before you could use the set that it was often overwhelming to even think about using one. Nevertheless, the protocol analyzer is essential to troubleshooting problems between equipment. Individual sections of your network might meet acceptable transmission performance criteria, but the total system does not function. Over the years, the vendors of analyzers have moved from firmware boxes to software and faster processors.

As the networks get faster and faster, analyzers face a problem of keeping pace with megabit rates. It takes very fast processors to handle the data and make decisions. The other problem is finding enough memory to record more than just a few seconds or minutes of data when you are looking for an obscure problem. Some of the things to consider when you look for an analyzer that fits your needs are as follows.

- It should provide filters that specify the protocol under test.
- Provide event triggers.
- Capture and record data.
- Ease of integrating into other network management displays.
- Remote operation capability.
- Level of expertise needed to operate.
- Modularity capability to add different protocols later.
- Protocol simulation capability for installation or long-term testing.

Transmission measuring sets

Your need for transmission measuring sets depends on several factors. If you lease the facilities, you don't need any sets with the following possible exceptions:

- The time for a telco repair person to reach your location is excessive.
- You lease many lines from a central location.
- Your technical staff is smarter than the telco's personnel.
- There is a need to verify what the telco provided.

When the facilities are your own, you do not need anything other than the instruments you used to install them. As mentioned in chapter 15, your personnel should be involved with any installation. Even if an outside contractor installed cabling or other transmission media, your personnel should assist. There is no greater training ground.

Today's transmission equipment is completely solid-state and has a very low degradation characteristic. When microwave radio used vacuum tubes for amplifiers, there was a monthly routine to adjust or replace components. Along came completely solid-state microwave amplifiers, and the routine went from monthly to yearly to just checking the operating frequency. Gone were all the adjustments and the trips at night to an isolated repeater tower. Technical skills went from highly trained to "jerk-n-jamb" technicians that pulled out the bad circuit board and put in a new one.

Sectionalizing troubles

After your (Network Management System) or individual subsystem reports a trouble, it is time to sectionalize the trouble. The worst trouble is when a high-capacity facility goes out and a great number of your circuits go open. This is when it seems the whole world is ringing alarms to tell something is wrong. Your equipment room is a blaze of red flashing lights and all those irritating alarms are screeching. While your world seems to be coming apart, the scene at the telephone company's office makes your situation look minor. At the telco, there are loud bells ringing and klaxon horns blaring that add to the confusion. People are moving around the floor to silence alarms, start restoration plans, and answer the phone calls from customers and the telco upper management. Remote centers also have seen the same alarms and start reconfiguring the switch-network around the cable break.

Sectionalizing troubles in your own facilities often requires analytical reasoning to reduce the number of places to look for the problem. You should have some database where you can quickly identify common transmission paths. This database can be as simple as a loose-leaf notebook, a software program to sort out the circuits, or the program built into NMS.

Services that have alternative routing paths might require greater reasoning skills. The services might automatically start taking alternative paths around a break or open circuit. If the section did not report an alarm back to a central site, the first indication of a problem is a higher utilization on other paths.

Locating troubles in equipment is easier than finding the exact location of a facility problem. For years, telcos used a Whetstone Bridge to locate the precise location of an open, in-wire facility. The introduction of coaxial cable reduced the estimation to four-mile spans and gas-pressure alarms. It was then the job of the cable maintenance personnel to track the problem down.

When it is not evident where the problem is, you must then divide the facility into sections. If you have limited access to the facility, start as close to the midpoint as possible to begin testing. Twisted-pair facilities require at least some type of continuity checker like an ohmmeter. The next level of testing is a transmission measuring set. Fiber testing requires an optic power meter. You now know which half of the facility has the problem. Again, divide the half in two as best possible and repeat the test. This bisecting continues until you can locate the cause of the problem.

Network management systems

Network management systems is a general term that takes on different meanings for a lot of vendors. Because network management is such a hot item, a vendor cannot say their product doesn't have some form. It is like the recent craze for oat bran, calcium, or being fat-free. All the products on the shelf made some claim to one or all items to be marketable.

Multi-vendor network management requires something more than individual vendor's claims to managing a network, however. Very complex networks can end up with several network managing systems or use one system that combines everything into a centralized location. Your network managing system will depend on the:

- Expertise of your technicians.
- Complexity of the network.
- Need for rapid restoration.
- Need for reconfiguration.
- Need for remote monitoring.

Internal to computing system

Computing systems have had network management programs to control their network architecture for years. The most notable network architecture is the IBM SNA using VTAM/NCP. It was always a mystery to telecommunication people that IBM users only spoke in acronyms. The other mystery was why they chose the acronym SNA, which is the Scottish word for snow.

While this type of system alludes to telecommunication management, the computer-oriented systems are after-the-event reporting and are rudimentary in reporting telecommunication troubles. The computer management systems are only capable of reporting on how well their own hierarchical levels are doing.

Internal to vendor's devices

Another form of networking management is the diagnostic capabilities of a particular vendor's equipment. This has advanced from simple alarm reporting to include performance monitoring and accounting or inventory management. The other advancement is the extension of the management system to a centralized display unit. At last, you can move your personnel out of the equipment room into an office atmosphere.

The biggest disadvantage to separate vendor management systems is that they usually have different operating systems. Some vendors have adopted AT&T's telecommunication management system to make them somewhat compatible in a multi-vendor environment. Now, systems like the Simple Network Management Protocol (SNMP), Common Management Information Protocol (CMIP), and Common Management Information Services (CMIS) are appearing in newer products. Vendors are adopting versions of the SNMP as a de facto standard, and some include the CMIP and CMIS capability. Whatever system you purchase, you should have a commitment from the vendor that they will upgrade any system to the finalized standard.

To be truly integrated, the NMS should check devices in the computing network as well as the communication system. If you are adding an integrated NMS to your existing system, you need to review Part-I and Part-II of this book to select the system that fits your needs and budget. You can offset the expense of an NMS by eliminating the need for additional personnel. Other advantages for a couple of the top-of-the-line NMS are as follows:

- Quicker trouble identification.
- Provides probable locations of troubles.
- Concentration of events to one console or split functions to separate consoles.
- Ease of restoring or reconfiguring services.
- Reduced level of technical skills needed to maintain the network.
- Automatic trouble-reporting to the telco.

Integrated computing and communication

The optimum integrated computing and communication NMS integrates all the data and voice equipment in addition to the carrier services. It should maintain a single inventory of the various components of the total network. Instead of personnel interpreting different reporting formats from individual NMS components, it should convert these into a single method. Going back the other way, the key strokes to perform a function should convert to the indi-vidual subsystem. Learning individual system function controls is difficult and leads to issuing wrong commands.

While the advantages are great when all network information converges into a single point, if the integrator is down for repairs, the risk of losing control increases. Contingency plans should be in place to either monitor the subsystems or pass the control to some other location. System control could be transferred to other locations for staffing reasons due to the time of day or extreme weather conditions. For those managers that are married to their network, they can have a terminal at home to monitor what is going on with the system. However, remote operation capability is recommended only if you can prevent unauthorized people from entering the system.

Summary

Testing and sectionalizing troubles is a matter of using the most expedient device to test with and looking for the section with the highest probability of failing. Often, your ears and eyes are the only tools you need to locate problem areas. Sectionalize the trouble area by dividing and redividing the testing distance until you can locate the actual fault.

Don't purchase expensive test equipment unless you have a real need and you have the level of expertise to operate it. When obscure problems appear, you can rent complex test equipment to solve the puzzle.

17

Making it work better

Never be satisfied with the present, because it can always be made better. Your goal is to improve the network's operation by increasing the traffic loading and handling within the constraints of the network. A technician goes about improving on how the equipment runs by tweaking the controls. Tweakers never leave anything alone. You can find them in hotels and motels around the country adjusting the TV set in the room. They always carry a small screwdriver on trips so they can adjust to their heart's content. The TV set happens to be the only electronic gadget they can get their hands on at night. Tweaking becomes a fetish to the technician, but everything they touch is a little better when they leave.

Now is the time to tweak and adjust the network. Making a minor adjustment will not make a dramatic impact. Add a coprocessor chip to a personal computer to help with the number crunching and the processing speed improves, but you lose the reference of how long it took before. You are able to crunch numbers in less time, which means an improvement. Nevertheless, the change is accepted as a matter of fact. It is not until you sit down at another PC without the coprocessor chip that you recognize how much slower the operation is.

Improving response times

One way to improve response time is to load-balance the network. The first thing is to make sure the traffic is evenly distributed over the high-speed facilities. While your planning process looked at existing traffic and forecasted growth, you must monitor the network management tools to remain current. The other process requires a way to dynamically reconfigure the network on the fly. Companies such as AT&T have locations where they can control their entire network. Pertinent information and various alarms from around the country home into a control site. From this point, they can issue commands to large switching machines to route calls around trouble areas or congested routes. Dynamic load balancing is an adjustment that speeds the traffic flow and utilizes the network to a higher degree.

Don't overlook simple things like the operating speeds of batch printers. If your new network has greater bandwidth, it might be possible to increase the operating speed of the terminal to run at full bore. An example of this was a batch printer in one location and the host in another city. The transmission line was running at 9600 bps and the printer was just loping. Doubling the speed of the transmission line automatically increased the speed of the printer. The printer then pumped out reports so fast that they had to build a cage to catch the paper as it flew out of the enclosure. People that were in the habit of waiting for a large printout were productive again in a shorter time.

Just because a terminal is running at a particular transmission speed does not mean it cannot run a little faster. Almost every synchronous device will automatically adjust to a faster clock. However, that is not to say that there is not a limit as to how fast it can operate. Everything has some limit. In the case of the printer, there was a mechanical limitation that prevented it from going any higher. When the equipment's operating manual does not specify its limitation, you should contact the engineer who designed the unit. You could, of course, experiment to see how fast the terminal can go, but you might void any guarantee if you operate it for periods above any stated rate. Again, contact the engineers; they are the only people that probably know what the unit's true limitations are. It might take some effort to get through several layers of vendor's hierarchy to talk to the engineer, but it might pay off in increased operational speed.

Restoration

Networks that bundle communications into high-speed facilities must have plans to restore and reconfigure the circuits. High-speed facilities are normally very good and have a high percentage of operational time (excluding errored second performance). Even if the carrier guaranteed a 99.9 percent operational time during a year, it still equates to 8.76 hours in that period. Hopefully, the eight plus hours are spread over the year in increments of minutes that only happen around 3:00 AM on Sunday morning. Realistically, this is not the case. As luck would have it, the eight-hour outage occurs during the most critical period of communications. Cable cuts normally happen only during the normal business hours of most companies. Freak outages caused by defective water mains or violent storms happen anytime, but rarely at 3:00 AM on Sunday.

It doesn't matter if you have a sophisticated NMS that can make rapid reconfigurations or if you make manual patches, you must prioritize your circuits to know what to restore first. Voice circuits usually have alternate routing based in the individual PBXs, and will seek other routes during facility outages. This leaves the data communication as the prime target for restoration. Typically, a company has many different data communication needs, and their priorities are different. You need to put everything into perspective as to how critical a circuit is before you can determine which circuit gets restored first. If you listen to individual groups, they will all have the greatest need over any other department. The needs must be rank-ordered as to the economic value to the total company. One value is the amount of money the company will lose from lost transactions, and the other is the amount of money lost by idle workers.

Before trying to restore or reconfigure your network, you need an estimate from the carrier as to just how long it will be before the facility is restored. It is not reasonable to start massive restoration plans if the prospect for restoral is five or ten minutes. If the telco is vague as to what happened, you should begin full restoration plans. In both instances, you should start with the restoration of the most critical communication path. Just remember that it takes a certain amount of time to actuate restoral plans and an equal amount to return things to normal. Sophisticated reconfiguration systems must go through sanity checks to verify that switches were made and all this takes time. Manual restoral still takes an equal amount of time for voice coordination to make patches.

After you have prioritized circuit restoration, the next step is to map out the network. Each facility segment in the network then has a list of circuits for restoration, from the most critical to the lowest circuit. Ideally, all this information is on a database where you can identify the circuits from a known facility outage or identify the facility outage from the known circuits not operating. Large NMS systems provide inventory and probable cause functions that reduce the time to respond to a restoration.

No matter what arrangement you have for restoration, it has little value unless personnel know how to go about restoration. Restoration of services must be practiced to make people knowledgeable and able to respond quickly. If your restoration plans are in a book somewhere, be sure everyone knows exactly where it is. Be sure they understand what their roles are during the restoration period. Last, be like the military and practice, practice, practice. Hold dry runs that simulate the real restoral as much as possible. The ultimate practice is making a complete wet-run and see if the actual restoration really works.

Telco or carrier performance

One of the most frustrating things for a telco is when a customer has nine out of ten circuits that are near perfection and exhibit only a couple of bits in error the whole year. The tenth circuit is not near perfection, but still far exceeds the stated error performance. It is difficult to tell the customer that the tenth circuit is fine when they compare it to the other nine. The telco will probably make a lot of tests because the customer complained about the service. If the circuit far exceeds the supported performance, there is little they can do. Swapping facilities or equipment to make that tenth circuit have the same performance as the other nine is not economical nor does it make good business sense to "gold-plate" services.

However, when that tenth circuit just meets the supported performance criteria, they should make every effort to improve the circuit. If a circuit just meets the performance level, it is a sick circuit because the supported level is way under what is realistic. The old analog circuit performance is well understated because the long-haul facilities are almost all digital carriers now. High-speed (i.e., 14,400 bps and higher) modems will operate smoothly as long as the digital carrier uses Pulse Code Modulation (PCM). If your equipment uses a different encoding scheme other than PCM, the high-speed modem will only operate at a much lower rate. Most telcos use PCM exclusively in their facilities because it is the better system.

Whenever you complain to a telco about a service, you should have as much history about the trouble as possible. It is like going to the doctor and just saying that you do not feel good. If you went to the doctor and said I do not feel good and here is a history of things leading up to it, the doctor can make an informed opinion of the problem. The time to arrive at a solution is drastically reduced. There is a reduction of tests to pinpoint the trouble, and less second-guessing what the trouble could be. Any service trouble history should contain dates, times, and events leading up to the problem. Some of the strangest problems have the most unusual explanations. One problem occurred only during certain parts of the day. The particular building was short on cable ducting between floors and the circuit's cable ran inside a little-used elevator shaft. However, the elevator was pressed into service only during rush hours and the power for the elevator radiated into the cable. When they tested the circuit, it was during the lull between rush hours, and it tested to be a very good circuit. Had the end user noted the time of the day when the circuit was bad, the solution would have been easier to find and the circuit fixed in a shorter time. As it was, the customer and the telco's nerves were worn very thin over several weeks of frustration.

Design changes

Some design changes can improve the performance of the network. As was the case of the batch printer being able to operate at a higher speed, it is also possible to increase the speed of other devices. PC manufacturers are starting to build modular systems. Changing operating speeds is now a board or chip replacement instead of replacing the whole unit.

Electronic devices have internal clocks that govern the speed of operation. Clocking starts from a very high frequency generator and then they divide the clock a number of times until it reaches the originally desired rate. Simple design changes to clock division can increase operating speed. The best time to incorporate a simple design change like this is during the original design period. Had the product manager explained to the engineer that the product should have variable operating speeds, the design could have movable straps or switches to quickly change operating modes.

The other issue about design changes is that the engineer is usually isolated from the customer and the real world. Their input is through a marketing-oriented person that has written a business case to develop a product that has potential sales. The product manager creates the design criteria that the engineer uses for the design. An end product leaves the engineers' hands and is never heard about again other than trouble reports. Your network needs are served better if you can get back to the product manager and engineer to express your feelings about the product. After a short time, you have an opinion about the likes and dislikes about how the product works. By sitting down with the vendor, you can go over the strong and weak points. Every vendor loves praise about the strong points. The weak points are often overlooked during the initial design. When these issues come up, the engineers usually respond by offering a quick and inexpensive way to make it happen. It is rare that they will admit it cannot be done. If the design changes are minor to make, the vendor is normally happy to improve the product. Major design changes will appear in the next model or in the "Series-II" version that corrects design faults.

Upgrades

Part of your risk analysis involved finding all you could about how the vendor handled upgrades for their hardware or software. The effort there concerned how the vendor let everyone know that an upgrade existed and how they treated the expense. If you are not in the loop to hear about upgrades, you might miss out on any improvement. Had you purchased hardware or software through a third party, your chances of knowing about changes are slim if you did not fill out the product registration card.

One thing to note about upgrades is that it might be predicated on a previous upgrade. Generic-III software may require that Generic-I and Generic-II upgrades be installed before using the latest version. Many years ago, the Bell System used a single-frequency (SF) unit for signaling and supervision on their toll circuits. One particular SF unit had about 20 changes to correct initial design problems. When they made an upgrade, a different problem developed. Each upgrade required checking to see if the previous change was made, because it required the other modifications to make it work.

Understand what the upgrade will do and what it is supposed to correct. Next, find out what the upgrade means in the way of taking the system out of service for the change, and if additional memory is required for software changes. After all the facts are in, you can decide whether or not to install the upgrade.

The biggest reason equipment and software is upgraded is because some end user has complained to the vendor. Instead of being unhappy about some feature or the lack of, you need to go on record and complain to the vendor.

One little letter outweighs 50 telephone calls because it gets the attention of the responsible people. Your letter should point out the change you think is desirable and why it would benefit the end user. Simple changes, like moving the "Caps Lock" key away from the "Shift" key, for example, would help prevent fat fingers from hitting the wrong key. This would reduce the number of times a person had to toggle strings of uppercase letters to lowercase letters. Just remember that improvements come from complaining about deficiencies. The squeaky wheel does get greased.

User groups

User groups are open forums for end users to make their concerns known to the vendor. Vendor-sponsored user groups have an unusual agenda in that the vendor really controls the event. They bring a group of the large users to a nice location, ply them with food and drink, and tell them what the vendor is ready to introduce. The vendor is not expecting to hear about complaints and is not equipped to do anything about them at that meeting.

The better user groups start from the end users having a common cause. They can set their own agenda for a meeting and be in control. Now the vendor expects to hear complaints and can bring the right personnel. As you read in chapter 10, meetings and vendor presentations must be controlled. In the case of the user group, someone from the user group must have full control and not let the vendor try to change the agenda. At the completion of the meeting, all open items should be assigned to the responsible party with an agreed upon interval for an answer.

Getting results

Getting people to respond to your needs goes back to the squeaky wheel. The best way to handle the telephone company is to start at your normal first level and work your way up the ladder. During that call, be sure to ask for the their supervisor's name and telephone number. If you do not get results in a reasonable time, your next call is to the supervisor. Repeat your request for the next supervisor's name and telephone number. It will be a rare instant that the first call does not get results, and even rarer to go up another rung on the ladder. A way to show displeasure about not getting results is to use the phrase "I am through talking to you—switch my call to your supervisor." This really gets things rolling, especially the higher up the ladder you go.

Dealing with vendors requires a different approach. Smaller-sized companies let you go right to the top of the company. Trying to telephone the president of the company is another story, however. Telephone calls are usually screened by the secretary or the telephone receptionist. Instead, compose a simplified letter and fax it to the president. Within minutes, your concern is in the hands of people who can make things happen. Trying to get a very large vendor to respond is a different story. A company like IBM has many levels of supervision that require going up the ladder to find the person who will make things happen. The other choice is to fax a letter to upper management and express your concern. A good place to locate names of people in upper management is in the company's financial statement. These people do not normally hear from customers. When they do, they respond quickly to get things corrected.

Planning for the future

Up to this point, you were concerned in getting a multi-vendor network installed and properly working. Now is the time to start gathering information for the next network. This information comes from two major sources. One is from internal needs and desires; the other from developments in the industry that change the way you will communicate in the future. As I said before, the **Engineering Times**, a weekly industry newspaper, is way ahead of other publications on new developments. Knowing what is being developed gives you an idea of what communications will offer in a few years.

Managing a network also requires that you know how your end user perceives the network. While you look for feedback from the end user after implementation, you need to stay in touch with them. After a year, interviews or another survey can be used. This lets you know how well the network serves the end user and also find out if there are unmet communications needs.

Summary

Minor adjustments to the network are usually low-cost items that can make the network work a little better. By analyzing voice and data traffic, the network can be optimized to load-balance or evenly distribute the transmission. Maintaining the network means finding ways to fine-tune the operation and reduce any downtime because of failures. Knowing how well your network performs requires analyzing traffic data and interviewing the end user.

Appendix A

Standard & technical suppliers

AMERICAN NATIONAL STANDARDS INSTITUTE (ANSI)
Attn: Customer Service
11 West 42nd Street
New York, NY 10036
(212) 642-4900 Fax: 212-302-1286

Documents available: EIA, IEEE, CCITT Blue Book, International Organization for Standards (ISO). International Electrotechnical Commission (IEC), and Underwriters Laboratories (UL)

AMERICAN TECHNICAL PUBLISHERS, LTD.
27/29 Knowl Place, Wilbury Way
Hertordshire, SG4 0SX England
ANSI documents available

AT&T
Customer Information Center (Technical Catalog PUB10000)
P.O. Box 19901
Indianapolis, IN 46209-1999
Phone: 1-800-432-6600

VISA, MasterCard, American Express; International money order drawn on a U.S. bank in U.S. dollars.

BELLCORE CUSTOMER SERVICE (CATALOG SR-NWT-000264)
60 New England Avenue - Room 1B252
Piscataway, NJ 08854-4196
1-800-521-CORE or (908) 699-5800 (for foreign calls)
FAX: 908-699-0936

VISA, American Express, or MasterCard; International money order drawn on U.S. bank in U.S. dollars.

ELECTRONIC INDUSTRIES ASSOCIATION (EIA)
TELECOMMUNICATIONS INDUSTRIES ASSOCIATION (TIA)
2001 Pennsylvania Ave. NW
Suite 1100 (EIA) Suite 800 (TIA)
Washington, DC 20006-1813
(202) 457-4900 (EIA) (202) 457-4939 (TIA)

GLOBAL ENGINEERING DOCUMENTS
2805 McGaw Avenue
P.O. Box 19539
Irvine, CA 92714
(714) 261-1455, 800-624-3974
Fax: 714-261-7892
See ANSI for alternative source

FEDERAL COMMUNICATIONS COMMISSION DOCUMENTS
U.S. Government Printing Office
Washington, D.C.
(202) 783-3238
Visa and MasterCard
(FCC Part 68 is contained in 47 CFR, Parts 40–69 ; FCC Part 15 is contained in
47 CFR, Parts 0–19)

IEEE
345 E. 47th Street
New York, NY 10017
(212) 705-7867
Documents available through ANSI

JAPANESE STANDARDS ASSOCIATION
1-24 Akasaka, Miato-Ku
Tokyo 107, Japan
ANSI documents available

STANDARDS COUNCIL OF CANADA
350 Sparks, Suite 1200
Ottawa K1P 6N7, Ontario
Canada

BELL REGIONAL COMPANIES' DOCUMENTS
AMERITECH SERVICES, INC.
Information Management
3040 West Salt Creek Lane 3-23
Arlington Heights, IL 60005
(708) 394-6406

BELL ATLANTIC NETWORK SERVICES, INC.
Document Coordinator—DIDS
13100 Columbia Pike, E-1
Silver Spring, MD 20904
(301) 236-2440

BELLSOUTH SERVICES
Documentation Operations
North W5A1
3535 Colonnade Parkway
Birmingham, AL 35243
(202) 977-8821

NYNEX
Telesector Resources Group, Inc.
Information Management
441 9th Avenue, 7th Floor
New York, NY 10001
(212) 502-6984

PACIFIC BELL
Information Exchange Administrator
2600 Camino Ramon, Room 1S450
San Ramon, CA 94583
(415) 823-0222

SOUTHWESTERN BELL TELEPHONE
Manager—Information Release
1010 Market, Room 810
St. Louis, MO 63101
(314) 235-8300

U.S. WEST
See Bellcore for all U.S. West publications.

Appendix B

Glossary of printed board definitions

additive process A method to deposit conductive material on top of an unclad base material.

art master The photographic representation of the circuit board's conductor patterns or foils. Used to define the areas that are etched from a clad-base material.

base The material that makes up the bulk of the circuit board. Also referred to as base insulation, base laminate, laminate, and substrate.

blister, foil Separation between the base material and the conductor material.

bridging Unintended connection between conducting paths. Usually seen as excessive solder flowing between conductors or wire leads that were not properly trimmed.

checking Fine, hairline cracks in the surface of the base laminate.

clinched connection Connection of a component to the circuit board that inserts the lead or wire through a hole in the base material, bends it towards the foil surface, and then solders the connection.

component side Side of the circuit board with the resistors, integrated circuits, etc.

conductor path Metallic foil bonded to the base material that provides the electrical connection between components.

contact finger The edge connector of particular conductor paths on the circuit board. It should have a microscopic plating of gold to ensure a good, electrical contact with the jack connector.

cosmetic defect Change in the appearance of an item, such as a color change.

cover coat Usually, a clear finish applied to the completed circuit board to prevent humidity and dust from creating a bridge between components and conductor paths.

delamination Separation between layers of the base substrate or between the conductor path and the base material.

drag soldering After the circuit board has all or most of its components mounted and clinched, the board's conductor side (i.e., the reverse of the component side) is dragged through a static bath of molten solder. Some components cannot stand the temperature of the molten solder and are added later.

dross Contaminants that form on the surface of the molten solder used in the solder machines.

etched foil Normal method to develop the complete conducting pattern on a circuit board. Artwork is photographed onto a blank base material that has its entire surface bonded with a metallic coating. The areas that were not shown to have a conducting path are then etched in acid.

flow soldering After the circuit board has all or most of its components mounted and clinched, the board's conductor side is brought in contact with a circulating flow of molten solder.

foil Metallic conductor path. It should be plated with a tinning material to promote good solderability. Its surface should be smooth and shiny. Pits and a dull appearance is a sign of poor manufacture. A pit is a small indentation in the conducting path.

jumper Strap of wire (not part of the etched conductor patterns) that spans between components or conductor paths.

measling White spots that are below the surface of the base material that indicate a separation of the fibers used in the laminate.

nonwetting Condition where the solder has not adhered to the conducting path.

plated-through hole Method to either connect conducting paths on either side of the circuit board or to ensure a good connection to nonclinched components. After the circuit board has the conducting paths defined, the board enters a second phase to have all the appropriate holes drilled. The holes then have a metal deposited on the surfaces of the hole to provide an electrical path.

solder mask Substance to prevent solder from adhering to certain areas of the conducting path during drag or flow soldering. Used when hand soldering heat-sensitive components after the mass soldering of other components.

twist Bend of the completed circuit board that appears between its opposite corners.

warp Bend of the completed circuit board that appears between its length or width. Twist or warp is the result of the expansion of the circuit board after the soldering operation. If the twist or warp is too great, it is difficult to insert and remove the circuit board from its mounting.

Appendix C

Quality evaluation checklist

I. Administration Policy

A. Management's commitment and quality organization: The vendor's quality control should have sufficient authority and freedom to perform appropriate quality related tasks.

Quality Item	Yes	No
1. Does the quality consciousness stem from the vendor's top management? Quality should start at the very top of an organization and not just from the quality control group.		
2. Has top management established policy which defines the quality-related responsibilities of the quality organization, engineering, manufacturing, purchasing organizations?		
3. Can the quality control group initiate corrective action and verify the resolution of the problem? They should have the freedom to identify, assess and report quality problems.		

Quality Item	Yes	No
4. Does the quality group have the final authority to determine whether manufacturing material will move on to its next operation?		
5. Does the quality process appear to be in constant use or is it only invoked when a quality problem arises?		
6. Do all areas of the manufacturing operation from the incoming inspection department through the shipping department have a thorough knowledge of their roles in the quality system?		

B. Documentation of the quality system is **critical.** The entire quality control system should be documented to cover all related activities. And once documented, the manuals should be readily available throughout the manufacturing process. Lack of quality control manuals or the only manuals located only in someone's office are a sign of ineffective control. The items below assume there is evidence of adequate and available manuals.

Quality Item	Yes	No
1. Does the quality manual(s) include the following: a. Description of responsibilities and procedures for control at all points. b. State the quality policy and objectives of the company.		
2. Are incoming material, in-process, and final product requirements for workmanship and engineering specifications well documented?		

Quality Item	Yes	No
3. Are quality levels documented for acceptable product and/or processes at each inspection station? Each inspection station should have a definition of the nature of the inspection, tolerance levels, gauges or test sets used, data recorded, sample sizes taken, and how to designate an inspected item.		
4. Quality manuals need review for possible updating Is there a method in place that periodically checks the documentation?		

C. A program should control how design changes are implemented in a smooth and timely way. It should also assure the design changes do not adversely affect the quality of the product.

Quality Item	Yes	No
1. Is there a method to assure the changes in design have all the appropriate quality and reliability requirements included?		
2. Does the quality organization review the design changes to assure the overall quality of the completed product will not change? Changes made for cost reduction require the most attention.		
3. Is there a formal method to update all testing and quality testing as a result of a design change?		

D. Control of incoming material should have a program to inspect purchased components or units to assure consistency of the finished product.

Quality Item	Yes	No
1. Do the specifications include the acceptable design and quality levels of all the parts and materials?		
2. If the purchased material relies on the manufacturer's quality information, has the vendor verified or observed a good quality history? The vendor can purchase high-quality components that have the assurance of the manufacturer that they performed the necessary inspection.		
3. Is there some method to make acceptance tests or inspect incoming material to assure the final product will perform properly.		
4. What happens when defective material is found? Detailed records of the defective number and frequency can show a need to find a different source. Is the rejected material placed in well marked containers to make sure they do not inadvertently get back into the manufacturing stream?		

II. Manufacturing Controls

Sufficient testing and inspection of the product during manufacture should exist to assure that the product conforms to the quality standards.

Quality Item	Yes	No
1. Each inspection point should have a quality standard for comparison. Are the results of the inspection recorded and analyzed?		

Quality Item	Yes	No
2. Whenever a new operator, new technique, etc. is used, do they make a critical examination of the first units in the process?		

3. A quality test is only as good as the accuracy of the test equipment used. Calibration of test equipment includes the following:
    a. A serial number and a tag or sticker with the next calibration date.
    b. Detailed records showing the calibration and maintenance of each test equipment.		

4. In-process and completed products should bear some identification showing the inspection status. Products that do not conform to the quality standards should be clearly marked and separated from good products.		
5. Individual circuit boards and major component parts should have a method or number that designates it sufficiently to enable identification when the product was manufactured. If the vendor changed the design because of poor reliability or operation deficiency, it is desirable to find the particular units and have them retrofitted.		
6. Final tests should simulate, as best possible, how you plan to use the product. The vendor should have written records of the final inspection.		

III. Collection and Analysis of Field Performance

Analysis of performance in the field is a useful way of determining the actual failure rate of the equipment. Units returned for repair should have the detailed recording of the defective parts. These records should also include the amount of time to repair and return the units to the field.

Quality Item	Yes	No
1. When products are returned for repair, there should be records identifying the reasons for failure and the frequency of product or component failure.		
2. When a particular product or component exhibits a failure rate, do they pass this information on to engineering or production to improve the product?		

IV. Corrective Action

As soon as a quality deficiency is noted, there should be a change in the quality control system and in the development, procurement of components, and production to reduce the recurrence of the quality problem.

Quality Item	Yes	No
1. The quality organization has the authority to initiate action to correct product deficiencies.		
2. The quality organization monitors the actions taken to verify they are adequate.		
3. Upper management is aware of open or delinquent cases or corrective action. Upon completion of the corrective action, a detailed report is circulated to all concerned parties.		

Quality Item	Yes	No
4. Are there recall procedures in place to swap out units in the field that exhibit a high failure rate?		

Appendix D

Risk analysis worksheet

Vendor: _____**Date:**_____

Product or Service:_____

Generic Description:_____

Reviewer:_____**Total Risk Points:**_____

A. Meeting the Absolute Needs

Missing Items	0	1	2	3
Risk Points	0	25	50	100

B. Quality of the Product or Service

Quality	Excellent	Good	Minor Problems	Major Problems
Risk Points	0	10	50	100

C. Meeting the Desired Needs

Missing Items	0	1	2	3
Risk Points	0	15	25	50

D. Uniqueness of the Product or Service

Uniqueness	Multi-Source	One-of-a-Kind	Beta Test
Risk Points	0	50	75

E . Extra Features

Missing Items	0	1	2	3
Risk Points	0	5	10	15

F. Safety Certification

Safety Certification	Indep. Lab Tested	Vender Tested	No Tests Made
Risk Points	0	25	75

G. Availability of the Product

Availability	Stock Item	Special Order	Prototype Test
Risk Points	0	20	50

H. Mean Time to Failure

Rank Order	1st	2nd	3rd	4th	5th
Risk Points	0	10	20	40	80

Subtotal This Page_____

I. Mean Time to Repair

Rank Order	1st	2nd	3rd	4th	5th
Risk Points	0	10	20	40	80

J. In-house Maintenance Availability

On Site Maintenance	< 2 Hours	< 4 Hours	< 8 Hours	< 24 Hours	> 24 Hours
Risk Points	0	10	20	40	80

K . Repair Availability

Factory Repair	< 3 Days	< 1 Week	< 2 Weeks	> 2 Weeks
Risk Points	0	10	20	30

L. Technical Assistance or Support

Rank Order	1st	2nd	3rd	4th	5th
Risk Points	0	10	20	40	80

M. Training and Operating Manuals

Rank Order	1st	2nd	3rd	4th	5th
Risk Points	0	10	20	40	80

Subtotal This Page_____

N. Power and Space Considerations

Changes Needed	Minimal	Some	Major
Risk Points	0	10	25

O. Environmental Considerations

Changes Needed	Minimal	Some	Major
Risk Points	0	10	25

P. Upgrade of Operating Hardware and Software

Changes Needed	Minimal	Some	Major
Risk Points	0	10	25

Subtotal This Page_____

Appendix E

FCC-Part 68 Registration

The following excerpts are from the Code of Federal Regulations Title 47, Part 68, Subpart D—Conditions for Registration. These excerpts cover registration of communications equipment connected to the public telephone network. There are no restrictions on reproduction of material appearing in the Code of Federal Regulations. All other sections of this book are covered by the copyright of McGraw-Hill, Inc.

Section 68.302 Environment simulation

Registered terminal equipment and registered protective circuitry shall comply with all the criteria contained in the rules and regulations in this subpart, both prior to and after the application of each mechanical and electrical stresses specified in the section, not withstanding that certain of these stresses may result in partial or total destruction of equipment.

(a) Vibration. The equipment shall be subjected to vibration while in the condition that it is normally shipped or transported. That is, during the following vibration test the equipment shall be vibrated while packaged if shipped packaged, or the equipment shall be vibrated while unpackaged if shipped unpackaged. The following sinusoidal vibration should be applied once in each three orthogonal directions, however, for large equipments, the unit should rest on the base or side on which it is normally shipped: One sweep at a level of 0.5g peak from 5 to 100 Hz, and one sweep at a level of 1.5g peak from 100 to 500 Hz. The 5 to 100 sweep should be conducted at a sweep rate of 0.1 octave/min. (approximately 45 minutes) and the 100 to 500 Hz sweep at a rate of 0.25 octave/min. (approximately 10 minutes).

(b) Temperature and humidity. Cycling at any convenient rate through the following temperature and humidity conditions three times: 30 minutes at 150° F and 15 percent humidity, followed by 30 minutes at 90° F and 90 percent relative humidity, followed by 30 minutes at -40° F and any convenient humidity.

(c) Shock.

(1) Registered Terminal Equipment and Registered Protective Circuitry Equipment Unpackaged:

Hand-Held Items Normally Used at Head Height:
18 random drops from a height of 60 inches onto concrete covered with 1/8 inch asphalt tile or similar surface.

Normally Customer Carried Equipment:
6 random drops from a height of 30 inches onto concrete covered with 1/8 inch asphalt tile or similar surface.

Equipment Not Normally Carried by Customers:
These tests are made onto concrete covered with ⅛-inch asphalt tile or similar surface.

0—20 lbs: One 6-inch face drop on each normal or designated rest face, one 3-inch drop on all other faces, and one 3-inch drop on each corner.

0—50 lbs: One 4-inch face drop on each normal or designated rest face, one 2-inch drop on all other faces, and one 2-inch drop on each corner.

50—100 lbs: One 2-inch face drop on each normal or designated rest face. One edgewise drop and one cornerwise drop from a height of 2 inches on each edge and corner adjacent to the rest face.

100—1,000 lbs: One 1-inch face drop on each normal or designated rest face. One edgewise drop and one cornerwise drop from a height of 1 inch on each edge and corner adjacent to the rest face.

Over 1,000 lbs: One 1-inch face drop on each normal or designated rest face. One edgewise drop and one cornerwise drop from a height of 1 inches on each edge adjacent to the rest face.

(2) The drop tests specified in the mechanical shock conditioning stresses shall be performed as follows:

FACE DROP—The unit should be dropped such that the face to be struck is approximately parallel to the impact surface.

CORNER DROP—The unit should be dropped such that upon impact a line from the struck corner to the center of gravity of the packaged equipment is approximately perpendicular to the impact surface.

EDGEWISE DROP—The unit should be positioned on a flat surface. One edge of the rest face should be supported with a block so that the rest face makes an angle of 20° with the horizontal. The opposite edge should be lifted the designated height above the test surface and dropped.

CORNERWISE DROP—The unit should be positioned on a flat surface. One corner of the test face should be supported with a block so that the rest face makes an angle of 20° with the horizontal. The opposite corner should be lifted the designated height above the test surface and dropped.

RANDOM DROP—The unit should be positioned prior to release to ensure as nearly as possible that for every six drops there is one impact on each of the six major surfaces and that the surface struck is approximately parallel to the impact surface.

(d) Metallic voltage surge. Two 800-volt peak surges of a metallic voltage (one of each polarity) having a 10-microsecond maximum rise time to crest and a 560(sic)-microsecond minimum decay time to half crest applied between (1) tip and ring of a 2-wire connection; (2) between tip and ring , and tip 1 and ring 1 of a 4-wire connection; (3) between tip and tip 1 (with tip and ring ties together and tip 1 and ring 1 tied together) of a 4-wire connection which uses simplexed pairs for signaling; and (4) any other pair connections on the which lightning surges may occur (with one of the connections of the pair under test grounded) with the equipment in the following states.

(i) Any operational state which can affect compliance with the requirements of Part 68;

(ii) Any state in which the equipment might be connected to the telephone network and from which it is capable of transferring to an operational state by an automatic or manual action required for proper use of the equipment and provided that any such state can affect compliance with the requirements of Part 68; and

(iii) Any state in which the equipment might be connected to the telephone network and from which it is capable of transferring to an operational state by an automatic or manual action under all reasonably foreseeable possibilities of disconnection of connections of such equipment with primary commercial power sources (including possible loss of equipment grounding through disconnection of a third-wire ground connection contained in a primary power source plug).

All other equipment leads (telephone connections, auxiliary leads, and terminals for connection to nonregistered equipment) not being surged or connected to those being surged should be terminated in a manner which is no less severe than that which occurs in normal use and affect compliance with Subpart D. Also, equipment states which cannot be achieved by normal means of power shall be achieved artificially by appropriate means, if necessary to comply with the above requirements. The peak current drawn from the surge generator must be limited to less than 100 amperes by the capabilities for the simplexed arrangement in case (3), which must not be limited to less than 200 amperes.

(e) Longitudinal voltage surge. With registered terminal equipment in each of the following states: first, any operational state which can affect compliance with the requirements of Part 68, second any state which the equipment might be connected to the telephone network and from which it is capable of transferring to an operational state by an automatic or manual action required for proper use of the equipment and provided that any such state can affect compliance with the requirements of Part 68 and third, any state in which the equipment might be connected to the telephone network and from which it is capable of transferring to an operational state by an automatic or manual action under all reasonably foreseeable possibilities of disconnection of connections of such equipment with primary commercial power sources (including possible loss of equipment grounding through disconnection of a third-wire ground connection contained in a primary power source plug):

(1) Two 1500 volt peak surges (one of each polarity) having a 10-microsecond maximum rise time to crest and a 160-microsecond minimum decay time to half crest applied separately between each of the following leads individually and (i) and (ii) below, and where available, also between all of the following leads tied together and (i) and (ii) below: Tip, ring, tip 1, ring 1, M (only for registered terminal equipment located on the "A" side of a Type I E&M interface).

(i) Earth ground; and

(ii) All leads on the registered equipment intended for connection to nonregistered equipment when these leads are connected together.

The peak current drawn from the surge generator must not be limited to less than 200 amperes by the capabilities of the surge generator.

(2) Two 1500 volt peak surges (one of each polarity) having a 10-microsecond maximum rise time to crest and a 160-microsecond minimum decay time to half crest applied between pairs of connections other than tip and ring on

which lightning surges may occur, connected together, and individually to (i) and (ii) below:

(i) Earth ground; and

(ii) All leads on the registered equipment intended for connection to nonregistered equipment when these leads are connected together.

The peak current drawn from the surge generator must not be limited to less than 200 amperes by the capabilities of the surge generator.

(3) Three 2500 volt peak surges (three of each polarity) having a 2-microsecond maximum rise time to crest and a 10-microsecond minimum decay time to half crest applied between phase and neutral terminals of the ac power line. The peak current drawn from the surge generator must not be limited to less than 1000 amperes by the capabilities of the surge generator. All other equipment leads (telephone connections, auxiliary leads, and terminals for connection to nonregistered equipment) not being surged or connected to those being surged should be terminated in a manner which is no less severe than that which occur in normal use and affect compliance with Subpart D. Also, equipment states which cannot be achieved by normal means of power shall be achieved artificially by appropriate means, if necessary to comply with the above requirements.

(f) Failure modes resulting from the application of metallic and longitudinal surges. Registered terminal equipment and registered protective circuitry are permitted to reach a failure-mode state in violation of longitudinal balance requirements of (Sect.) 68.310, and for terminal equipment connected to Local Area Data Channels a failure-mode state in violation of the longitudinal signal power requirements of (Sect.) 68.308, after application of the electrical surges specified in paragraphs (d) and (e) herein, provided that: (1) Such failure results from an intentional, designed failure mode which has the effect of connecting telephone or auxiliary connections with earth ground; and (2) if such a failure-mode state is reached, the equipment is designed in such a manner that it would become substantially and noticeably unusable by the user, or an indication is given to the user (e.g., an alarm), in order that such equipment can be immediately disconnected or repaired.
NOTE: The objective of this subsection is to allow for safety circuitry which diverts lightning-like transients to earth ground, but which may continue to maintain the earth ground connections after the transients have ceased. Such a failure-mode has the potential for causing interference resulting from the longitudinal imbalance, and therefore designs must be adopted which will cause the equipment either to be disconnected or repaired rapidly after such a state is reached, should it occur in service. This section does not apply to tie trunk interface leads.

Section 68.304 Leakage Current Limitations

Registered terminal equipment and registered protective circuitry shall assure that, if a voltage source is connected to the combinations listed in the table below, of(sic) the following points on such equipment:

(a) All telephone connections,

(b) All power connections,

(c) All possible combinations of exposed conductive surfaces on the exterior of such equipment or circuitry excluding terminals for connection to other terminal equipment,

(d) All terminals for connection to nonregistered equipment,

(e) Points having a conducting path to secondaries of any power supply,

(f) All auxiliary lead terminals, and

(g) All E&M lead terminals,

(h) All PR, PC, CY1 and CY2 leads,

and is gradually increased, from zero to the values listed in TABLE E-1, over a thirty second time period, then applied continuously for one minute, the current in the mesh formed by the voltage source and these points shall not exceed 10 milliamperes peak at any time during this 90 second time interval.

Table E-1. Voltage for
various electrical connections

Voltage sources connected between	Value*
(a) and (c) note 5	1000
(a) and (d) note 5	1000
(a) and (f) note 5	1000
(a) and (g) note 5	1000
(a) and (h) note 5	1000
(b) and (c)	1500
(b) and (d)	1500
(b) and (e)	1500
(c) and (f)	1000
(c) and (g)	1000
(d) and (f)	1000
(d) and (g)	1000
(f) and (h)	1000

*Values to which test voltage is gradually increased, rms, 60 Hertz.

NOTES:

(1) If, in any operational state, one of the telephone connections, auxiliary leads or E&M leads has an intentional conducting path to earth ground, that

lead may be excluded from the leakage current test in the operational state. Connections excluded for this reason must comply with the requirements of (Sect.) 68.306(c) in addition to other applicable rules. However, leakage current tests between telephone connections and auxiliary leads, and between telephone connections and E&M leads are required unless both points have intentional conducting paths to earth ground.

(2) Terminal port connections to registered protective circuitry shall be treated as point (d) leads for the purposes of leakage limitation.

(3) Leakage current limitations shall be met between each point (d) and point (f) leads and all pairs of tip and ring telephone connections. (Testing all pairs may be done by a sequence of appropriate combinations of pairs.)

(4) Equipment states which cannot be achieved by normal means of power shall be achieved artificially by appropriate means, if necessary to comply with this section.

(5) For multi-unit equipment interconnected by cables, which is evaluated and registered as an in connected combination or assembly, the specified 10 milliamperes peak maximum leakage current limitation, other than between power connection points, may be increased as described here to accommodate cable capacitance. The leakage current limitation may be increased to (10N+0.04L) milliamperes peak where L is the length of the interconnecting cable in the leakage path in feet and N is the number of equipment units which the combination or assembly will place in parallel across a telephone connection. However, all combinations of electrical connections requiring the increased limitation and involving point (c) (exposed conductive surfaces) surfaces must comply with the requirements of Sect. 68.306(c) in addition to applicable rules.

(6) Leakage current limitations shall be met between each of the point (h) leads and all pairs of tip and ring telephone connections.

Section 68.306 Hazardous voltage limitations

(a) **General.** Under no condition of failure of registered terminal equipment or registered protective circuitry, or of equipment connect thereto, which can be conceived to occur in the handling, operation or repair of such equipment or circuitry, shall the open circuit voltage exceed 70 volts peak for more than one second, except for voltages for network control signaling and supervision, which, in any case, should be consistent with standards employed by the telephone companies.

(1) Registered terminal equipment shall assure that at the MR channel interface, no continuous ac or dc voltage appear across the tip (MR) and ring (MR) leads, from the tip (MR) lead to PBX ground, or from the ring (MR) lead to PBX ground.

(2) Registered terminal equipment shall assure that during normal operation, at an AOID data channel interface, (i) no significant ac voltage to ground other than data transmission appears on the tip (AI) and ring (AI) leads; (ii) no open

circuit dc voltage to ground appears on the tip (AI) and ring (AI) leads other than the range from 0 to –56.5 volts.

(3) Registered terminal equipment shall assure that at either the MR channel interface or an AOID data channel interface, voltage transients appearing on either the tip (AI or MR) or ring (AI or MR) to ground as a result of inductive components in the registered terminal equipment shall not be capable of delivering more than 2 joules to a 500 ohm resistive termination.

(4) Type I E&M leads. Conditions for "A" side of interface with conditions for the "B" side in parentheses. Registered terminal equipment shall assure that (i) the dc current in the E lead does not exceed 100 milliamperes, (ii) no significant ac or dc voltage to ground appear on the E&M leads*, (iii) no significant ac or dc voltage to ground appear on the (E) & (M) leads*, (iv) the open circuit dc voltage to ground on the E&M leads does not exceed 56.5 volts and is not positive. M lead protection shall be to assure that voltages to ground do not exceed 80 volts. For relay contact implementation a power dissipation capability of 0.5 watt shall be provided in the shunt path. If the registered terminal equipment contains an inductive component in the E lead it must assure the transient voltage across the contact as a result of a relay contact opening, does not exceed the following voltage and duration limitations: (i) 300 volts peak, (ii) a rate of change of one volt per microsecond, and (iii) an 80 volt level for more than 10 milliseconds.

(5) Type II E&M leads. Conditions for "A" side of interface with conditions for the "B" side in parentheses. Registered terminal equipment shall assure that (i) the dc current in the E and (SB) leads does not exceed 100 milliamperes and no significant ac or dc voltage to ground appear on the E and (SB) leads*, (ii) no significant ac or dc voltage to ground appear on the M, SG, SB (E), SG, and (M) leads from sources in the registered terminal equipment*, and (iii) the open circuit dc voltage to ground on the E and (SB) leads does not exceed 56.5 volts and is not positive. If the registered terminal equipment contains an inductive component in the E or (M) lead, it must assure the transient voltage across the contact as a result of a relay contact opening, does not exceed the following voltage and duration limitations; (i) 300 volts peak, (ii) a rate of change of one volt per microsecond, and (iii) an 80 volt level for more than 10 milliseconds.

* The ac component should not exceed 5 volts peak or the dc component 5 volts, where not otherwise controlled by Sect. 68.308

(6) Off-premise station voltages.
    (i) Talking battery or voltages applied by the PBX (or similar sys-tems) to OPS interface leads for supervisory purposes must be negative with

respect to ground, shall not exceed 56.5 Vdc for Classes A, B, and C, and shall not have a significant ac component. *

(ii) Ringing signals applied by the PBX (or similar system) to OPS interface leads shall be applied for the purpose of station alerting only, and shall comply to the requirements in paragraph (d) of this section. Ringing voltages shall be applied between the ring conductor and ground.

(7) For Local Area Data Channel interfaces, during normal operating modes indicating terminal equipment initiated maintenance signals, registered terminal equipment shall assure, except during the application of ringing (limitations specified in paragraph (d) of this section), with respect to telephone connections (tip, ring, tip 1, ring 1) that:

(i) Under normal operating conditions, the rms current per conductor between short-circuited conductors, including dc and ac components, does not exceed 350 milliamperes. For other than normal operating conditions, the rms current between any conductor and ground or between short-circuited conductors, including dc and ac components, does not exceed 350 milliamperes for no more than 1.5 minutes.

(ii) The dc voltage between any conductor and ground does not exceed 80 volts. Under normal operating conditions it shall not be positive with respect to ground (though positive voltages up to 80 volts may be allowed during brief maintenance states);

(iii) Ac voltages are less than 42.4 volts peak between any conductor and ground. (Terminal equipment shall comply while other interface leads are both (A) unterminated and (B) individually terminated to ground); and,

(iv) Combined ac and dc voltages between any conductor and ground are less than 42.4 volts peak when the absolute value of the dc component is less than 21.2 volts, and less than (28.8 + 64 × Vdc) when the absolute value of the dc component is between 21.2 and 80 volts.

(8) During normal operation, registered terminal equipment for connection to ringdown voiceband private line interfaces or voiceband metallic channel interfaces shall assure that:

(i) Ringing voltage is used for alerting only, does not exceed the voltage and current limits specified in paragraph (d), and is: (A) applied to the ring conductor with the tip conductor grounded for 2-wire interfaces, or (B) simplexed on the tip and ring conductors grounded simplexed on the tip (1) and ring (1) conductors for 4-wire interfaces.

(ii)   Except during the signaling mode or for monitoring voltage, there is no significant positive dc voltage with respect to ground (not over +5 volts): (A) for 2-wire ports between the tip lead and ground and the ring lead and ground, and (B) for 4-wire ports between the tip lead and ground and the ring lead and ground, the tip 1 lead and ground, and the ring 1 lead and ground

(iii)   The dc current per lead, under short circuit conditions shall not exceed 140 milliamperes.

(b)   Connection of nonregistered equipment to registered terminal equipment or registered protective circuitry.

(1) **General.** Leads to, or any elements having a conducting path to telephone connections, auxiliary leads or E&M lead shall:

(i)   Be reasonably physically separated and restrained from and be neither routed in the same cable as nor use the same connector as leads or metallic paths connecting power connections;

(ii)   Be reasonably physically separated and restrained from and be neither routed in the same cable as nor use adjacent pins on the same connector as metallic paths to leads to nonregistered equipment, when specification details provided to the Commission pursuant to Sect. 68.200(g) do not show that interface voltages are less than non-hazardous voltage source limits in Sect. 68.306(b)(4).

(2)   **Connections to registered terminal equipment.** The voltage measurable between auxiliary leads, auxiliary leads to ground, E&M leads and ground, tip and ring, tip to ground, ring to ground, tip 1 to ground, and ring 1 to ground shall not exceed 70 volts peak for more than 1 second, with tip to ring, tip 1 to ring 1, and auxiliary lead each terminated with 1500 ohms center-tapped through 1000 ohms to ground and each E&M lead terminated in 1500 ohms to ground, if 120 volts rms 60 Hz, ac is applied between all connections to other equipment tied together (except connections to non-hazardous voltage sources) and ground. The source shall not be limited to less than 20 amperes continuously, not to less than 50 amperes for 1 minute, and shall not be interrupted by an overcurrent device permitting less total energy flow than a 20 ampere time delay fuse or breaker.

(3)   **Connections to registered protective circuitry.** The voltage measurable between auxiliary leads, auxiliary leads to ground, E&M leads and ground, tip and ring, tip to ground, ring to ground, tip 1 to ground, and ring 1 to ground shall not exceed 70 volts peak for more than 1 second, with tip to ring, tip 1 to ring 1, and auxiliary lead each terminated with 1500 ohms center-

tapped through 1000 ohms to ground and each E&M lead terminated in 1500 ohms to ground, if 120 volts rms 60 Hz, ac is applied:

(i)   Between all protective circuitry connections other than telephone connections (and connection to non-hazardous voltage sources), tied together and ground; and

(ii)   Across all protective circuitry connections, other than telephone connections (and connection to non-hazardous voltage sources) which have a transmission path to the telephone connections, with alternative leads grounded; under all reasonable applications of earth ground to the protective circuitry. The source shall not be limited to less than 20 amperes continuously, not to less than 50 amperes for 1 minute, and shall not be interrupted by an overcurrent device permitting less total energy flow than a 20 ampere time delay fuse or breaker.

(4)   **Non-hazardous voltage source.** A voltage source is considered a non-hazardous voltage source if it conforms with the requirements of Sects. 68.302, 68.304, and 68.306(b)(1), with all connections to the source other than primary power connections treated as "telephone connections," and if such source supplies voltages no greater than the following under all modes of operation and of failure:

(i)   Ac voltages less than 42.4 volts peak;

(ii)   Dc voltages less than 80 volts; and

(iii)   Combined ac and dc voltages between any conductor and ground are less than 42.4 volts peak when the absolute value of the dc component is less than 21.2 volts, and less than $(28.8 + 64 \times Vdc)$ when the absolute value of the dc component is between 21.2 and 80 volts.

(c)   **Hazards from exposed surfaces** (to be applied for intentional conductive paths to ground as required by Sect. 68.304). The voltage measurable between auxiliary leads, auxiliary leads to ground, E&M leads and ground, tip and ring, tip and ground, ring and ground, tip 1 and ring 1, tip 1 to ground, ring 1 to ground, shall not exceed 70 volts peak for more than 1 second, with tip to ring, tip 1 to ring 1, and auxiliary lead each terminated with 1500 ohms center-tapped through 1000 ohms to ground and each E&M lead terminated in 1500 ohms to ground, if 120 volts rms 60 Hz, ac is applied between conductive exposed surfaces and ground. The source shall not be limited to less than 20 amperes continuously, not to less than 50 amperes for 1 minute, and shall not be interrupted by an overcurrent device permitting less total energy flow than a 20 ampere time delay fuse or breaker.

(d) Ringing Sources. Ringing sources, except for class A OPS interfaces, shall meet all of the following restrictions:

(1) The ringing signal shall use only frequencies whose fundamental component is equal to or below 70 Hz. (33 Hz may be the highest frequency necessary for OPS service.

(2) The ringing voltage shall be less than 300 V peak-to-peak and less than 200 V peak-to-ground across a resistive termination of at least 1 megohm.

(3) The ringing voltage shall be interrupted to create quiet intervals of at least one second (continuous) duration each separated by no more than 5 seconds. During the quiet intervals, the voltage to ground shall not exceed the voltage limits given in paragraph (a)(6)(i) of this section.

(4) As specified below, ringing sources shall be required to (a) include a series current-sensitive tripping device in the ring lead which will trip ringing as specified in Figure 68.306(d), and/or (b) provide a voltage to ground (monitoring voltage) on the tip to ring conductor with a magnitude of at least 19 volts peak (but may not exceed the voltage limits given in paragraph (a)(6)(i) of this section) whenever the ringing voltage is not present (idle state). Tripping devices and/or monitoring voltages are required dependent upon the current flow through a specified resistance connection between the ringing source (R(OPS)) and ground as follows:

(i) If the current through a 500 ohms (and greater) resistor does not exceed 100 mA peak-to-peak, neither a tripping device nor a monitoring voltage are required, or

(ii) If the current through a 1500 ohms (and greater) resistor exceeds 1000 mA peak-to-peak, the ringing source shall include a tripping device. If the tripping device meets the operating characteristics as specified in Figure 68.306(d) with R = 500 ohms (and greater), then no monitoring voltage is required. If, however, the tripping device only meets the given operating characteristics with R = 1500 ohms (and greater), then the ringing source must also include a monitoring voltage as described above, or

(iii) If the current through a 1500 ohms (and greater) resistor exceeds 1000 mA peak-to-peak, but does not exceed this value of current with a 1500 ohms (and greater) termination, the ringing source shall include either a tripping device which meets the operating characteristics as specified in Figure 68.306(d) with R = 500 ohms (and greater), or a monitoring voltage.

Section 68.308 Signal power limitations

(a) General. Limits on signal power shall be met at the interface for all 2-wire network ports and, where applicable to offered services, both transmit and receive pairs of all 4-wire network ports. Signal power measurements shall be made using terminations as specified in each of the following limitations. The transmit and receive pairs of 4-wire network ports shall be measured with the pair not under test connected to a termination equivalent to that specified for the pair under test. Through gain limitations apply only in the direction of transmission toward the network.

(b) Voice band metallic signal power — (1) Limitations at the interface on internal signal sources not intended for network control signaling.

(i) For registered terminal equipment or registered protective circuitry which is registered to interfaces associated with services contained in Section 68.2(a)(1)(2), and (7), other than data equipment or data protective circuitry which is registered in accordance with Section 68.308(b)(4), the maximum power of other than live voice signals delivered to a loop simulator circuit shall not exceed −9 dB with respect to one milliwatt, when averaged over any 3-second interval. No manufacturing tolerance is allowed which would permit this power to be exceeded by any unit of equipment.

(ii) For tie trunk type interfaces, the maximum power of other than live voice signals delivered to a 600 ohm termination shall not exceed the maximum power with respect to one milliwatt, when averaged over any 3-second interval, as shown in TABLE E-2.

Table E-2. One milliwatt maximum power for a three-second interval.

Two-wire	Four-wire lossless	Four-wire CTS[b]
−15 dB[a]	−15 dB[a]	−19 dB, nom.

NOTES:
(a) The maximum signal power may be exceeded by as much as 1.0 dB by a single unit of equipment or circuitry, provided that the power averaged over all units of production, complies with the specified limitations.
(b) The 4-wire CTS shall meet the requirements for Tie Trunk Transmission Interfaces as defined in Section 68.3.

(iii) For OPS lines, the maximum power of other than live voice signals delivered to an OPS line simulator circuit shall not exceed –13 dB with respect to one milliwatt, when averaged over a 3-second interval.

(iv) For AOID channels, the maximum power of other than live voice signals delivered to an AOID data channel simulator circuit in each of the following states shall not exceed –4 dB with respect to one milliwatt, when averaged over any 3-second time interval (TABLE E-3).

Table E-3. Maximum
AOID channel power.

Simulator circuit operating state	Tip and ring[1]
1	–42.5 – 56.5
2	0
3	0

(1) Remote terminal equipment open circuit DC volts to ground on AOID tip and ring.

The maximum signal power may exceed –4 dB with respect to one milliwatt by as much as 1.0 dB provided that the power averaged over all units of the equipment complies with the specified maximum.

NOTE: The maximum signal power may be exceeded by as much as 1.0 dB by a single unit of equipment or circuitry, provided that the power averaged over all units of production, complies with the specified limitations.

(v) For registered test equipment or registered test circuitry the maximum signal power delivered to a loop simulator circuit shall not exceed 0 dBm when averaged over any 3-second interval. No manufacturing tolerance is allowed which would permit this power to be exceeded by any unit of equipment.

(vi) For voiceband private lines using inband signaling in the band 2600 ±150 Hz, the maximum power delivered to a 600-ohm termination shall not exceed –8 dBm during the signaling mode. The maximum power delivered to a 600 ohm termination in the on-hook steady state supervisory condition shall not exceed –20 dBm. The maximum power of the other than live voice signals during the non-signaling mode and for other inband systems shall not exceed –13 dBm when averaged over any 3-second interval. The maximum signal power may be exceeded by as much as 1.0 dB by a single unit of equipment or circuitry, provided that the power averaged over all units of production, complies with the specified limitations.

(2) Limitations on internal signal sources primarily intended for network control signaling, contained in voice and data equipment.

(i) For all operating registered terminal equipment or registered protective circuitry, the maximum signal power delivered to a loop simula-tor circuit shall not exceed one milliwatt when averaged over any 3-second interval.

(ii) For tie trunk type applications, the maximum power delivered to a 600 ohm termination for registered terminal equipment and registered protective circuitry under all operating conditions shall not exceed the maximum power with respect to one milliwatt, when averaged over any 3-second interval (TABLE E-4).

Table E-4. Maximum tie-trunk power

Two-wire	Four-wire lossless	Four-wire CTS
–4 dB	–4 dB	–8 dB, nom.

(3) Registered one port and multi-port terminal equipment and protective circuitry with provision for through transmission from other terminal equipment, excluding data equipment and data protective circuitry which are registered in accordance with Section 68.308(b)(4).

(i) Where through-transmission equipment provides a dc electrical signal to equipment connected therewith (e.g., for powering of electro-acoustic transducers), dc conditions shall be provided which fall within the range of conditions provided by a loop simulator circuit unless the combination of the through-transmission equipment and equipment connected therewith is registered as a combination which conforms to Section 68.308(b) (1) and (2).

(ii) Through-transmission equipment to which remotely connected data terminal equipment may be connected shall not be equipped with or connected to either a Universal or Programmed Data Jack used in data configurations. (See Sections 68.308(b) (4) and 68.502(e)).

(4) Limitations on registered data terminal equipment and registered one-port protective circuitry with provision for through-transmission

from data equipment. When such equipment or circuitry is used for transmission of data signals to the telephone network, it shall assure in all operating conditions, other than network control signaling (see Section 68.308(b)(2) of this section), that one of the following limitations is met, depending upon the means of connection of the equipment or circuitry to the telephone network. The transmitted signal power, averaged over any 3-second time interval, delivered to a loop simulator circuit, shall not exceed:

(i) A maximum level adjustable to no greater than -4 dB with respect to one milliwatt, for connection to a Universal Data Jack used in the "fixed loss loop" configurations of Section 68.502(e).

(ii) A maximum level determined by means of connections in the Programmed Data Jack or Universal Data Jack, used in the "programmed" configurations of Section 68.502(e), which level can be programmed in 1 dB steps from −12 dB to 0 dB with respect to one milliwatt by means of programming connections made within the jack.

(iii) A nonadjustable level no greater than -9 dB with respect to one milliwatt for connection by means other than those which implement the limitations of paragraphs (b)(4)(i) and (ii) of this section. Equipment or circuitry designed in accordance with this −9 dBm limitation shall be treated as non-live voice equipment within these rules.

The maximum signal power specified in (paragraphs (b)(4)(i) and (ii) of this section may be exceeded by as much as 1.0 dB by a single unit of equipment or circuitry, provided that the power is averaged over all units of production. The maximum signal power specified in paragraphs (b)(4)(iii) of this section may not be exceeded any units of production.

(5) **Registered one port and multi-port terminal equipment and protective circuitry with provision for through-transmission from ports to other equipment which is separately registered for the public switched network, or ports to other network interfaces.**

(i) Registered terminal equipment and protective circuitry shall have no adjustments that will allow net amplification to occur in either direction of transmission in the through-transmission path within the frequency range of 200 to 4000 Hertz that will exceed that shown in TABLE E-5.
NOTES:
(A) The source impedance for all measurements shall be 600 ohms. All ports shall be terminated in appropriate loop or private line channel simulator circuits or 600 ohm terminations. The numerical "avg." and "max." requirements mean that the net gain for each type of connection through such equipment or circuitry shall be designed not to exceed the average gain for

Table E-3. Maximum allowable amplification between ports (A) (D) (E) (F).

To → From ↓ (F)	2-Wire (C)	4-Wire lossless (C)	4-Wire CTS (C)	Subrate 1.5 Mbps satell. (C)	Subrate 1.5 Mbps tandem (C)	OPS ports (2-wire) (B)	PSN ports (2-wire)	NCC digital PBX-CO
2-wire (C)	0 dB avg. 1.5 dB max.	0 dB avg. 1.5 dB max.	−4 dB nom.	0 dB avg. 1.5 dB max.	3 dB avg. 4.5 dB max.	−2 dB avg. −0.5 dB max.	—	—
4 wire lossless (C)	0 dB avg. 1.5 dB max.	0 dB avg. 1.5 dB max.	−4 dB nom.	0 dB avg. 1.5 dB max.	3 dB avg. 4.5 dB max.	−2 dB avg. −0.5 dB max.	—	—
4-wire CTS (C)	−4 dB nom.	−4 dB nom.	−8 dB nom.	−4 dB nom.	−1 dB nom.	−6 dB nom.	—	—
Subrate 1.5 Mbps satellite 4-wire (C)	0 dB avg. 1.5 dB max.	0 dB avg. 1.5 dB max.	−4 dB nom.	0 dB avg. 1.5 dB max.	0 dB avg. 1.5 dB max.	0 dB avg. 1.5 max	—	—
Subrate 1.5 Mbps tandem 4-wire (C)	−3 dB avg. −1.5 dB max.	−3 dB avg. −1.5 dB max.	−7 dB nom.	0 dB avg. 1.5 dB max.	0 dB avg. 1.5 dB max.	0 dB avg. 1.5 dB max.	—	—
RTE (B)	−2 dB avg. −0.5 dB max.	−2 dB avg. −0.5 dB max.	−6 dB nom.	−3 dB avg. −1.5 dB max.	−3 dB avg. −1.5 dB max.	0 dB avg. 1.5 dB max.	0 dB avg. 1.5 dB max.	−3 dB avg. −1.5 dB max.
OPS 2-wire (B)	−2 dB avg. −0.5 dB max.	−2 dB avg. −0.5 dB max.	−6 dB nom.	0 dB avg. 1.5 dB max.	0 dB avg. 1.5 dB max.	0 dB avg. 1.5 dB max.	0 dB avg. 1.5 dB max.	0 dB avg. 1.5 dB max.
PSN 2-wire	—	—	—	—	—	0 dB avg. 1.5 dB max.	—	—
HCC digital PBX-CO 4-wire	—	—	—	—	—	0 dB avg. 1.5 dB max.	—	—

(C)—Tie-trunk-type ports.

such paths in all units; however, the gain for any path of any single unit may exceed the average by as much as the maximum provided that the net gain, averaged over such paths in all units of production, is no greater than the average. The term "nom." allows for variations encountered in conventional terminating set losses as defined in Section 68.3.

(B) These ports are for 2-wire on-premises station ports to separately registered terminal equipment.

(C) The 4-wire CTS shall meet the requirements for Tie Trunk Transmission Interfaces as defined in Section 68.3.

(D) These through gain limitations are applicable to multiport systems where channels are not derived by time or frequency compression methods. Terminal equipment employing such compression techniques shall assure that equivalent compensation for through gain parameters is demonstrated in the registration application.

(E) Registered terminal equipment and registered protective circuitry might have net amplification exceeding the limitations of this subsection provided that, for each network interface type to be connected, the absolute signal power levels specified on this section are not exceeded.

(F) The indicated gain is in the direction which results when moving from the horizontal entry toward the vertical entry.

(G) Registered terminal equipment or protective circuitry with the capability for through-transmission from voiceband private line channels or voiceband metallic channels to other telephone network interfaces shall assure that the absolute signal power levels specified on this section, for each telephone network interface type to be connected, are not exceeded.

(H) Registered terminal equipment or protective circuitry with the capability for through-transmission from voiceband private line channels or voiceband metallic channels to other telephone network interfaces shall assure, for each network interface type to be connected, that signals with energy in the 2450 to 2750 Hertz band are not through-transmitted unless there is at least an equal amount of energy in the 800 to 2450 Hertz band within 20 milliseconds of application of signal.

    (ii) The insertion loss in the through connection paths for any frequency in the 800 to 2450 Hertz band shall not exceed the loss at any frequency in the 2450 to 2750 Hertz band by more than 1 dB (Maximum loss in the 800 to 2450 Hertz band minus minimum loss in the 2450 to 2750 Hertz band plus 1 dB).

(6) **For tie trunk type interfaces — Limitation on idle circuit stability parameters.** See unabridged version of 47 CFR Ch.I, Part 68.308, Page 143-144.

(7) **Registered terminal equipment and registered protective circuitry shall provide the following range of dc conditions to off-premise station (OPS) lines.**

(i) DC voltages applied to the OPS interface for supervisory purposes and during network control signaling shall meet the limits specified in Section 68.306(a)(6)(i).

(ii) DC voltages applied to the OPS interface during the talking state shall meet the following requirements:

(A) The maximum open circuit voltage across the tip (T(OPS)) and the ring (R(OPS) leads for Classes A, B, and C shall not exceed 56.5 volts

(B) Except for class A OPS interfaces, the maximum dc current into a short circuit across the tip (T(OPS)) and the ring (R(OPS) leads shall not exceed 140 mA, and

(C) Except for class A OPS interfaces, the dc current into the OPS line simulator circuit must be at least 20 mA for the following conditions:

(8) For message Registration the requirements of Section 68.308(b) do not apply.

(9) For connections to 1.544 Mbps digital services, the permissible code words for unequipped Mu-255 encoded subrate channels are limited to those corresponding or signals of either polarity, of magnitude equal to or less than X48, where code word, XN is derived by:

$$XN = (255 - N) \text{ base } 2$$
$$-XN = (127 - N) \text{ base } 2$$

(c) **Signal power in the 3995-4005 Hz frequency band — (1) Power resulting from internal signal sources contained in registered protective circuitry and registered terminal equipment (voice and data) not intended for network control signaling.** For all operating conditions of registered terminal equipment and registered protective circuitry which incorporate signal sources other than sources intended for network control signaling, the maximum power delivered in such sources in the 3995-4005

Hertz band to an appropriate simulator circuit, shall be 18 dB below maximum permitted power specified in paragraph (b) of this section, for the 200-4000 Hertz band.

(2) **Terminal equipment with provision for through-transmission from other equipments.** The loss in any through transmission path of any registered terminal equipment and registered protective circuitry at any frequency in the 600 to 4000 Hertz band shall not exceed, by more than 3 dB, the loss at any frequency in the 3995 to 4005 Hertz band, when measured into an appropriate simulator circuit from a source which appears as 600 ohms across tip and ring.

(3) For message Registration the requirements of Section 68.308(c) do not apply.

(d) **Longitudinal voltage at frequencies below 4 kHz.** *

(e) **Voltage in the 4 kHz to 6 Mhz frequency range-general case** *

(f) **LADC interface***

(g) **Requirements in paragraphs (d), (e) and (f) apply under the following conditions:** *
  * NOTE: See unabridged version of 47 CFR Ch.I, Part 68.308, Page 145-148.

(h) **Interface limitations for transmission of bipolar signals over digital services-**

(1) **Limitations on Terminal Equipment Connecting to Subrate Digital Services.**

(i) Pulse repetition rate: The pulse repetition rate must be synchronous with 2.4, 4.8, 9.6 or 56.0 kilobits per second.

(ii) Template for maximum output pulse. When applied to a 135 ohm resistor, the instantaneous amplitude of the largest isolated output pulse obtainable from registered terminal equipment shall not exceed by more than 10% the instantaneous voltage defined by a template obtained as follows: The limiting pulse template shall be determined by passing an ideal 50% duty cycle rectangular pulse with the amplitude/pulse rate characteristics defined in TABLE E-6 through a single real pole low pass filter having a cutoff frequency in Hertz equal to 1.3 times the bit rate. For bit rates of 2.4, 4.8 and 9.6 kbps, the filtered pulses shall also be passed through a filter providing the additional attenuation in TABLE E-7.

Table E-6.
Driving pulse amplitude

Pulse rate (R) (kbps)	Amplitude (A) (volts)
2.4	1.66
4.8	1.66
9.6	0.83
56.0	1.66

Table E-7. Minimum additional attenuation

Pulse rate (R) (kbps)	Frequency band 24 to 32 kHz (dB)	Frequency band 72 to 80 kHz (dB)
2.4	5	1
4.8	13	9
9.6	17	8

The attenuation indicated may be reduced at any frequency within the band by the weighting curve of Figure 68.308(d). Minimum rejection is never less than 0 dB; i.e., the weight does not justify gain over the system without added attenuation.

(iii) Average power. The average output power when a random signal sequence (0) or (1) equiprobable in each pulse interval is being produced as measured across a 135 ohm resistance shall not exceed 0 dBm for 9.6 kbps or +6 dBm for 2.4 kbps, 4.8 kbps and 56 kbps.

(iv) Encoded analog content. If registered terminal equipment connecting subrate services contains an analog-to-digital converter, or generates signals directly in digital form which are intended for eventual conversion into voiceband analog signals, the encoded analog content of the digital signal must be limited. The maximum equivalent power of encoded analog signals for other than live voice as derived by a zero level decoder test configuration shall not exceed −12 dBm when averaged over any 3-second time interval. The maximum equivalent power of encoded analog signals intended for network control signaling shall not exceed −3 dBm when averaged over any 3-second interval.

(2) Limitations on Terminal Equipment Connecting to 1.544 Mbps Digital Services.

(i) Pulse repetition rate: The pulse repetition rate shall be within ±75 pulses per second of the 1.544×10^6 pulses per second.

(ii) Output pulse templates. The registered terminal equipment shall be capable of optionally delivering three sizes of output pulses. The output pulse shall be selectable at the time of installation.

(A) Option A output pulse. When applied to a 100 ohm resistor, the instantaneous amplitude of the largest output pulse obtained from the registered terminal equipment shall fall within the pulse template defined in TABLE E-8.

Table E-8. Output pulses

Pulse height (volts)	2.4 to 3.3
Pulse width (half amplitude) (nsec)	324 ±45
Maximum rise or fall time: from 10% to 90% points (nsec)	100

(B) Option B output pulse. When applied to a 100 ohm resistor, the instantaneous amplitude of the largest output pulse obtained from the registered terminal equipment obtained when Option B is implemented shall fall within the pulse template obtained by the bounding pulses permitted by Table II through the following transfer function.

$$\frac{V_{out}}{V_{in}} = \frac{n_2 S^2 + n_1 S + n_0}{d_3 S^3 + d_2 S^2 + d_1 S + d_0} \tag{E-1}$$

where:

$n_0 = 1.6049 \times 10^6$

$n_1 = 7.9861 \times 10^{-1}$

$n_2 = 9.2404 \times 10^{-8}$

$d_0 = 2.1612 \times 10^6$

$d_1 = 1.7223$

$d_2 = 4.575 \times 10^{-7}$

$d_3 = 3.8307 \times 10^{-14}$

$S = j2\pi f$

$f = $ frequency (Hertz)

(C) Option C output pulse. When applied to a 100 ohm resistor, the instantaneous amplitude of the largest output pulse obtained from the registered terminal equipment obtained when Option B is implemented shall fall within the pulse template obtained by passing the pulses obtained in Option B through the transfer function in Option B a second time.

(iii) Adjustment of signal voltage. The signal voltage at the network interface must be limited so that the range of pulse amplitudes received at the first Telephone Company repeater is controlled to ±4 dB. This limitation is achieved by implementing the appropriate output pulse option as a function of Telephone Company cable loss as specified at time of installation (TABLE E-9).

Table E-9. Output pulse options

| Cable loss at 772 kHz (dB) | Terminal equipment | |
	Output pulse	Loss at 772 kHz
15 to 22	Option A	0
7.5 to 15	Option B	7.5
0 to 7.5	Option C	15.0

(iv) Output power. The output power in a 3 kHz band about 772 kHz when an all ones signal sequence is being produced as measured across a 100 ohm terminating resistance shall be within the following shown in TABLE E-10.

Table E-10. Output pulse options.

Output pulse option	Power in 3 kHz band approx. 772 kHz (dBm)
A	12 to 19
B	4.5 to 11.5
C	–3 to +4

The power in a 3 kHz band about 1.544 Mhz shall be at least 25 dB below that in a 3 kHz band about 772 kHz.

(v) Encoded analog content. If registered terminal equipment connected to 1.544 Mbps digital service contains an analog-to-digital converter, or generates signals directly in digital form which are intended for eventual conversion into voiceband analog signals, the encoded analog content of the subrate channels within the 1.544 Mbps signal must be limited. The maximum equivalent power of encoded analog signals for other than live voice that are not intended for network control signaling as derived by a zero level decoder test configuration shall not exceed -12 dBm when averaged over any 3-second time interval. The maximum equivalent power of encoded analog signals as derived by a zero level decoder test configuration for signals intended for network control signaling shall not exceed –3 dBm when averaged over any 3-second interval.

Section 68.318 Additional limitations

(a) General. Registered terminal equipment for connection to those services discussed below must incorporate the specified features.

(b) Registered terminal equipment connecting to 1.544 Mbps service.

(1) Until December 18, 1989, terminal equipment connecting to 1.544 Mbps service shall contain circuitry that assures continuity of output signal. This equipment shall assure that either the outgoing signal meets the minimum pulse density requirements below or one of the specified keep alive signals is transmitted. Power to operate this equipment may come from the line or premises power. Line powered functioning shall be achieved as follows: A direct current connection shall be provided between the simplexes of the transmit and receive pairs. The line power to operate the equipment which assures continuity of the output signal shall be derived from the direct current connection between the simplexes of the transmit and receive pairs. For circuits placed in service prior to February 18, 1988, the telephone company will drive 60 mA through the connection from a constant current source. With 60 mA between the transmit and receive pairs, the voltage drop between the transmit and receive pairs shall not exceed 67 volts. The minimum acceptable average pulse density is 0.125. The maximum acceptable length of a continuous sequence of "zeros" is 80 pulse positions. The keep alive signal inserted when the pulse density drops too low shall be one of the following:

(i) Type 1 Keep Alive Signal. This signal is a consecutive sequence of all "ones".

(ii) Type 2 Keep Alive Signal. This signal is a sequence of 193-bit frames consisting of a framing bit plus 192-bit sequence of consecutive "ones". The framing bit executes the following repetitive pattern every 12 frames: 1 0 0 0 1 1 0 1 1 1 0 0

(iii) Type 3 Keep Alive Signal. This signal sequence is the regenerated received signal connected to the transmit port through a loopback circuit.

(2) For circuits placed in service on or after February 18, 1988, and for all circuits as of December 18, 1989 whenever such circuits were placed in service, the telephone company is not required to provide line power to operate continuity of output functions in terminal equipment, connecting to 1.544 Mbps service. As of December 18, 1989 such terminal equipment is

not required to contain continuity of output capability, provided, however, that telephone companies by tariff may require that such equipment contain the continuity of output capability described in this paragraph up to December 18, 1992. Applications for registration of terminal equipment for connection to 1.544 Mbps service which does not contain the continuity of output capability shall be accepted as of December 18, 1988, but eligibility for connection to 1.544 Mbps service shall be governed by this paragraph.

(c) Registered terminal equipment connecting to the public switched network.

(1) Limitation on automatic dialing. Automatic dialing to a particular number must cease after 15 successive attempts. This rule does not apply to manually activated dialers which dial a number just once following activation.

Index

request for quote (*see* RFP/RFQ)
response times 169-170
RFP/RFQ, 3, 6
  absolute needs 59-60 114-115
  clarifying responses, 76 108-109
  cover sheet, 62
  desired needs 61 115-116
  extra features, 61 116-117
  issuing, 75
  overview 61-62
  risk analysis items, 63
  selecting vendors to send to 71-74
  specification lists 62-67
  vendor's verifying receipt, 75
  writing 59-67
risk analysis, 63, 76 113-123
  weighing the risks 117-123
  worksheet 191-194
RJ-45 connectors, 30

S

safety
  AT&T tests, 37
  Bellcore tests, 37
  hazardous voltage limitations 201-207
  requirements 37-45
safety certification, 64
  risk analysis, 117
safety wire, 42
seminars, 90
services selecting 71-77 çsignal power
  limitations 207-218
Simple Network Management Protocol
  (SNMP), 166
singing point (SP), 142, 160
Society of Telecommunication Consultants
  (STC), 74
software
  Lotus 1-2-3, 130
  upgrading 66-67
standards 7-8
  ANSI, 8, 11, 21, 31, 35, 41
  AT&T, 21
  Bellcore, 14, 18, 21
  cabling 33-36
  caution statement 9-10
  CCITT, 8, 11, 26 31-32
  De facto, 8
  EIA, 8, 21, 22
  EIA/TIA, 23-28
  engineering 23-36
  environmental, 39-40 43
  FCC, 8, 20, 195
  IEEE, 8, 21, 34, 35
  ITU, 8
  manufacturing quality, 56
  originators of 7-8
  TIA, 21
  transmission 11-22

understanding terminology 8-9
static noise, 158
Stratum Level-1, 12
Stratum Level-2, 12
Stratum Level-3 12-13
Stratum Level-4, 13
suppliers 177-179
synchronization, 12

T

T1 line requirements
  AMI 14-15
  B8ZS, 15
  CCC, 14
  continuity of output signal, 20
  error performance 18-19
  jitter 16-17
  ones density 13-14
  signal format 17-18
  ZBTSI, 15
technical support, 65, 85-86 94 120-121
Tele-Communications Association (TCA),
  73
telecommunications
  clocking accuracy 11-13
  DS-3 digital service, 21
  45 Mb/s digital service, 21
  Stratum Levels 12-13
  T1 line requirements 13-20
  transmission requirements 11-22
  voiceband applications, 21
telecommunications consultant, 6, 74
telephone companies
  brochures, 90
  dealing with, 75 87-94
  equipment performance 171-172
  getting results from complaints, 174
  maintenance/repair 92-93
  personnel hierarchy 88-90
  presentations, 90
  questions to ask 91-93
  seminars, 90
  technical support, 94
  vs. vendors 87-88
telephone interfaces 32-33
temperature, 39, 43
10-Base F, 34
10-Base FL, 34
10-Base FP, 34
test equipmenÙ 157-159
  analog voice-grade transmission 158-159
  breakout box, 163
  data checkers, 162
  protocol analyzers 163-164
  test levels 158-159
  transmission measuring sets, 164
test level points (TLP), 159
testing
  burn-in, 55

drop, 40 43-45
tests
    analog circuits 160-162
    arranging system 143-144
    correcting design problems, 144
    digital circuits 162-164
    equipment acceptance 150-151
    identifying problems, 144
    types of 142-143
TIA, 21
trade shows, 72
training
    during installation process 152-153
    end user, 153
    manuals, 65, 84-85 90-91 121
    on-the-job (OJT), 91
transmission measuring sets, 164
troubleshooting (*see* maintenance/repair)

U

Underwriters Laboratories (UL), 39, 117
US Sprint, 8
user groups, 174

V

vendors
    checking quality 82-85
    choosing 71-74
    clarifying responses, 76 108-109
    dealing with, 75 79-86
    dealing with product managers, 82
    getting results from complaints, 174
    limiting number of 73-74
    making final choice 76-77
    manufacturing quality 47-55
    missing parts checklist, 110
    personnel hierarchy, 82
    professional ethics 79-81
    reliability 55-57
    repairing products, 85
    requesting presentations 81-82
    responses from 107-111
    returning products to, 85
    reviewing responses 109-111
    selecting equipment/services 71-77
    technical support 85-86
    vs. factory representatives, 81
    vs. telephone companies 87-88
    warranties, 85, 111
voice interfaces 32-33

W

warranties, 85, 111
white noise, 158

Z

Zero Byte Time Slot Interchange (ZBTSI), 15